The USA from a Chevrolet

The USA from a Chevrolet

Scenes from a Forty-Year Drive in a '65 Biscayne

JAMES A. WARD

McFarland & Company, Inc., Publishers
Jefferson, North Carolina, and London

LIBRARY OF CONGRESS ONLINE CATALOG DATA

Ward, James A., 1941–
    The USA from a Chevrolet : scenes from a forty-year drive in a
'65 Biscayne / James A. Ward.
        p.   cm.

Contents: Table of contents — Preface — Introduction — Phoebe's
youth — Phoebe's ancestry — Storm of the decade — The seething
sixties — Steamy red stick — The Diary Queen klan — Long hot
march — Literary connections — Sugar-boy — Road writings — Back
roads — Out on the blue roads again — Home again, lickety-split —
Decision time — Chapter notes — Bibliography — Index

    Includes bibliographical references and index.

    ISBN 0-7864-2588-1 (softcover : 50# alkaline paper) ∞

    1. Ward, James Arthur, 1941– — Travel — United States.
2. Biscayne automobile.   3. Automobile travel — United States.
4. United States — Description and travel.   5. United States —
History — 1961–1969 — Miscellanea.   6. United States — History —
1969– — Miscellanea.   7. United States — Social life and customs —
20th century — Miscellanea.   I. Title.

E169.Z8 W+   2006
                                            2006014335

British Library cataloguing data are available

On the cover: Phoebe at Fall Creek Falls State Park, Tennessee,
March 1996

Manufactured in the United States of America

McFarland & Company, Inc., Publishers
  Box 611, Jefferson, North Carolina 28640
    www.mcfarlandpub.com

Table of Contents

Preface 1
Introduction 5

PART I: PHOEBE'S YOUTH

1. Phoebe's Ancestry 25
2. Storm of the Decade 45

PART II: THE SEETHING SIXTIES

3. Steamy Red Stick 65
4. The Dairy Queen Klan 74
5. Long Hot March 89

PART III: LITERARY CONNECTIONS

6. Sugar-Boy 111
7. Road Writings 123

PART IV: BACK ROADS

8. Out on the Blue Roads Again 147
9. Home Again, Lickety-Split 166
10. Decision Time 187

Chapter Notes 201
Bibliography 207
Index 211

To Anne's boys,
Theodore Ward Chambers and Henry Ward Chambers,
to whom Phoebe has been entailed

Preface

This book is a prime example of history that makes no pretensions to being objective, all-inclusive, or even chronological. Rather, it is an idiosyncratic, sometimes narrow, oftentimes anecdotal look at some events that convulsed the United States in the 1960s, viewed through numerous eyes, including mine, Phoebe's (my car's), reporters', authors', and commentators'. A former colleague accused me of writing a disguised memoir and, to some extent, she was right. I was an observer in what follows and the book's viewpoint in many ways flows from my proximity and my personal, political and social proclivities. I still believe, however, that what follows is good primary history telling a coherent and interesting story that illuminates something about national conditions then and now. In a sense, this is an exploration of America over the last forty years.

These are huge topics that I have anchored to some very slim reeds. Viewing history through one middle-aged historian's eyes and those of his faithful automobile of forty years at first blush appears ludicrous; many of my colleagues and students have told me so. They usually admit, though, that such a novel approach has benefits not usually found in most histories. I just hope those gains outweigh the drawbacks.

This is not really a history of my car — that would not be worth telling. I use Phoebe as a narrative thread throughout, for to some degree she was responsible for my presence at a Ku Klux Klan rally, my attendance at a civil rights march, my drive across the nation's back roads thirty-five years later, and my experiences in the eye of a major hurricane. She was always the facilitator; she made possible the connections. And as a product of the mid–1960s, she embodies the technological conventional wisdom of that decade. Phoebe is a rolling manifestation of accepted national attitudes towards safety, speed, beauty, efficiency, and corporate capitalism. Her technological sophistication, or lack of same, offers poignant insights into America's history, values, organizational structures, dreams, and fears. Phoebe stands as a most minor monument to the nation's ebullience in the mid–1960s before race riots, war, and assassinations sowed the seeds of doubt that have bedeviled Americans since.

This quasi-memoir in conjunction with Phoebe highlights the incredible resiliency of humans (and machines) to absorb blows, storms, damage, and changes, yet emerge substantially intact. When Phoebe rolled off the assembly line in July 1965 and began touring America's back roads, Lyndon Johnson presided over the White House. The world's problems did not differ in great degree from those George W. Bush grapples with forty years later. Both presidents faced implacable problems in the Middle East, both pondered their relations with Communist China, both worried about racial divisions in the country, both championed the build-up of American armed forces, and both attacked enemies far removed from America's borders.

Hurricane Betsy, which leveled New Orleans and battered Baton Rouge in September 1965, has been followed by dozens of others — most recently Katrina, Rita, and Wilma in 2005 — that have mangled Louisiana, Florida, Texas, and the Atlantic Coast. Preparations for their arrivals, plywood nailed over windows, National Guardsmen directing the chaotic evacuations from the threatened areas, runs on grocery stores for bread, milk, medicines, batteries, and ice, have changed little in forty years. The National Hurricane Center installs more sophisticated electronic devices in its airplanes that it sends into the eyes of such storms, but the information it releases to the public about the storms' probable wind speeds and directions is still plotted on the TV news and in newspapers in much the same manner as it was when Betsy blew the motel roof off onto the brand-new Phoebe.

The Ku Klux Klan is not as noticeable and powerful as it was in the midst of national racial turmoil when Phoebe was new, but the organization, although badly splintered, still exists. It occasionally mounts public displays, and continues to spew racial hatreds that attract disaffected, frightened, and angry Americans who fear they have been marginalized. Although I never attended another Klan gathering, I strongly suspect the group has not altered its rituals, rightly conducted under cover of night.

The 1967 civil rights marchers from Bogalusa to Baton Rouge suffered violence in their attempts to secure equal rights for all people. They succeeded to a degree not readily apparent on that miserably hot, humid September day, but fell far short of their goals of forcing meaningful integration of people of all colors into one social and political body. A peek inside most popular gated communities in the early twenty-first century confirms that America, for all her rhetoric about social amalgamation, remains racially and economically segregated.

Driving Phoebe across America early in the new century I discovered, especially in small towns and rural areas, that much of the culture and many of the attitudes that prevailed in the 1960s are alive and cherished. Folks still tote their lawn chairs to town to watch Fourth of July parades, farmers in pickup trucks still wave to everyone they pass even if they don't know them, small cafes still advertise home-cooked meals and attract a morning coffee klatch in which locals catch up on gossip and complain about the weather. County museums still display dinosaur bones unearthed locally, the World War I uniforms the county's boys wore when they trooped off the make the world safe for Democracy, and old photographs of Main Street before the 1927 flood. Virtually every town still has family motels that still offer a surprise behind every door and feature rooms often bedecked with notes advising guests to hold the toilet handle down for twenty minutes, or to lock the door, or not to run the air conditioner and a hair dryer at the same time.

On the national level, Americans over these forty years tinkered with their national pastime and introduced the designated hitter and free agency. Probably as much ink was expended debating the pros and cons of these two revolutionary changes as was used to cover the entire civil rights struggle. Withal, the Yankees continued to win the World Series. College football caught up with national racial trends when black students broke into big-time "white" universities' teams in the 1960s. Nevertheless, forty years later, most of the same schools — Notre Dame, Oklahoma, Nebraska, Alabama, Tennessee, and the like — still dominate the game.

Phoebe's story is about contrasts between violence and calm and between passionate desires for change and the power of inertia. It is part of the ongoing quest to divine who Americans are and what they want. And underneath it all appear to lie certain constants, such as the very nature of humans and their institutions, against which the contests and storms are arrayed. Phoebe draws a connecting thread through all this, becoming in the process a participant in the history that plays out across these pages.

Introduction

"Cars aren't just molded hunks of metal anymore. These days, cars have personality. They're extensions of who we are.... Protective. Practical. Expressive. Whatever your personality, Ford has the car for you." — Ford Motor Company advertisement, August 2005.

Lisa Jardine observed in *The Curious Life of Robert Hooke* that "biography is the art of giving shape and coherence to the life of an individual." She follows that mundane definition with the thought that when the subject "has a major achievement to his or her name" then that person's story can be written as a before or after tale "around that beacon moment." When the subject has been "varied in his endeavors ... without leaving his lasting mark on history," however, it is much more difficult to put him or her in a proper historical context.[1]

Writing the biography of an automobile is on first blush even more fraught with difficulties. It is a cold, mechanical contrivance, less lively than even the Tin Woodsman, one that does not act without outside physical intervention. Phoebe has done nothing to change the course of history; she has no before and after. Worse, anthropomorphically she is still alive, which lends the biographer a whole separate set of problems, not the least of which is that she has not completed her "varied endeavors." She still has a future — a history that will change as she continues to age.

Writing Phoebe's biography, however, is not so very different from dealing with a human subject. She has, for example, a traceable lineage — physical, intellectual, and organizational — just as we all do. Her mechanical configuration and technical sophistication is a tribute to those who preceded her, to some seventy years of evolutionary dead-ends and successes. Her design, contours, shape, and size are the outgrowth of her ancestors' physical attributes. Her "family," in her case General Motors, decided whether and when she would be conceived and born.

Phoebe even has a DNA of sorts. The chemical composition of her "bones," cast iron, sheet steel, and aluminum, were all predetermined before she was created and were predicated on combinations that were found "fit" enough, to quote Herbert Spencer, the famous 19th century Social Darwinian, to survive in her rough and tumble world. Likewise her "flesh," plastic, fabric, and rubber parts, are all susceptible to decay into their elemental components.

Like her more human sisters, Phoebe features milestones in her life. She has known birth dates, plural because her major parts were manufactured at different times during 1965, but those that can be definitely dated were cast in a forty-five day period that summer. Her conception, that day when humans formed her and brought her to life, can be narrowed to a two-day window in July. The date of her delivery is attestable because like human babies, she arrived in a blizzard of paperwork and bills. We even know the date we took her home.

Like most people Phoebe has regional antecedents. She is the product of the southern rim of the Great Lakes, from Detroit to Buffalo, America's industrial heartland where so much of its automotive manufacturing takes place. But she drew her first sustenance and air in New England — Framingham, Massachusetts, to be precise — where she coughed to life. And in a gestational divergence from her human friends, she was delivered to her family in Utica, New York, only a few weeks later. If she had a passport, it would sport the blue cover that marks her as a native American.

Phoebe is a girl; all cars are. So are locomotives, eighteen wheelers, airplanes, gigantic yellow Euclid earth movers, ocean-going ships, blimps, and all other manner of mechanical contrivances. For some reason people don't feel absurd standing in front of a 1934 twelve cylinder Packard with a 148 inch wheel base that appears about as long as a first down in football and weighs close to three tons, or beside a massive Union Pacific Railroad 4-8-8-4 articulated steam engine capable of 7,500 horsepower and, with its tender, tipping the scales at a earth-squashing 1,120,000 pounds, and exclaiming "she's a pretty little thing."[2]

The whole question of mechanical things' gender is a complex psychological one that probably dates back into the prehistoric mists when man first made tools which he later used to create mechanical devices. Such man-made contrivances, especially those that provide transport, are often unpredictable, volatile, hot, beguiling, powerful, lithesome, and colorful. They are also passive, at least until they impetuously exert their occasionally destructive independence; in short, automobiles and their fellow wheeled, keeled, and winged kin are freighted with many of the stereotypes men have historically stamped upon females. The feminist movement and the political correctness of the last third of a century have not yet intruded into the ofttimes brutal world of mechanical creatures, often capricious and violent, that we name in an attempt to make them more friendly.

Automobiles are intensely personal. Roland Barthes, the late French critic, noted that a car is "a purely magical object," not unlike a beloved woman. He also observed that ownership is "a special sort of relationship. More attention goes into selecting car than a pet." He could have added that some people take more care in picking out a car than they do a mate. K.T. Berger in his *Where the Road and the Sky Collide* concluded that a "car is a close friend, a family member, a part of the family home. It even has its own room in the house — the garage."[3]

It is not surprising that Berger discovered "that nearly half of the drivers gave their cars names such as Honey, Old Bitch, the Zephyr, Patty Wagon, Hank the Tank, Gray Ghost, and LeMans from Hell." This penchant to personalize suggests that about the same percentage of drivers talk to their automobiles. Berger found they "offer them encouragement and a pat on the dashboard to start in cold weather, or to cuss them out for breaking down in traffic," just as they do to people.[4]

I never considered a masculine name for my "little" 3,720 pound Chevrolet after her delivery; I wanted something that denoted plainness and perhaps Puritanical habits, knowing full well the Puritans were anything but colorless and priggish, a name that suggested primness, pursed lips, plain dress, proper morals, sternness — a girl without make-up, short skirt, and sparkly stiletto heels. Phoebe is not exactly a moniker guaranteed to strike envy in the hearts of drivers stopped next

Arguably the homeliest automobile in the world, Phoebe looks much more attractive in front of spectacular scenery such as Watts Bar Lake in Tennessee.

to her at red lights or to elicit challenges to drag race. In thirty-nine years nobody has tested Phoebe's obvious utter lack of dash; she looks too deliberate.

She looks like Phoebe. Holden Caulfield's little sister of the same name calls forth notions of wisdom, insistence, common sense, and devotion, all attributes that in some ways describe the car — Phoebe. She was not named after J.D. Salinger's character, however. Her name is wholly descriptive. A plain vanilla variety, four-door sedan, the cheapest full-sized Chevrolet manufactured in 1965, with a minimum of chrome, one accessory, blackwall tires, the homeliest vinyl upholstery ever foisted upon the public, and a barely adequate power plant never suggested names such as "Flash," "The Blonde Bombshell," or "Roxxy."

I was a good deal more intuitive than Max in Lizbie Brown's novel *Broken Star,* where he calls his car "her ... it ... Phoebe because she's yellow." That bit of information is followed by a discussion over whether or not he ought to call her Phoebus, who was the sun god, rather than Phoebe, who was the goddess of the moon. Another character explains that Max says that his auto is "definitely female, very changeable, and that the moon's yellow as well, so it hardly matters." The authority on such matters, Edith Hamilton, attests that Phoebe was one of the Greek moon goddesses. If Biscayne-Phoebe were conceived on Framingham's night shift my chosen name for her would ironically close the circle.[5]

Like humans, Phoebe was delivered with a fixed number of physical attributes. Her greenish-blue skin tone, lack of knockout beauty, four silverish eyes, oversized, curved rump, short legs/wheels, weight, agility, noisiness, and pep were all genetically pre-programmed. I have had little inclination to perform any cosmetic surgery. As she aged I developed pride in what she lacked, never had, and never would have. For years I bemoaned, for example, that Phoebe has an interior light that does not turn on when I open her doors. I cursed her on cold winter nights when I had to stash our baby daughter's paraphernalia in her back seat before we brought Anne out to the car. It is just as dark in her now, but it has become an asset; her lack of light acclimates my old eyes to the dark which enables me to see better at night. For about $10 I could buy and install the switches in her doors' frames, the holes are already there, capped with small rubber grommets, but there is not a chance that I will. She is one of the few cars around her age that stay dark — the moon goddess.

Phoebe's odd name recognizes that she has an unique personality; men never forget cars they owned that were allergic to cold and hot weather, or that were oil leakers, prone to swerve left, tire eaters, or whatever. They can recite their cars' faults with a wistfulness and humor usually reserved for stories about demented great uncles. I would be as wealthy as a 1999 e-entrepreneur if I had a buck for all the folks who have said to me they had a car just like Phoebe and then prated on with great specificity to explain how it was really quite *unlike* her; theirs was a Caprice coupe with a 327 cubic inch V-8, powder blue with the big, full chrome hubcaps, and a dozen other detailed differences no other human should bother to remember. They then explain that they are sooooo sorry they sold it for it was the best car they ever had and proceed to rationalize all the circumstances that led to its sale. Their stories indicate they subconsciously recognize a genetic similarity between their Caprice and Phoebe that draws forth stories and emotions usually reserved for former romantic relationships.

Introduction

From the moment of her delivery Phoebe had to be taught what her family expected of her. During her break-in period I taught her how to drive on the New York Thruway, how to run-in her brake linings, and how to digest low-octane gas. In my more windy moments I have spun the tale that I take Phoebe to a local junkyard once a year, pull in so her headlights face the automotive carcasses, and carefully explain to her that she will join her sisters in there if she lets me down. I don't, of course, but I have occasionally mentioned to her that almost all of her siblings have been cannibalized, stripped, burned, baled, and melted to drive home to her the reality of death. My admonitions have worked so far. I also praise her as I would a good child, especially when she starts at one a.m. in a dark, deserted parking lot or burps to life after being left in the garage for three months during the summer.

She doesn't hear me and has never replied, but I have talked to people who swear *their* cars speak to them; maybe Phoebe is just the silent type. She has a voice though, a pair of horns that are deceptively high pitched for a car of her bulk, just right for a girl. I rarely honk at anybody, however, and I think she appreciates that—she is not the rude type. I suspect I talk to her because I spend so much time alone in her. Besides, she has no radio.

I believe some inanimate objects, like humans, harbor spirits. Abandon a house and it will deteriorate faster than if it had been lived in but never maintained. And motorcars are the same. They should be sat in, driven, stroked, dusted, anything that brings them into human contact. Our relationships with them are symbiotic and they do respond, to a degree, to the manner in which we treat them. Phoebe, for example, always runs better when she is clean and shiny and after she has had an oil change and grease job.

Like our children, cars absorb some of their owners' attributes; they take on our smells, clutter, and personal dirt. Moreover, they wear in odd places as do our shoes, gloves, pants, shirts, and skirts. Blindfold any half-aware auto owner and have him sit in a dozen different cars and the odds are high he can identify his own, if he has had it for more than a week. Phoebe has her own distinctive scent that like a human's has changed as she has aged. She used to smell of newness like a baby, a clean odor of new paint, vinyl, sealants, and nylon carpeting.

Now she smells like my grandfather used to, of age, dirt in her crevices, something redolent of mold and unpasturized milk.

Cars can become an integral part of us. The playwright William Saroyan understood something of this when in 1963 he purchased a 1941 Lincoln limousine in New York City and with his cousin drove it across the country to Fresno, California. After crossing Lake Michigan on a ferry, Saroyan decided to drive on deep into the night. When cousin John offered to take his turn at the wheel, the writer snapped, "You don't know how to drive *this* car. This is a car only I know how to drive.... It would be unthinkable that anybody else would drive it." A short time later John hesitantly inquired, "Are you identifying yourself with the car?" Saroyan retorted, "I am. I was identifying myself with the car while the salesman was showing it to me.... I have got to identify with everything that becomes a part of my life." How often true.[6]

That sense of identity helps to make us what we drive. Berger claims, "The car is practically braided into our genetic code." Film critic A.O. Scott believes "the car is a bold statement of individual identity." So are our children. Our autos, chock full of our most personal characteristics, serve as outward displays of who we think we are and maybe who we wish to be. Much of this we never think about; when I bought Phoebe all I was looking for was a commodious, cheap car with few accessories that would last long enough to get me through graduate school. I was not trying to tell the world anything; I was so young and poor I had nothing to tell. But later, as we both aged, I rather basked in the thoughts of the money I saved by not replacing her. She remained the family's only car for twenty-two years, a rolling billboard advertising my cheapness. She was plain and naked; as my hair fell out we shone together.[7]

Cars, like houses and children, are a wonderful advertisement for our economic and social status. In our consumption-driven society, especially one with a broadly based middle class, we rely upon small but noticeable distinctions to trumpet our status. As fabrics and clothing became increasingly democratized and luxurious homes disappeared down winding, gated driveways and communities, the auto became our principal plumage. Early in the century well-to-do Americans purchased expensive automobiles such as the Peerless, Packard, Pierce

Arrow, Duesenberg, Cadillac, or the big Marmons and Franklins, and were noticed. In the last third of the 20th century, however, the distinctions among automobile brands shrank and became more subtle. We have to look harder to discern the shades of prices, styles, colors, and model years, which is why some drivers resort to vanity license plates to proclaim their social, economic, and political standing. People also cheat with their cars; they boost their status through the simple expedient of borrowing enough money to buy a more showy vehicle. Then there are those who choose the opposite path. Sam Walton, the billionaire founder of Wal-Mart, drove a battered 1970s Ford pickup that severely underrepresented his financial standing. He would have loved Phoebe.

Phoebe's social contradictions are part of the fun of owning her. Even though she is in pretty good shape and as aficionados say "has a straight body," she sends wonderfully mixed signals about her driver-owner. Her condition speaks to someone willing to pay to keep her up, a task that demands more than a modicum of neurotic attention. Her plainness, or as some claim, ugliness, hints at her owner's aesthetic blindness, his inability to recognize the beauty of pleasing curves and clean lines. Her advanced age denotes a driver who seems to care little about his personal safety and is oblivious to the urge to boost his social standing.

My students think I am just odd. Two generations of them have escaped my tutelage and when I meet them afterwards, they invariably remind me of their names, announce that they had my class in 1973 or whenever, and immediately ask, "Are you still driving *that* car?" When I say "Of course," they shake their heads and break out in those knowing little smiles that wordlessly announce that all professors are nutty and I have rolled farther from the tree than most.

I never intended to keep Phoebe all these years to prove anything, it just happened. Nobody normal ever collected Chevrolet Biscaynes. It was the quintessential family hack designed to provide the most basic transportation at an affordable price. Many of Phoebe's sisters went into taxi and police work that demanded big, cheap, reliable cars that could be worked to death and replaced at minimal cost. In Phoebe's case, I assumed I would keep her until she was no longer dependable, but she fooled me and kept chugging along almost unnoticed — every day.

In the early 1980s, however, she began to look her age. And she *was* old. The average auto owner in the 1960s and 1970s kept his car about eight years. Assuming a 75 year human life span, a car aged about 9.3 years for every human year, making Phoebe in 1981 almost 150 years old. Worse, the neighbor's cat had scratched her front seat upholstery into shreds. Cheap nylon seat covers hid the damage but could not disguise the pronounced sag that had developed on the driver's side of her bench seat. I effected a temporary repair by filling the depression with old *National Geographics,* but they did little to make driving more comfortable; they did, however, keep my chin above the dashboard. Phoebe's paint, after sixteen years of southern summer sun, had badly faded and an ant family had established a colony under her front seat. Any reasonable soul would have sold her but everything vital on her still worked. Moreover, we had eased her duties and relegated her to only around-town driving and a few short winter trips. Every year from 1970 through 1984 we drove up to the Adirondacks where we spent three months at a private lake to escape Tennessee's heat. Returning home in 1972, around Knoxville we hit a traffic snarl known locally as "malfunction junction." As we sat stock still in the middle of the interstate with the thermometer boiling above 100 degrees, Anne, then eight months old, turned red as a rhododendron. Roberta laid down the law that that would be the last time we drove Phoebe up to New York's woods; thereafter, every summer we rented an air conditioned car for the trip.

Even though Phoebe had 115,000 miles on her odometer when she turned sixteen in 1981, it made some economic sense to put a thousand dollars into her for new upholstery and a paint job. With that decision Phoebe won a long-term reprieve from the junkyard; we made a commitment to keep her as long as she ran. With our new investment, which came to almost one-half her original price, we had to drive her for years to realize a return on our money.

Looking back, however, I think our decision to refurbish her was driven mostly by the fact that she had ingratiated herself into the family. She shared a history with us, figured in every significant event of our married lives, and was central to much family lore. She took us on our honeymoon, brought Anne home from the hospital after she was born, and carried her to school on her first day and every day thereafter until

Phoebe has insinuated herself into forty years of family history. Here she brings newborn Anne home on December 16, 1971.

she graduated from high school. I drove Phoebe to teach my first class and have every intention of letting her take me to my last. She is such a family constant that when one of Anne's college application essays asked her to describe how she handled disruptions in her life, she wrote that for eighteen years she had the same parents, same cat, same house, and same car; what did she know about disruptions? The money we saved by keeping Phoebe helped to pay Anne's college tuition. Phoebe did not take her to Indiana University because a heat wave engulfed the Midwest that weekend, but the following May, in 1990, we did drive Phoebe to Bloomington to retrieve Anne and her junk for the summer.

The stories of that journey, which Anne still calls "the trip from hell," are frequently passed around our dining room table. Most of the problems were my fault; before we left I had Phoebe's oil changed and put in the new, more expensive, heavily advertised synthetic oil. Five hundred miles later some of her valve lifters collapsed. On the way home with Anne, Roberta, her mother, who was almost stone deaf and did not see all that well either, and Phoebe stuffed with Anne's possessions, we stopped at a restaurant on I-65 in Louisville where I asked a state trooper where I could get Phoebe fixed. He gave us the name of a garage a few miles down the road and in pouring rain we lumbered off. We found it, a decaying two-story brick building surrounded by a junkyard, both squatting in the middle of a muddy parking lot. While I waited inside for the proprietor, I noticed that men kept coming downstairs fiddling with their trousers and belts. Then I spotted the siren on the short-wave radio luring the truckers. Had Phoebe not stumbled Anne would have missed the rare opportunity to watch a brothel in action, one recommended by a state trooper. A can of lifter gunk temporarily solved the problem and Phoebe brought us home slowly, but without further mishap.

I have owned her well over one-half of my life. She graces pages in the family photo albums. We rarely make a conscious effort to photograph her, she just manages to edge into them. Her trunk is so large

This was one of Phoebe's grandest moments as she takes Anne and husband Tom Chambers from the church after their wedding to their reception on October 21, 1995. The groomsman was chosen to drive Phoebe because he had spent the summer wrestling a UPS truck around Jackson Hole, Wyoming, good training for driving Phoebe.

that we can fit any Christmas tree, up to nine feet tall, in it. She has brought home every one since 1965, save the one in 1981 when she was being reupholstered. They have not all been beauties, but that was not Phoebe's fault. Our aesthetic appreciation for Christmas trees is equaled only by our demonstrated appreciation for automotive beauty and well-proportioned Halloween pumpkins, all of which resemble Woodrow Wilson.

As with any family member, Phoebe makes demands. She must have insurance, gas, oil, grease, and occasional repairs. She has survived all these years because she has been given good nutrition. Fresh oil every 2,000 miles, grease jobs at closer intervals, and relatively high-octane gas after the government removed lead from gasoline have kept her internally clean. Phoebe gives us a break on her insurance for nobody will write collision on her; her $100 book value is less than the deductibles. She likes new tires and for decades rapidly ran through her nylon ones. Only after I bought her steel-belted radials did she stop wearing her shoes out. Now her tires rot before their tread wears down. Radials are not recommended for old cars whose suspensions were not designed or tuned for them; the mantra is that older vehicles become "squiggly" and dangerous. Phoebe easily adjusted to the new tire technology, however, and is dicey only on ungrooved, wet cement floors, the kind found in parking garages. Otherwise, her larger "feet" enable her for the first time in her life to stop with some assurance. She also likes to be clean, and driving around in a freshly washed and waxed old car of no obvious value is a major part of our confusing public image. I keep her dusted and shiny; she prances better that way.

A venerable family automobile develops idiosyncrasies that make her as crotchety as some blood relations — and both have to be tolerated. Phoebe has a host of quirks, some of which were gifts from Chevrolet's engineers. Her glove compartment door, for example, is a technical marvel. The key must be turned and pushed in to unlock it, but the door must be pulled out to open it and there is nothing on which to pull. For a quarter of a century it stayed locked; each year I slid Phoebe's registration through the crack around the door and swore if a cop ever stopped me I would let him figure out how to get it out. Finally I noticed that a credit card fit into the crack and could be used to pry the door open as I turned the key. I found an historical treasure trove inside: the GM book that describes her features, her maintenance booklet complete with its protecto-o-charge plate, a stack of road maps of the eastern United States, all of which showed only small portions of the interstate highway system completed, old pencils, matchbooks, a couple of replacement light bulbs, and all those registration slips. It was an automotive archives.

General Motors' body designers inset Phoebe's back window to make it even with the metal around it. A trough encircles the glass, collects water that runs off the roof and window, and traps it. It has no place to drain out. For decades rainwater sat under the chrome strip that runs around the window, rusted out the channel, and began to drip into the trunk. All 1965 Chevrolets share this clever design and most have trunks with their floor pans eaten away and trails of rust running down the inside of their trunks. I had Phoebe's channel repaired when she was repainted and devised a clumsy technique for stopping further deterioration. There is a crevice around the chrome strip just wide enough to admit a hypodermic needle. I visit the university's chief nurse periodically to beg the biggest hypodermic she stocks. Each time I explain why I want it and she gives me that same knowing look that conveys she's not as stupid as she may seem and that I am probably a lot cruddier than I look. When Phoebe gets wet, I suck the water out of her dammed up channel; it is surprising how often it rains.

And for almost forty years every time it rains water leaks into the car about half way down the front edge of the driver's side door. The weather-stripping on that door edge is another engineering coup. It has a sharp bend in it that does not seal against the door frame. The rug gets wet and eventually rots out, although it took a quarter of a century for that to happen. About ten years ago I had the weather stripping replaced because it had hardened and was flaking. The replacement has the same kink that invites the water to drip in.

The little wing windows on the front doors help keep the inside puddles topped up. When driving in the rain with the quarter windows open, water blows against them and drips into the car. General Motors designers neglected to put a small rain gutter on the bottom of the window frames to channel the water down the outside of the car. I have the option of closing all the windows and driving a foggy, muggy, but almost-dry Phoebe, or opening them and inviting nature's elements inside; I usually opt for the latter.

Phoebe hates water. When she was about ten years old she developed eccentric windshield wipers. They work just fine, but when I turn them off, they frequently, but not always, return to their "rest" position and then hiccup, rising up about two inches and falling back until I shut off the engine. No amount of fiddling with the wiper switch will stop them; neither did a new switch. Mechanics shake their heads and advise me to live with it. The tic does not appear to hurt anything, but it is maddeningly distracting to drive with her wipers humping up and down two feet from my nose.

Phoebe does not like the water inside her engine either. She eats water pumps; she dropped her first one at 27,000 miles and has maintained that tradition to the present. She is very methodical about it; there is never a sudden ear-piercing squeal so common with dying pumps. Phoebe's just become "floppy"; the fan blade wiggles as the bearing gets looser. Chevrolet, however, has been very accommodating over the decades; the water pumps on its modern V-6 engines fit Phoebe exactly. They are easy to find, easy to install, and relatively cheap. I have some hope, however, that Phoebe has finally reformed. Her present one has 27,000 miles on it and its bearing appears still to be tight.

Phoebe is not overly fond of her steering wheel bearings either. She does not have power steering and steers like a truck, especially at low speeds or when I try to park her. While she was still under her munificent 24 month/24,000 mile warranty, her steering wheel stopped returning after turning corners, a disconcerting — and dangerous — habit. I took her to a Baton Rouge Chevy dealer and two days later picked her up, assured the warranty work had been done. I turned out of the service area and the wheel refused to spin back. After some loud and heated conversation they admitted they changed the top bearing but did not check the lower one in the steering box; after they replaced that one, she drove normally. Thirty-six years later, when her mechanic took the steering column apart to fix another problem, he found her top bearing again mangled. A defect that occurs only every thirty-six years is tolerable, but why she eats her bearings is an open question.

Her idiosyncrasies shape her personality; they help to define her and her relationship with me. We appear to have reached an unspoken agreement that I will tolerate her bothersome nature to some level, which she appears to have divined. Her quirks usually do not endanger either of us or threaten to end her usefulness. She has never left me stranded, she just irritates the hell out of me from time to time to let me know she has a mind of her own.

As Phoebe aged she developed very human-like symptoms. She has become afflicted with rattles and squeaks, mostly around her doors where her rubber bumpers have, like the material between our joints, hardened, thinned, and become stiff. They are easy and cheap to replace, however, and that usually solves the annoying noises. Like a human she also slowed down, probably because she has lost compression over the years thanks to valve recession caused by the unavailability of the leaded gas she was designed to drink. Likewise, her springs have lost some of their elasticity and she tends to wallow more than a new car, although extra-stiff shock absorbers have ameliorated the problem to a degree. And, of course, she looks old. With her vertical, squarish face Phoebe does not slice or slip through the air; she pushes it along in front of her like a wall.

In a few cases, however, her aging problems have the potential to become more structural, dangerous, and difficult to repair. In 2002 an "ear" on her outer steering column case broke off, allowing the column and the steering wheel to wiggle up and down several inches. She remained drivable but her elastic steering system was a bit disconcerting. The sheet metal ears are the only fasteners that hold her entire column in place, another engineering wonder. Dozens of phone calls to junkyards and replacement firms all over the country elicited only the information that everyone's "ears" broke and most of them had failed years ago. Chevy owners had stripped the yards and suppliers' shelves so that unless I could find someone who was parting out a car with good ears, I was in trouble. To further complicate the problem, Phoebe has a standard column shift which has its own peculiar casing and Chevrolet manufactured many fewer of them than it did cars with Powerglide transmissions. After two fruitless weeks of searching it dawned on me that perhaps the broken ear could be welded back on. A magnet proved it was not made of pot metal and a local specialty metals shop did a quality job reattaching it. It solved the problem but pointed up the difficulties of keeping an aged car on the road.

Phoebe's advancing age, however, has its positive side. Unlike other members of the Ward clan, she appreciates with age, becomes more desirable, and is even, judging from random comments, becoming better looking. People frequently ask if she is for sale; nobody has *ever* asked if I were. A few years ago when she was resting outside a restaurant someone left a note under her wiper offering me exactly what I paid for her in 1965. Of course modern dollars are worth less than they were in the Viet Nam era, but it was a singular coincidence.

Like old people, Phoebe attracts a certain amount of deference, much of which is instinctive. People like to touch her. A couple of years ago I was eating in a cafe and had parked Phoebe on the street outside. I watched a well-dressed man, wearing an ID tag that marked him as an employee at nearby TVA, walk by and look Phoebe over very carefully. He went a few steps past her, stopped, returned, and ran his hand lightly down her front fender. Then he turned and walked off. It was almost a reverential touch.

Earlier we had driven Phoebe to Atlanta where we spent a weekend and attended a Neil Simon play at the Fox Theater. When we arrived at the theater, there was a long line of Mercedes, Jaguars, BMWs, Lincolns, and the like, waiting to enter the Fox parking garage. The attendant looked at Phoebe and told us we should not park her in a regular slot. Instead he directed us to a wide handicapped spot just inside the door on the ground level where no one would open his door on her. We protested that we did not think that was fair, not to mention legal, but he assured us that he had a surplus of handicapped spaces. The expensive luxury cars, he squeezed into his regular parking places.

On our way north to pick up Anne on the trip from hell, we stopped in Paoli, Indiana, at about dusk to have Phoebe's clattering lifters checked. The mechanic at a local garage thought we needed to replace at least two but since it was almost five o'clock he told us he did not have time to do it. Then he hesitated a moment and said, "I haven't worked on one of these in years" and offered to check with the local parts store to see if it was still open and whether it had the lifters. He did, they were and did, and he stayed two hours late to put in several new lifters and did not charge for his overtime. When he finished, he did what mechanics have done for the last thirty years, he carefully wiped off the grease, oil, and fingerprints from the motor, the engine compartment, and the fenders and hood. They all do that; it is almost as natural as tucking a comforter around someone who is wheelchair-bound.

The deference to Phoebe's age extends to road manners. Drivers have a greater dollop of tolerance for Phoebe than for other cars on the road. As with most aged folks, Phoebe has lost a step or two over the years and is not able to keep up comfortably at modern turnpike speeds. She can still step up to seventy or so miles per hour but she makes it obvious with her cacophony of clatters and other strange sounds that she is not fond of such strenuous exercise; she is much more comfortable humming along at fifty-five miles per hour, at which speed she only chatters a little. Even when she backs traffic up, nobody honks angrily or shakes a fist and she's not been on the receiving end of the singular international sign of disrespect — not once. Instead, people fly by and salute her with short honks, smiles, and waves. We often get thumbs up, Churchill's victory sign, or some hand motion such as a thumb to forefinger circle that denotes approval — or perhaps pity. When parked, people often walk over to us to say hello and comment on her. Taking her out is akin to walking a three legged dog. Everyone will stop to make some charitable comment about the mutt, inquire about its pedigree and age, and wonder why anyone would own it.

Phoebe is the three-legged dog of the automotive world. Her birth year was a particularly good one for Chevrolet stylists and many of their offerings, especially the Impala SS two-door hardtops and convertibles, have become collectibles that forty years later fetch prices well into the thirty and forty thousand dollar range. Even the cheaper Malibus and Novas were quite attractive and those with odd options, such as large engines, still do well in the marketplace. Bluish-green, four-door Biscaynes equipped with the smallest engine Chevrolet offered, spartan interiors, and few accessories were the dogs of the year. Phoebe's body, like that of some dogs and many adolescents, is too big for her frame. She has too much overhang, her wheels look too small. From the front she has a four-eyed mopey look that is not improved by having had three of her original headlights replaced with ones that feature different designs on their lenses that makes Phoebe look slightly dyslexic. From the rear she looks as if she is trying to tuck her tail between her wheels

This is not Phoebe's most attractive angle. Her rear overhang is so long she looks as if she is trying to tuck her tail between her wheels but cannot quite bring it off. Her two small brake lights do not afford much protection; the 1965 Impala had four such lights, proving that money buys safety.

but cannot quite bring it off. Her polished aluminum accents do not shine. It's just all wrong. But she is so wrong, so awkward, so unattractive, she is cute and as she ages she becomes more beguiling. If we really are what we drive, Phoebe radiates hope that as she ages her transformation from beast to beauty will somehow rub off on her owner.

PART I

Phoebe's Youth

1

Phoebe's Ancestry

"The fascination of the petrol engine to the man who is born with an engineering instinct is largely due to its imperfections and its eccentricities. In these respects, it possesses a soul that has much in common with the human." — Quoted in Gijs Mom, *The Electric Vehicle: Technology and Expectations in the Automobile Age* (Johns Hopkins University Press, 2004, 41).

Phoebe's DNA is complex. It mirrors General Motors' Byzantine corporate structure and Chevrolet's place in it, contemporary styling trends, automotive technology of the turbulent mid–1960s, Phoebe's price niche, and popular tastes of her era. She is a rolling historical artifact that four decades later advertises the strengths and weaknesses of the automobile industry and the country that birthed her.

General Motors was itself a pastiche built of William Crapo Durant's dreams to control the automobile industry and his penchant for indiscriminately absorbing auto companies and suppliers. Born a year before shells rained down on Fort Sumter, Durant was a quintessential American success story. He left home at sixteen to work for what became the Durant-Dort Carriage Company in Flint, Michigan, and thus became one of the many auto pioneers who emerged from the carriage, bicycle, or cash register businesses to dominate Detroit.[1]

By his early forties Durant had made his fortune in the carriage trade and was semi-retired, working off his legendary energies playing the New York stock markets. David Dunbar Buick, however, changed Durant's life and became responsible for Phoebe's conception. A manufacturer of plumbing supplies, Buick switched to building cars in Detroit. Like many newcomers to the business, he survived thanks to the willingness of his suppliers to extend him credit until he assembled and sold his cars. He was soon heavily indebted to Benjamin and

Frank Briscoe, who sold him his sheet metal and who left their own mark on the automobile world with their Briscoe and Maxwell automobiles. Buick's works soon passed into the hands of James M. Whiting, a Flint carriage manufacturer, who moved the plant to his hometown. After he failed to rejuvenate Buick he hired Durant to take it over.[2]

In 1904 Durant drove a new two-cylinder Buick and was so impressed he agreed to manage the company. Buick's valve-in-head engine, whose legacy powers Phoebe, designed by a pair of brilliant engineers, Walter Marr and Eugene Richard, was the company's most valuable asset. Ironically, Phoebe indirectly met Marr years afterward. After a short career detour to build his own automobile, which he not surprisingly called the Marr, he returned to Buick as its chief engineer. When he retired he moved to Chattanooga where he built an impressive home on Signal Mountain. His granddaughter still lives next door and she and her husband, Bill Close, own the two extant Marrs. In 2003 I drove Phoebe up to their house and Bill took me for a ride in his 1904 Marr. History is full of close misses; had events transpired differently Phoebe might have been a Marr.[3]

Durant hit Buick like a whirlwind and by 1907 had moved it into second place in national sales behind Henry Ford, who was only a year away from building his first Model T. Durant believed that Buick, which manufactured only middle priced cars, was vulnerable to market vagaries and he bought other auto manufacturers so he could offer cars in all price ranges. The Briscoes, who were heavily involved in Maxwell-Briscoe, teamed up with Durant in a scheme to dominate the industry. The three men were short of cash, however, and when Henry Ford and Ransom E. Olds, who was then at REO, each demanded three million dollars in real money for their companies, the Durant-Briscoe partnership folded. The Briscoes formed the United States Motors which, after buying some 130 companies, plunged into bankruptcy in 1912.[4]

Durant's consolidation attempt, which eventually led indirectly to Phoebe's birth, folded even more quickly. He chartered General Motors with a munificent capitalization of $2,000 in 1908. Using GM stock he quickly bought Henry M. Leland's Cadillac company; Leland went on to create Lincoln, which Henry Ford purchased in 1921. In three years Durant purchased thirteen motor vehicle companies and nearly a dozen auto supply firms, upped GM's capitalization to almost sixty million dollars, and listed its stock on the New York exchange, the first auto company to do so.[5]

Unfortunately, by then Durant had lost control of GM. He was overextended and was forced to appeal to eastern bankers for a bailout. A consortium of Boston and New York banks loaned GM the necessary money on the condition that Durant step down. He left in 1910 and the trust that replaced him pared GM down to Buick, Cadillac, Oakland (which later became Pontiac), Oldsmobile, and General Motors Truck. In so doing, GM left the lower priced field to Ford because Charles Nash, Buick's president, ended production of Buick's low priced entry in the market in 1910. During the bankers' five years at GM's helm, the company's share of auto sales fell from 21 percent to a skimpy 8.5 percent.[6]

Durant had tasted the heady flavor of empire building, however, and began to lay plans to win back control of GM. He recognized that if GM was to gain supremacy it had to be competitive at the bottom of the price market that Ford had captured with his Model T. Durant created such a company to leverage himself back into possession of GM.[7]

The former GM president hired Louis Joseph Chevrolet to design his economical car. Born in Switzerland but a French resident, Chevrolet emigrated to the United States around 1900. He had the mechanical aptitude that Durant lacked and had made his name as the race-car driver who had bested Barney Oldfield, the country's best known speed demon, three times in 1905. When Buick created a racing team in 1907 it hired both Louis and his brother Arthur as team drivers. Louis was more successful and Arthur became Durant's chauffeur.[8]

Durant hoped to capitalize on Chevrolet's racing reputation to sell a car to compete with the Model T. The Frenchman had his own ideas, however, and the first car he designed, the Model C, was big, heavy, and expensive. Chevrolet wanted his name associated with a quality car that would bring him personal prestige. His six cylinder vehicle bore a price tag of $2,150, $25 more than Phoebe's in 1965. Model T's sold in the four to five hundred dollar range and eventually became much cheaper.[9]

In 1913 Louis quit the company that bore his name, organized the Frontenac Motor Company that later became a part of Stutz, and with Arthur manufactured racing accessories for the Model T. During the depression it was reported that he worked on the Chevrolet assembly line. He died in 1941.[10]

As Chevrolet's personal fortunes withered, his namesake company prospered. Durant reorganized the firm in 1913, downsized its offerings to four cylinder cars, and sold them for between $750 and $925. By 1915 Chevrolet showed a profit on sales of 16,000 cars and Durant again reorganized Chevrolet, chartered it in Delaware, and capitalized it at eighty million dollars. He then offered to trade five Chevrolet shares for each share of GM stock. Within a year Durant owned forty-four percent of GM and with his ally, Pierre S. duPont, controlled a majority of its shares. In May 1916 Durant assumed the presidency of GM, a company actually owned by Chevrolet.[11]

That ludicrous situation lasted only until 1918 when Durant rechartered GM to include Chevrolet and another Durant creation, the United Motors Corporation, which included Delco and the Hyatt Roller Bearing Company. Hyatt's president, Alfred P. Sloan, soon became GM's president and rationalized its operations. Durant resumed his normal frenetic expansion, paying thirty million dollars for the Fisher Body Company, which is why Phoebe's aluminum step plates on each doorsill sport the Fisher Body logo, a black oval with a luxurious horse-drawn carriage in it.[12]

Durant's meteoric comeback did not last long, however. The sharp recession that began in 1919 shook the whole automobile world and soon cost Durant his presidency. The following year, when Durant discovered he was about thirty million dollars in debt, Pierre duPont and the House of Morgan raised the funds to bail him out in exchange for two and one-half million GM shares and Durant's promise to leave the company. Pierre duPont took over his job, but GM was really run by its executive vice president, Sloan.[13]

Phoebe owes a debt of gratitude to the always ebullient auto pioneer who begot Chevrolet to regain GM, but it was Alfred Sloan who created the company's divisional structure in which each automobile brand became autonomous under a centralized authority that made the overall critical corporate policies. Sloan believed that GM was too big for one man to run; he insisted that decisions at all levels be the product of group consultations, thus imprinting on the automotive giant its vaunted layers of committees that served it so well for decades but nearly brought about its ruin in the 1980s.[14]

Sloan's decentralization policy enabled the Chevrolet division to chart its own destinies within the boundaries of overall corporate policies. Sloan's oft repeated dictums — that GM should build a car for every pocketbook, offer the customer a little bit more in every price class for only a slightly higher price, and be improved yearly with major redesigns on a three year cycle, roughly the average life of the firm's dies — meant that Chevrolet was free to do anything as long as it adhered to Sloan's guidelines.[15]

GM slotted Chevrolet in the lower price range between Ford's Model T, which had about 70 percent of the auto market in the early 1920s and the lower rungs of the middle price categories. Sloan recognized that by the 1920s many auto buyers were purchasing their second or third cars and the country was full of Tin Lizzie owners who were ready to move up to a car that was mechanically more sophisticated and more attractively appointed but would not crush their pocketbooks. Later Sloan intended to entice Chevy owners to buy more expensive GM automobiles and eventually his pricey Cadillac. After drivers tired of their Model T's, Ford had no other more expensive cars they could buy, except after 1921 the Lincoln. Not until Ford created the Mercury in 1938 did the company produce a car in the popular mid-price range, where GM was already comfortably ensconced.

It took Chevrolet almost a decade to find its place in the crowded auto market. Its sales lagged far behind Ford's in the 1920s until Henry closed his manufacturing plants for six months in 1927 to retool for his Model A. For the first time Chevrolet surged into the sales lead, besting Ford by almost six to one. It held its place in 1928 against Ford's new car by a very slim margin.[16]

In 1929 Sloan's Chevrolet division surprised the automotive world when it introduced a six cylinder engine, advertising "A Six for the Price of a Four," a not-so-subtle slap at Ford's four cylinder Model A. Chevy's new overhead valve engine remained its mainstay for twenty-six years and an improved version has powered Phoebe for almost four decades. From 1931 until the start of World War II, Ford outsold

Chevrolet only in 1935, despite the fact that Henry Ford personally designed a new seventy horsepower, flat-head Ford V-8 that he introduced in 1932 and offered for only $460. Chevrolet remained contented with such mundane innovations as four wheel mechanical brakes in 1928, rubber engine mounts in 1932, hydraulic brakes in 1936, and a column shift in 1939, all of which, except for the mechanical brakes, were standard items on Phoebe.[17]

Ford and Chevrolet maneuvered to outstrip one another in the booming 1950s. Chevy offered its Bel Air two door hardtop and Powerglide automatic transmission in 1950, only to be countered by Ford's Victoria and Ford-O-Matic the following year. Chevrolet attempted to inject some pizzazz into its dowdy lineup when its engineers grabbed parts off their shelves and cobbled together the Corvette in 1953, making it one of the first "dream cars" from a Motorama to go into production. It was a great deal less than a true sports car, however; it rested on a standard Chevrolet frame and was powered by the company's trusty six that had been tweaked and drank from three carburetors to produce 150 horsepower. Two years later Ford replied with its Thunderbird; it was not much of a sports car either, but its "Thunderbird" OHV V-8 churned out 193 horsepower. The mid–1950s competition for sportiness and comfort with hardtops, bigger V-8s, automatic transmissions, and domestic sports cars presaged the flashy 1960s, when the horsepower race began in earnest.[18]

Chevrolet lagged in the horsepower contest after Ford introduced its first OHV V-8 in 1954 that featured 130 horsepower and was designed with eventual increases in mind. More important, Cadillac's introduction of its OHV V-8 in 1949 had caught the public's fancy and became synonymous in consumers' minds with acceleration, speed, flash, and technological sophistication. Chevrolet was caught in the slow lane, offering only its traditional six cylinder engines through 1954.[19]

Seven years later when I became a junior at Purdue University, which forbade out-of-county freshmen and sophomores from driving in Tippecanoe County, I bought a used 1954 Chevrolet. This car never graced any undergraduate's dreams, even in a cameo role. It was a four door, gray, two-ten, the middle range model, powered by a "blue-flash" 125 horsepower six cylinder engine mated to a two-speed Powerglide.

It was stodgy and sluggish, which may have said much about its owner. Seven winters of Utica's salt and snow had peppered the car with disintegrating fenders, holes in the floor pan, rusted parking lights, and peeling chrome.

It was, however, the consummate Chevrolet of the era, dependable and almost indestructible. One Christmas I drove it 800 miles from West Lafayette, Indiana, to Utica with a main bearing shot and almost no oil pressure. Over sixty miles per hour I could not hear the engine knocking so I drove it that fast as often as possible — and it brought me home. In the winter of 1962 Lafayette had a stretch of thirteen days when the thermometer never got up to zero. The whole town slowly congealed; every day there were fewer cars on its streets. The gray beast, however, despite sitting outside all night, started every morning. By the end of the freeze I was running a taxi with the faithful old clunker.

The gray two-ten was the last year Chevrolet offered only such cars to its buyers; in 1955 the company went after the growing youth and speed markets. It brought out its own OHV V-8, a 265 cubic inch motor that put out 162 horsepower, and restyled its entire line. Although at the time I did not think Chevrolets were as attractive as the all-new 1955 Fords, car collectors, who avidly snap up any decent Chevies for the years 1955–1957, have judged otherwise.[20]

The 1957 Bel Air Chevrolets have become classics of the era. GM engineers bored their V-8 out to 283 cubic inches that milked 185 horsepower from the power plant. Becoming ever more adventuresome, the company also introduced fuel injection on the 283, which raised the motor's output to the magic figure of one horsepower per cubic inch. The 1957 Bel Air hardtops, convertibles, and Nomad station wagons have developed a cult following over the years. A convertible in good condition will now command $50,000. In 1974 Chevrolet recognized the unique appeal of its 1957s when it advertised them as "the most popular used car in history." It pointedly did not mention Phoebe.[21]

Chevrolet's later offerings did not fare as well. The 1958 models were solid, rather oddly styled cars but they looked terrific next to the 1959 models with their horizontal tail fins. Even Ford, which fielded no beauties that year, outsold them. GM quickly dropped that styling approach and retooled for the next three year cycle that included their fiftieth anniversary 1962 model. To fend off inroads in the lower price ranges Chevrolet brought out the Corvair in 1960, the Chevy II in 1962, and its Malibu two years later.[22]

By 1965 Chevrolet offered cars from the mid market range down to the most basic transportation. James Flink in *The Automobile Age* quotes a Yale physicist who "whimsically calculated" that in 1965 "Chevrolet offered 46 models, 32 different engines, 20 transmissions, 30 colors, and 400 options [that] could be purchased in almost as many permutations as there are atoms in the universe."[23]

Chevrolet's "super-store" approach to building and selling automobiles proved a bonanza; in 1965 it sold a record number of cars, 2,587,490 to be exact. Phoebe was one of them, but in many respects she was a technological throwback to over a decade earlier. Her mechanicals are very similar to those of my 1954 gray beast. Through the vagaries of merchandising and production scheduling, Phoebe, who shares a body with the more expensive Bel Airs, Impalas, and Caprices, drew a production sheet void of almost all product choices. She was not a bespoke car, a popular option in the 1960s when a customer could fill out a sheet at the dealer listing everything he wanted and his order was forwarded to the appropriate factory to build that car for him. Phoebe instead was built in the hope that someone looking for commodious, cheap, basic transportation would take pity and buy her — which is exactly what happened.

The Biscayne was far from the most popular Chevrolet model in that halcyon automotive year. Chevrolet manufactured just over 144,000 of them, about five and one-half percent of the company's total production for the year. Almost three-quarters of them, including Phoebe, were powered by the standard Chevrolet six cylinder engine. In 1965 that engine had 230 cubic inches with a compression ratio of 8.5:1 and boasted 140 horsepower, a decent size motor. Phoebe has only ten fewer horsepower than the 1953 Corvette and only five fewer than a 2002 Ford Taurus. What she has though, is weight; at almost two tons her power plant struggles to overcome her built-in inertia. And her engine is a great deal less sophisticated and efficient than modern motors of her size. She has no computer or electronic controls, everything in her engine compartment, which is so cavernous that bodies could easily be stowed on either side of her engine, operates on

Phoebe's engine indisputably shows its Chevrolet heritage, right down to its orange paint. With 140 horsepower, it is simple and slow, but almost indestructible.

levers, springs, vacuum, gravity, whimsy, or luck. Coupled with her gear ratio, which is perfectly calculated for a taxi operating in a city without hills, Phoebe's engine has to turn just over 2400 rpm at sixty miles per hour; a similar sized V-6 in a modern Taurus, by contrast, can maintain that speed at just under 2000 rpm.[24]

Phoebe's major cast parts are stamped with production codes that give a detailed history of her creation. Those codes which grace her engine, transmission, intake manifold, axle, and vehicle identification number (VIN) plate indicate that her major components were cast, stamped, shipped, and assembled between June 6 and July 14. Her three biggest and most vital parts, however, were manufactured in the very short period of a week.

Phoebe's earliest casting mark is on her intake manifold and it indicates that it came out of the foundry on Sunday, June 6, 1965. Evidently working weekends enabled the manifold casting plant to run far ahead of final production schedules that year. Her transmission housing was made next and was coded SO628, meaning it was cast in Saginaw, Michigan, the O stands for a three-speed, and the numbers indicate it was made on Monday, June 28, a cloudy, cool, rainy day in Michigan, good weather in which to labor in a foundry.[25]

On the right side below the distributor Phoebe's engine is stamped F0707FA, which when decoded indicates it was cast in Flint, Michigan, on the seventh day of the seventh month. The FA identifies the engine as a 230 six cylinder. Ordinarily, buyers are warned to shy away from purchasing anything made in Detroit on Monday or Friday or around a holiday. In 1965, July 7 was a Wednesday, two working days past the Fourth, which allowed everyone time to sober up and settle down to work. The weather in Flint that day encouraged sobriety and attention to task, for the city had intermittent showers and nice, cool summer temperatures that kept conditions in the foundry tolerable.[26]

Perhaps summer cars built on cool, rainy days are of better quality than those assembled in the more typical blistering upper Midwest summertime temperatures. It was certainly a great deal hotter far away from Flint the day Chevrolet cast Phoebe's engine. The Viet Nam War was escalating and B-52 bombers, many of which would fly in President George W. Bush's Iraq II War, flew in from Guam and bombed an area 35 miles north of Saigon in what the Pentagon termed a "spoiling mission." A force of South Vietnamese, United States, and Australian troops searched for Viet Cong "but found little except abandoned tunnels and huts." In Europe, France played the spoiler in the European Economic Community by withdrawing its permanent representative in a diplomatic snit to try to make the EEC more responsive to its demands. In Flint, however, the GM foundry cast at least one engine block on July 7 that lasted for almost forty years of constant driving and ran 141,000 miles before it required any major work.[27]

Three days later and several hundred miles to the east, Chevrolet's Buffalo casting plant stamped DA0710B on Phoebe's rear axle housing. Not surprisingly, that day the Lake Erie port city enjoyed almost a half an inch of rain and a high temperature of only 73 degrees. The rear end is still under the car and with over 200,000 miles on it, it's as quiet as the day it came out of the plant. Strangely though, Chevrolets that year had no drain plug to draw off and replace the differential grease. Perhaps engineers were satisfied that they had achieved a design that would last forever, or as long as it took the average owner to pay off his car, or with luck to the warranty expiration.

Or maybe Chevrolet pinched a few cents off each car by forgetting the drain plug. In any event, Phoebe's original grease remained in her differential for thirty-one years before I had it pumped out and replaced.[28]

The heavy castings manufactured in Flint and Buffalo were shipped immediately to Chevrolet's assembly plant in Framingham, Massachusetts, quite a feat decades before "just-in-time inventory" became a mantra in the automobile business. According to her VIN plate, Phoebe was "conceived" on 07B, meaning July's second week. In 1965 that would have been between Thursday the 8th and Wednesday the 14th. Since the axle housing was not cast until Saturday, July 10, Phoebe probably was not assembled until late in the second week. Most likely she came down the assembly line on either Tuesday the 13th or Wednesday the 14th and with luck, it rained on both days.[29]

Chevrolet aficionados know that factory build sheets are usually found under the back seat. Somebody forgot to slip Phoebe's under there, maybe because her sheet was nearly blank. She must have slipped past dozens of assembly stations on Framingham's line where workers sat contentedly on their stools and watched her creep by. She passed the power steering, power brake, radio, clock, air conditioning, power window equipment, lap belts, floor carpets, hood insulation, trunk floor mat, even the interior light station without a worker at any one of them twitching.

Ironically, the devices Chevrolet used to cover up missing accessories on Phoebe have become valuable. A classic example is the gap where her radio belonged. The factory inserted a black, rectangular piece of plastic faced with "Chevrolet" written out in silver script, called a delete plate. Almost forty years later delete plates are selling for over $100. The same is true for the delete plate in the round pod where her clock would have been, had she had been well fitted out.

In several respects the cost-cutting and styling decisions at Chevrolet made Phoebe more unsafe than her sisters. To distinguish her from her more classy relatives, she has only two small brake lights. The more expensive Impalas and Caprices have four such lights to make them more expensive looking and they cast twice the light to attract the attention of tailgating drivers. Moreover, Phoebe's brake drums are not a square inch too big. At times they are just plain scary. Coupled with the "2 ply — 4 ply rated" original tires that put a minimum of tread surface on the road, I had to be extremely cautious when stopping the car, especially in wet weather. Not only were the factory tires the minimal size for Phoebe's fourteen inch wheels, but they wore out quickly, even with careful driving. I had to get rid of them after only 14,597 miles and I replaced them with the biggest nylon tires I could fit on her wheels. Chevrolet soon afterwards recognized its 2 ply tires were disasters and returned to the more traditional 4 ply nylon tires that lasted twenty thousand or more miles. I kept one of the 2 ply tires as a spare for thirty years until I began to worry that it probably had a terminal case of dry rot. Nevertheless, I saved the tire and may be the only United States citizen to own such a poorly designed, cheap piece of original equipment.

I also am the proud owner of about one inch of the original windshield washer fluid. The washers were standard equipment and the factory attached a small glass bottle in a metal clamp to the inside of the left fender in the engine compartment to hold replacement fluid. For some reason I never used all the washer liquid that came with the car. After about twenty years the neoprene gear in the washer pump stripped and the washers stopped working. I replaced the gear but still did not use that last inch. Unfortunately, in 2002 the helpful young man who changes Phoebe's oil filled the glass bottle with fluid while I was not watching. Now only about ten percent of it is original.

An anonymous factory inspector prominently scrawled a big "K" on Phoebe's firewall. I have often wondered how long he worked in Framingham making his indelible mark on every Chevrolet that rolled off the line and what exactly it was that he checked. In my darker moments when something on Phoebe is broken I envision an angry German-American scrawling a big "K" for kaput.

After Phoebe was completed she was parked in a storage lot from where she was trucked to the C. Weaver Chevrolet dealership then located on Genesee Street in Utica. Phoebe could not have been there long because within a month of her assembly she became a part of our family. I was engaged to be married on August 28, 1965, and in mid-September was scheduled to start my Ph.D. studies at Louisiana State University, where I had financial support to defray my tuition and books with just a bit left over to keep body and soul together. My parents took pity on their impecunious son and his almost-bride and promised to buy us a new car for a wedding gift.

Their generous offer prompted a real conundrum because they did not indicate how much they were willing to spend and there were many cars that were beguiling. On the other hand we needed something cheap to operate that had a reputation for dependability. And my bride-to-be made it very clear that it had to have four doors. Our choices were further narrowed because my parents were friends of C. Weaver's former owner who, when he had a few drinks under his belt, was a veritable font of stories about how he made his fortune after World War II selling places on his new car waiting list. He claimed he made more money from the list than he ever did selling Chevrolets. My parents also knew Weaver and had bought several of my mother's Chevrolets from him, although my father remained a dedicated "Buick man."

On August 11, 1965, Father and I went down to Weaver's dealership. It was clear and dry with temperatures in the mid sixties, a beautiful day; it could not have been otherwise for a young man about to be married and get a new car. I do not remember noticing that the world was going to hell all around us on such a nice day. My Pittsburgh Pirates had lost the night before after the Giants' Juan Marichal struck out a murderer's row of Roberto Clemente, Willie Stargell, and Donn Clendenon to wrap up the game. Richard Nixon, looking ahead to the 1968 presidential election, had traveled to West Branch, Iowa, the day before to celebrate Herbert Hoover's ninety-first birthday and there called for the United States to step up its air and sea attacks on North Viet Nam. Congressmen voted 393–1 to prescribe jail and a $10,000 fine for anyone who burned his draft card, protesters whom Congressman William G. Bray, R-Indiana, called "generally filthy beatniks."[30]

With a draft card safely stamped 2S (student deferment) for another year tucked in my wallet, my father and I looked over Weaver's offerings. A beautiful yellow convertible with a black top on his showroom floor immediately caught my eye. Unfortunately it was short two doors and I rather thought my father, the quintessential engineer, might object to its impracticality. We looked at other cars on display and walked outside to the storage lot, which was surrounded by a chain link fence. It was full of cars lined up bumper to bumper in rows and there at the very back Phoebe sat on the end, against the fence. The rear of the lot sloped down towards the fence so that Phoebe in all her Artesian Turquoise glory leaned towards the fence looking as if she was either casually resting or was trying to peer around the other cars to see what was going on. Or, she was trying to attract my attention. I remember wondering how Weaver would ever get her out of the lot if someone was dull enough to show an interest in her.

After looking at everything my father and I decided that a basic four door, six cylinder model would probably be the smartest buy. So we started over and just looked at those cars and when we again saw Phoebe the thought crossed my mind that if I didn't buy her nobody would and she would lean in that corner forever. And, the more I looked at her, the better she looked; she was so plain, so dowdy, so much more severe than anything else on the lot, she had a certain flair. She was the cheapest full-sized car there, which ameliorated some of the guilt I felt in accepting a free car.

I also hoped that my trade-in would further lower my father's out-of-pocket costs. We had driven my four-door 1956 Buick Roadmaster and parked it right in front of the showroom window. I had appropriated the car from my father, who had been in Germany for four years overseeing Sperry Rand's manufacturing plants there. Although my mother and sister also lived in Frankfurt, they kept our Utica house. When my 1954 gray rust bucket finally conked out, I "borrowed" the next oldest car in the family's garage, Father's Buick.

This car had a checkered career. In the summer of 1958 Mother crashed head on into a 1957 Ford station wagon, hitting it so hard that it drove the Ford's motor back into its third seat. Miraculously nobody was killed. For some reason Father, who was usually practical about such things, wanted his Buick rebuilt. It spent an interminable time in a body shop where everything from its windshield to its radiator was replaced. In the meantime Father, who was then general manager of UNIVAC, drove my black and yellow 1950 Ford with its leaded nose and glass packed muffler, roaring into the executive parking lot and burbling into his reserved space. He twitted his employees that they drove much newer and more expensive cars than he did. In the meantime I was on foot.

The principal reason my mother and sister survived their horrendous crash without seat belts was because the Buick was so heavy. New York assessed license plate fees by weight and the Buick squashed the scales at 5,470 pounds, dry, which placed it at the very top of the fee scale. Not only was it heavy, but it was huge with a 127 inch wheel base. By contrast Phoebe, who is too big for most standard parking spots, has a wheel base of only 119 inches. Of course, she also has a three foot overhang at the back which sticks out into the driving lane of most parking garages.

Father's Buick was far from the perfect college student's car even though it was equipped with every imaginable gadget, including air conditioning, a radio search button on the floor, a power antenna, and what must a been a ninety-seven-way power seat. It had a huge 322 cubic inch V-8 with a four barrel carburetor that produced 255 horsepower; with its Dynaflow transmission the car needed every one of those horses to move. On my trips back and forth to Purdue the Buick gulped high-test gasoline at the rate of one gallon for every eight miles. Gas was cheap; it was the repairs that killed me. The car had, as I recollect, four mufflers and two resonators and at any given moment at least one had a hole in it. Power steering and brake pumps and hoses went south practically daily.[31]

I lived in a classic dumbbell tenement in West Lafayette, fortuitously located right across the street from a gas station run by a nice guy who took pity on me and charged me very reasonable repair rates. His station was a gathering spot for several elderly locals and one, a retired professor of poultry science from the University of Iowa, or maybe it was Iowa State, took me under his wing and imparted daily grandfatherly advice, usually about women. He reminded me daily not to waste my time with coeds and girls in their twenties (he needn't have worried on either account); I needed, he asserted, a good woman between 32 and 37, the age span when females reached the peak of their sexual prowess. I had not a whit of experience from which to judge the truthfulness of his contention and at the tender age of twenty-two all women at their "peak" ages reminded me of my mother. I rather feared he was confused and was really talking about chickens, as he often did.

While I spent a lot of time at the gas station soaking up Dr. Chicken's wisdom and watching mechanics fix my car, unbeknownst to me it was also suffering from Utica's salt. It looked good on the outside but when I took it in for its New York inspection, the fellow hooked a long plastic alignment box on the headlight's nipples and watched as the box slowly pulled the whole light assembly out of the fender. It cost $1,100 to get both front fenders rebuilt so that the car was no longer cross-eyed.

The C. Weaver salesman was less than impressed with my trade-in. He walked over to the showroom window, took a long look at it, and asked if it ran. I assured him that's how it got there and, without even going outside, he allowed us $300 on it all the while opining that he knew a poor family in desperate need of a car to whom he would donate it. I hoped the new owner was a mechanic.

The salesman asked us to return the next day to pick up Phoebe and pay for her. Now when it came to money in the Ward house, Mother was queen and she needed no court. On August 12 she and I went back to close the deal. The listed price for six cylinder Biscaynes was between $2,417 and $2,524; the agreed-upon price for Phoebe, with my trade-in, was $2,150, which Father and I thought fair. Mother, who stood 5 feet tall on her tiptoes and weighed perhaps ninety pounds when fully outfitted against Utica's wintry blasts, looked Phoebe over carefully, sort of mumbling to herself, and walked over to the salesman, who had a very pleased look on his face, and asked him why she should pay an extra $11 for glove compartment and trunk lights she did not need. She imperiously informed the poor sod that she wanted them taken off the car; he reasonably suggested he would just delete the $11 from Phoebe's purchase price. She then mentioned that she had not seen a car without carpeting in years and asked how he could sell such cheap stuff. He explained he could install carpeting for a price but mother cut him short and told him that he would have to carpet the car *before* she bought it, for she was not going to pay for rugs the car *ought* to have. While she had the poor guy on the ropes, Mother moved in for the kill, explaining that she was not going to pay $2,150 for *that* car, it was too much. By then I was perfectly willing to forgo a new car and moseyed over to check out the yellow convertible. The salesman kept plodding off to see whether his boss would accept Mother's offers and made counter offers. After they were both finally exhausted, mother wrote out a check for $2,125 and we drove Phoebe,

with her new rugs and two accessory lights, home. I found the rigma-
role of buying a car so distasteful that I did not buy another one for
twenty-two years.

Perhaps in retribution for Mother's closeness, C. Weaver did not
fill Phoebe's gas tank. They put in just enough to get us off their lot
and out of sight. I picked up my sixteen year old sister, Sharon, and
took her for a ride down route 5S to Rome, enjoying the sunshine
glinting off the brand new, clean, Artesian Turquoise paint. I filled
Phoebe up in Rome, putting in 14.6 gallons for a total of $4.52 or 30.9
cents a gallon, which in terms of "real" dollars was only marginally
cheaper than gas forty years later. The Rome fill-up became the first
entry in the little spiral notebook in which I have recorded every one
of Phoebe's expenses.[32]

Chevrolet had obviously closely calculated its own costs in light
of its products' quality when it offered a generous warranty of 24
months or 24,000 miles. Quality control standards in 1965 were much
more lax than on modern Detroit cars that compete with well-
engineered and well-built European and Japanese automobiles that
have established quality standards worldwide. A fine example of 1965
acceptable quality is the welds that attach Phoebe's roof to her three
pillars on each side. They were welded by hand and Phoebe passed to
the next station where someone else ground them down, smeared hot
lead over the seams, and sanded them flush. The welder and sanders
must have been having a bad day. The job they did on both sides on
the C pillars, the ones in front of the back window, was positively rot-
ten; the seams are still visible and rough to the touch — yet Phoebe
passed her final inspection.

Phoebe was mechanically in much better shape, however. I had
only two warranty repairs, one on the steering bearings and the other
to replace a faulty speedometer cable. Phoebe did not suffer a breakdown until she was two months shy of three years old. We were on a
dissertation research trip from Baton Rouge to Yale through Washington, D.C., and on June 4, 1968, just two days before Robert F. Kennedy
was gunned down, we were driving about seventy miles an hour around
the capital when Phoebe's engine suddenly began making the most
unholy racket, as if a gnome was inside her valve cover banging it with
a ball peen hammer. She made it to a dealer who, after lots of head

Phoebe sat for her first portrait in New Hartford, New York, around August 20, 1965. She had been in the family fewer than eight days.

scratching, diagnosed a timing gear problem. He discovered a 20 cent fiber bushing in the timing chain sprocket had failed, allowing the sprocket to slip out of alignment, but not quite off.

I have spent much more time having Phoebe serviced than repaired. Unlike modern automobiles she demands frequent maintenance. Cars are now are guaranteed to run 100,000 miles without a tune-up; Phoebe made it all the way to 9,376 miles before I had to replace her plugs and points. New cars have no grease joints; Phoebe has an even dozen that have been greased perhaps 150 times. Her front wheel bearings require checking, repacking, and often replacement at about every 10,000 miles.

Some of Phoebe's original parts were designed to last not much longer than her warranty. Her tires and fan belt did not make it even two years. At twenty-eight months her muffler rusted through and her tailpipe rotted off. Only ten months later her water pump began dripping water. By then all of her hoses had outlived their life expectancies. On the positive side, however, her Delco battery lasted over five years, as long as modern ones, and she did not need brakes, shock absorbers, and a carburetor until 1970.[33]

Detroit's quality slipped badly after 1965 and reached all time lows in the next decade, when auto makers glued on exterior trim and vinyl tops that trapped water and rusted roofs, substituted cheap aluminum window moldings that corroded, bowed, and fell off as the buyer drove off the lot, and built bigger and less efficient engines that got ten or twelve miles to the gallon just as OPEC's oil embargoes hit. Meanwhile, Honda and Toyota revolutionized the automobile business by building attractive, well engineered cars with thrifty appetites, replete with better fit and finish than anything Detroit turned out and priced about the same as the Big Three's offerings. American automobile companies did not catch up until the 1990s, when they introduced redesigned cars, manufactured to more exacting standards, that far surpassed the quality of their 1965 offerings.

Chevrolet's record sales in 1965, however, were proof that its styling met with public approval. The year was a watershed for the GM division's exterior design. It softened its big cars' lines, curved their side glass, and gave them a kick-up over their rear wheels for a more rounded shape, sometimes called the "crouching cougar" look. The crease down their sides from their head lamps to their tail lights accentuated their length and visually lowered the belt line. From most angles, the cars were attractive. The least flattering view was from their rear quarter, where their huge overhang made them look tail-heavy and droopy. The Impala's and Bel Air's trim enhanced the new styling nicely. The Biscayne's accents, however, worked less well; the cheapest full-sized line was supposed to be the least attractive. When posed next to a 1965 four door Impala, Phoebe looks big, plain, and ugly. When viewed by herself, however, she appears big, plain, and less ugly. Appreciation for her Artesian Turquoise paint is an acquired taste and over four decades I have become accustomed to it. It makes her easy to spot in a crowded parking lot. Surprisingly, the color enjoyed a resurgence in the 1990s, especially on Hondas.

The 1965 styling messages set the tone for Chevrolet's future. While the 1966 models differed little, over the next few years Chevrolets changed more perceptibly. In the following decade full-sized Chevrolets became heavier, wider, and fatter looking, but retained essentially the same lines. The kick-up over the rear fenders disappeared in 1969 and styles into the mid–1970s emphasized the heaviness of the cars' front ends.

Chevrolet lost its way in 1977 with a boxy offering that had a long run into the 1980s. Ford, by contrast, built an all-new car it christened the Taurus, whose oval shape changed styling trends at all companies. GM took longer than most to see the future, however, and stuck with its squarish designs from Chevrolet to Cadillac until they became bait for advertising sneers, the most famous being a Lincoln ad that intimated that all GM products looked alike. Not until the end of the century, after GM's domestic market share had fallen from its once mighty almost sixty percent to a meager twenty-eight percent, did GM finally untangle its complicated and confused organizational layers and set to work on a generation of new cars that began appearing in the early 21st century. The evolutionary pace of change is swifter in automobiles than in humans; the redesigned Chevrolet Impalas, for example, are roughly four generations removed from Phoebe and are almost a new specie; they exhibit little of her engineering and design DNA. They are much lighter, smaller, fuel efficient, powerful, and comfortable. They are "high steppers" compared to Phoebe, who increasingly looks and drives like the antique that she is.

2

Storm of the Decade

Phoebe's "first step" was a long one. Eleven days after I brought her home I took her out on the New York Thruway for her first trip to Logansport, Indiana, where I was to be married in five days. Following the commonly accepted break-in advice I varied her speed on the highway from the closely enforced limit of 55 down to about 40 miles per hour and in the process probably drove other drivers nuts. She made the 800 mile trip in one day without a problem, however.

As we celebrated at our rehearsal dinner on the night before our nuptials, buried in the news, well below the fold, was the U.S. weather bureau's announcement that a tropical depression, with winds of 30 miles an hour, had formed in the Atlantic, 200 miles north of French Guinea. The hurricane season was full-blown in those remote parts but in the swirl of our wedding preparations nothing seemed farther away. Besides, the odds that the squall would affect our lives was minuscule; in an average season only 10 tropical depressions form in the Atlantic and only slightly over one-half of them develop wind velocities of over 75 miles an hour needed to qualify them as hurricanes. Not all of those hit land and only a few that do roar ashore in the continental United States. Had we even seen the small article announcing the new tempest's birth, we would not have paid much attention to it. We soon did, though.

The tropical depression gathered strength; its winds that swirled 35 miles an hour on our wedding day increased to 75 mile an hour blasts a few days later as we happily drove Phoebe from Fort Wayne to the Sands Motel in Dearborn, Michigan. While we spent two carefree days wandering among the artifacts Ford had collected to recreate the midwestern rural world of his youth, which his Model T had done so much to destroy, the tropical depression became a hurricane named

Betsy, signifying the season's second storm. It steered a north-northwesterly course away from South America's coast. When we checked out of the Sands at the end of August, Betsy stood well to the west of Hispanola, a location which promised to take it harmlessly into the Atlantic, away from the east coast.[1]

Betsy packed a greater punch than did our finances as we retreated on September 2 to Logansport, Indiana, to pack for our move to Baton Rouge. By then Betsy had gained speed and punch. The Baton Rouge *States-Times,* always alert to tropical storms frolicking in its backyard, first mentioned Betsy on that day and noted that her winds exceeded 100 miles per hour as she "roared with increased fury toward the southeastern Bahaman Islands." Although her northward thrust lessened her threat to the southeast coast of Florida, Miami's chief storm forecaster warned "we are not quite ready yet to take south Florida off the hook." With the hurricane moving at 10 miles per hour and spawning gales 200 miles in every direction, the best meteorological bets were that she might eventually threaten the U.S. Atlantic coast somewhere.[2]

We knew exactly where we were going as we stuffed our small U-Haul trailer with everything we owned. Betsy by contrast kept everyone guessing, but no weather forecaster was predicting any scenario that might threaten us. Three days before our departure the storm skirted the Bahamas and the Associated Press guessed "there was a good chance its 150 mile per hour winds would never strike land." The weather men, however, were less certain; Betsy was dangerously fickle and had already changed course a half a dozen times. Floridians, scarred veterans of such erratic storms, heeded their own counsel and even after Betsy had passed to their north, Miami housewives crowded grocery stores to stock up on supplies. Some wary fishermen on Cat and Eleuthera islands had "sunk their boats in secluded harbors to protect them from the rough water."[3]

As we packed and mooched free food and lodging from Roberta's parents, Betsy abruptly swung about in the Atlantic and headed for the Carolinas. A hurricane-hunter reported on September 4 that the storm's eye was 35 miles in diameter and swirled at 125 miles per hour. Florida was safe, the weather bureau predicted, but Betsy had drawn a bead on Charleston, South Carolina, some 500 miles north.[4]

We had no plans to go to Charleston — and neither did Betsy. The following night she just stopped "and churned around in the same position nearly 24 hours before starting to move south again at 8 miles an hour." Forecasters noted that it was not unusual for hurricanes to stall and change course but such restlessness made them nervous, for they were unable to predict a new direction until the storm moved along. A northeastern high pressure system slowly forced Betsy southward and weather men put out small craft advisories for the Bahamas and Florida Keys.[5]

On Labor day, September 6, Betsy "sat astride" Nassau with 135 mile an hour winds and stalled there for two hours before she made up her mind to visit Florida, where tides had already risen 4 to 6 feet above normal. After what the newspapers labeled her "freakish turnabout," Floridians along the southeast coast began boarding up their windows.[6]

Storms were brewing everywhere else too; President Lyndon Johnson was at his Texas ranch keeping his eye on the fighting between Pakistan and India and frightening accompanying reporters half to death with mad dashes across his property in his Lincoln Continental. Secretary of State Dean Rusk reaffirmed America's commitment to all its obligations in Southeast Asia and the former head of the Ku Klux Klan in Bogalusa, Louisiana, testified in court the Klan no longer existed there; he swore he was president instead of something called the Anti-Communist Christian Association, which was sponsoring the white rally in Bogalusa on the workers' holiday.[7]

We turned Phoebe south the next day; with everything we owned stuffed in the car and trailer we felt and looked like Steinbeck's Joads. And we did not go much faster; Phoebe is under powered at the best of times and she staggered under the load we imposed on her. We do not remember passing a single vehicle on the 1,046 mile trip into the subtropics.

As Phoebe sputtered South, Betsy turned west and aimed her 140 mile per hour winds at Florida's southeast coast, pushing a 6 foot wall of water in front of her. It was the most water that south Florida had seen since the 1926 hurricane. Three feet of salt water coursed down Phoebe's namesake, Biscayne Boulevard, in Miami. Luckily, however, Betsy unexpectedly dropped her wind speed to a positively puny 105 miles per hour when she finally struck the coast. The bad news for us, however, was that she then headed straight for the Gulf of Mexico where weather men warned, "Over the warm-subtropic waters which feed fury into a hurricane, it could grow even more." Gordon Dunn of the Miami weather bureau wisely observed, "Once in the gulf, it must hit another coast.... There is no other escape."[8]

That caught our eye; as we drove down through Indianapolis and on U.S. 31 until we met I-65, which was finished just north of Columbus, Indiana, it dawned on us that we might be driving into the teeth of a major hurricane. We chatted lightly about it as we chugged through downtown Louisville, picked up I-65 again to just below Elizabethtown, then turned Phoebe southwest on the Western Kentucky Turnpike. There we discovered one of the peculiarities of interstates; their off and on ramps are always built in valleys where the towns were located and the turnpike constructed its toll booths at the lowest points for fifty miles around, guaranteeing that it would take Phoebe a half an hour to get up to speed after we stopped to gas up, eat, or pay tolls. Highway designers seem impervious to the laws of inertia, which weigh more heavily on Phoebe than on most automobiles.

We straggled across Western Kentucky to U.S. 641 and into Tennessee on U.S. 79, where we spent the night at a Holiday Inn at Milan, a memorable stop because at $8.00 it is the cheapest Holiday Inn in which we have ever slept. The following day, September 8, we picked up unfinished I-40 to the Memphis bypass and headed into Mississippi on I-55, which was completed to just north of Grenada. We knew we were in the South for the temperature that day soared quickly to 90 degrees and the humidity was only a few percentage points lower. Had Phoebe been air-conditioned she would have coughed to a stop when we turned it on.[9]

We had our first taste of a South that was straining every sinew and law to perpetuate segregation when we stopped for gas in Canton, Mississippi. Never have I been more aware of Phoebe's bright blue and orange New York State license plates. The only person we saw around the station was a black man asleep with his rump buried in a stack of old tires. As we wondered what to do, a white fellow strode from the station and without looking at us, walked over to the stack of tires and gave it a swift kick that popped the sleeping attendant into the air as if he had been sitting in an ejection seat.

We were always leery of southern race relations in the hinterlands. There the races openly abraded each other, occasionally to the point of violence. Nothing seemed to infuriate rural whites more than strangers with northern accents, handy targets to blame for forcing integration upon them; we drove the backroads warily. Three years later, when we were returning from upstate New York and Indiana, we stopped for lunch somewhere on U.S. 51 in Mississippi. The cafe was in a pleasant brick building and promised good, satisfying, home-cooked southern food. It delivered, but we were a bit put off by the piles of segregationist literature stacked everywhere and the constant chatter about the horrors of the federal government and Yankees' inability to understand the true nature of southern "coloreds." My New York nasal twang and Roberta's glacial-scour Hoosier accent made us more than a little nervous. After we paid, the cashier pressed a George Wallace for president bumper sticker on us. Anywhere else we would have refused to take it and explained in graphic language just why. In rural Mississippi that did not strike us as being politic or safe; we thanked her and took it with us. Phoebe never wore it, however.

On our first trip south in 1965 Jackson, Mississippi, was the most pleasant town we saw. We later learned it had the highest percentage in the nation of college graduates for cities its size, because a couple of colleges and the state's government were the only significant employers in the town. Unfortunately when we arrived that Wednesday, the temperature was striding well into the nineties and the heat and humidity were working on our tempers. Roberta was driving and stopped for a red light located in the middle of a long hill. When it changed she killed the motor; the trailer's weight made take-offs much more difficult. She killed it on her second and third tries as well. Each time we rolled backwards a bit and the cars behind us all jockeyed to back up and take up the slack behind them to avoid being hit by a runaway U-Haul and two incompetent Yankees. I pleasantly mentioned to my new bride that if she were coordinated we might not be on the verge of wiping out a platoon of sons and daughters of the Confederacy. She failed to appreciate my humor but finally caught enough of the clutch to put to rest my fear of starting Civil War II right in the heart of Dixie. We rode in silence down to Hammond, Louisiana, turned right on U.S. 190, and arrived at dusk in Baton Rouge where we booked a room on Airline Highway.

The semester was scheduled to start at Louisiana State University the following week. We had to find a place to live, I had to register for classes, and Roberta had to find a job. We were out early on Thursday, September 9, to buy a newspaper for its apartment rental ads. We were shocked to see headlines screaming that Betsy was coming — soon. While we had been absorbing the culture of Mississippi gas stations, the storm had swung around the southern tip of Florida, regained her footing in the Gulf, tacked in a more northerly direction, and sped up to 18 miles per hour. As we ate breakfast and planned our assault on the city's housing market, the weather bureau was broadcasting hurricane warnings from the mouth of the Mississippi River to Mobile. That put us awfully near Betsy's projected bullseye.[10]

The locals thought so too and were taking the warnings seriously. An estimated 100,000 people in south Louisiana and Texas were preparing to flee Betsy's 140 mile per hour winds and "possible killer tides." Total evacuation of Cameron Parish, long a hurricane interstate, began as we finished our breakfast. Baton Rouge called out its civil defense forces, oil workers were taken off Gulf rigs, black and red hurricane flags flew from the Mississippi's mouth to Galveston and the newspaper was full of news items about Betsy's destruction in Florida. The Baton Rouge weather forecast called for afternoon rain with winds escalating to 73 miles per hour. Residents were urged "to take precautions."[11]

All we wanted was an affordable place to live, preferably close to the university. We had not driven a block before we realized it might be a bad day to hunt for an apartment. People everywhere were nailing plywood over their windows, bringing in everything from their lawns, and crowding grocery stores to stock up on batteries, kerosene, bread, milk, raw oysters, and hot boudin. The weather was stifling; the temperature by noon was near 90 degrees, the humidity felt higher, and the barometric pressure must have been around 2. Everything was so still we rather looked forward to some wind.

We soon discovered that apartments near the university were dumps — typical student housing. As we turned on the lights in one a corps of cockroaches paraded across the floor into the walls. Roberta swore she would never live with bugs; the landlord retorted that "if you live in Louisiana, you will live with bugs." We were determined, however, that we were not going to live with *that* many.

By lunch we had found nothing; we were sweaty and irritable, and everyone in the restaurant was speculating about how much of the town Betsy was likely to blow away. Over sandwiches we decided to change our strategy and search for apartments farther out and gamble on figuring out some way for Phoebe to deliver us to two places at the same time.

We got lucky. The first one we looked at was about two miles from campus, across the street from Baton Rouge High School, and it looked across the huge expanse of the school's front lawn crowded with live oaks draped with Spanish moss. The landlady was a throwback, way back, to an earlier era. Probably in her mid-sixties, Mrs. Bailey spent her whole day preparing for Fred, her husband who held a state civil service job, to take her out to dinner. To fill her hours she combed her Pomeranian's coat and brushed his teeth; never has a dog lived so well.

When we met Mrs. B the wind had already started to blow and our moods could not have been lower. She had quite a nice place, however, a fair-sized apartment that overlooked a central driveway with a

Phoebe and Roberta pose in November 1965 in front of our "hurricane-proof" and "bug-proof" apartment in Baton Rouge. Note that Phoebe still had her New York license plates. The KKK burned its cross at the end of our driveway, behind where the photographer was standing.

small house on either side. Mrs. B lived in one and she rented the other to a forty-something Canadian woman, a professor of sociology at LSU. She was the most gullible person we had ever met, but we became good friends. Once, over a few drinks, I convinced her that my mother was a blimp pilot with Trans Idaho Blimp Lines. On the back of her lot, Mrs. B, who we quickly realized was a shrewd, shrewd woman, had built a three car garage with an apartment above it. It was clean and was bug-free. When Roberta mentioned what the fellow had told her that morning, Mrs. B showed us that her garage had a sheet of aluminum cemented between its lower brick courses to prevent bugs from crawling up the walls; in our four years there we saw one bug inside and its life span was considerably shortened. Moreover, Mrs. B pointed out, with the winds whipping her housecoat about, she had set the apartment on 14 or 17 or some number of I-beams to make it hurricane proof. That sold us — we shook on the deal.

We could not move in because the utilities were turned off, but she suggested we store our trailer in the garage to shelter it from the oncoming storm, which we did. Afterwards we picked up the afternoon newspaper and drove back to our motel to ride out the promised 73 mile per hour winds. The storm did not sound as serious to us as the natives seemed to be taking it, especially when we read the *State-Times* editorial captioned "The B-Girl Boils Along." We were further reassured by a lengthy article reporting that LSU's chancellor had welcomed 4,000 freshmen to campus that afternoon, which we took to mean that the "old heads" in the bayous were doing normal things in the face of the oncoming threat. The paper did mention, however, that "the state is battening down with the advance warnings of the mad dance of this B-girl from the islands." When the editor extracted his tongue from his cheek he warned "hurricanes are not things to fool around with and the wise are readying for the wild wind."[12]

There was not much we could do to protect ourselves. Our trailer was tucked under our guaranteed hurricane-proof apartment, Phoebe was sitting out in the parking lot, and our room was on the second floor of a two-story motel. We did the only things we could: ate a hearty dinner; returned to the room; and watched the local television stations' continuous storm coverage. One announcer advised everyone to draw water for emergency use, which seemed like a good idea, except we had nothing to put it in except the bath tub, which we filled half full. Water pressure all over town must have been close to nil that evening. We watched TV as Betsy smashed into New Orleans with winds reported at 155 miles per hour, which the weather bureau later confirmed.

Winds raging at those velocities would have qualified Betsy as right on the border between a category 4 and 5 hurricane, the two highest levels. The Saffir-Simpson scale, named after a consulting engineer, Herbert Saffir, and the director of the National Hurricane Center, Bob Simpson, was not established until four years later. Their ratings judged a storm a category 3 when its winds were measured between 111 and 130 miles per hour. A category 4 blast registered winds between 131 and 155 miles per hour.[13]

Outside of our room it sounded like a category 10 storm. The wind roared at a noise level that was almost painful and the rain slashed across the parking lot and crashed against our window. Highway traffic dwindled to a few lonely cars picking their way around the trash and debris that swept across the road and an occasional eighteen wheeler racing the storm to get out of town.

Around midnight we lost power and with it our friendly faces on the TV screen. We sat in our darkened room while the primeval forces of an angry nature screamed their welcome to our new home. I ventured out once on the balcony to check on Phoebe and felt the cement undulating under my feet. Luckily, we did not have a picture window in our room, but we did have a sliding glass opening about two feet high and perhaps four feet wide. We closed the drapes over it so that if the window burst, we would not be slashed with glass shards.

Outside, in the winds later reported to have been between 120 and 140 miles per hour, all manner of things were happening. The Baton Rouge cops were looking for two men who were looting stores where windows had been blown in. The National Guard ordered 150 men to their armory to help the police control what they feared would become an epidemic of lawlessness. By 3 a.m., an hour before Betsy's eye passed, electricity was off in an estimated 90,000 homes, water pressure was very low, and power lines were down everywhere.[14]

And there were odd, unexpected occurrences. The city recorded its first death when a merchant seaman's body was found "in the storm blasted wreckage of a batture shack on the banks of the Mississippi River." At the governor's mansion, not far from our motel, the chief executive's daughter had left her pet deer outside. A state trooper was sent out in the teeth of the tempest to find the poor animal and bring it into the mansion's cellar. Out on the river, the tugboat *Marian M.* sank just south of LSU's campus but all crewmen made it to shore. At the Angola state prison Betsy leveled the penitentiary's sugar cane crop, upon which it had hoped to gross $800,000. Far from Betsy's havoc it was a memorable night too. The Los Angles Dodgers' left-handed ace, Sandy Koufax, pitched a perfect 1–0 game against the Chicago Cubs to register his 22nd win of the season. He faced only 27 batters and struck out 14, including the Cubs' last six.[15]

Back at the Holiday Inn I opened the drapes sometime after 3 a.m. just in time to see a nearby drive-in theater's screen slowly lean over and take flight across the field behind the motel. The rains were torrential and the fierce winds separated the sheets of water into individual drops and drove them against the motel like BBs. Water blew in beneath our door and soaked the carpet to the middle of the room. We packed towels against the bottom of the door in a vain attempt to stem the incoming tide.

Betsy's full fury pounded us for at least two hours until 4 a.m., when her eye passed about 20 miles west of the city. The wind ceased as if it had been switched off. The interminable roar was replaced by absolute silence; the quiet was as painful as the noise had been. Inside Betsy's eye the barometric pressure was so low and the humidity so high it was hard to breathe, especially in a sealed room with no fan. Gulf States Utilities sent its crews out in the eye to begin preliminary repairs and a company spokesman later boasted they made "considerable progress."[16]

Although the hurricane's center was estimated to be only 60 to 80 miles in diameter, it seemed much larger to us; the calm seemed to last forever. When the wind suddenly shrieked anew, signaling the storm's back side, we began to think that we had survived the worst that Betsy had to throw against us. If she failed to blow our motel down despite her best efforts in the first half, she was unlikely to do so her second time around. Besides, we were exhausted; I announced I was going to bed, about the only dry spot left in the room. Roberta thought I was nuts but with all hell breaking loose just outside the door, she soon joined me and we slept through Betsy's rerun.[17]

When we woke up a couple hours later, the wind still gusted to 75 miles an hour but by contrast with what we had experienced all night, it felt merely like a breezy day. Most noticeable was the decline in the noise level; Betsy was reduced to a moderate roar that was close to tolerable. We awoke very hungry and scrambled out to see if the motel's restaurant was open.[18]

From our balcony we were mortified to see that the roof over the motel's walkway had blown off and a large section of it had landed on top of Phoebe. Luckily, it was a flat sand and tar paper roof that was not unduly heavy. It did not dent her top but functioned like sandpaper, badly scratching her paint in spots. We collected about a hundred dollars from our insurance company to have Phoebe's top repainted but we were so poor that I bought a can of touch-up paint, covered the bare spots, and pocketed the rest. A decade or so later, after the brutal southern sun had taken its toll on her paint, it was almost impossible to see the damaged areas.

We left the roof problem for later and leaned into the wind to walk to the restaurant, which was open but had no water or electricity. It was crowded with folks the Holiday Inn had allowed to spend the night on the floor. The staff, trapped there all night, had brought all the food out from the kitchen and set it out in a buffet. The selection put a European breakfast to shame, everything from deli sandwiches to the dining room's entire dessert menu. Despite the fact that the inn would have to throw it all away, it charged all the traffic would bear, double or triple its pre-storm tariffs. We felt lucky, however, to find anything to eat at all.

By noon the winds were down to 30 to 40 miles an hour with occasional gusts up to 60. We sat in our dank, miserably hot room for as long as we could stand it, using water from the bathtub to drink and to flush the commode. Baton Rouge's water pressure had fallen to almost zero because the city had no electricity to purify or pump water to its towers. We were anxious to discover the fate of our worldly possessions but the telephone lines were down. As we listened to the wind gradually subside, we finally decided to venture out to see if we still had a place to live.

We went down and cleared the debris off Phoebe and drove carefully out into the disordered world. Electrical wires snaked everywhere; trees lay across the roads; garbage cans, lawn chairs, and everything else people kept on their porches had migrated into the streets; and all stop lights were out. Fortunately not many fools ventured out and after many detours we finally reached our new home. Our trailer was tucked under our apartment which had not even lost a shingle; Mrs. B had indeed built a Betsy-proof building.

We were stunned to find that the water company had already sent someone out that morning to turn on our service. We quickly decided that it made more sense to live where we had water than where we had none; besides, it was cheaper. I made the long, convoluted drive back to the motel to check out and set out to find food. All over town grocery store employees were busy emptying their inoperative coolers and freezers and were carrying all their perishables to the curbs. The heady aromas of charcoal grills announced that families were cooking their thawing meat before it spoiled. In some neighborhoods these grill-fests went on for almost a week until power was restored. Most stores were not open but I found one on Government Street that sold me vegetables, meat, and milk they would have otherwise thrown out. I also discovered that the Baton Rouge *Morning-Advocate* had printed its edition that morning and I bought a copy. When I returned to the apartment, Roberta was all smiles; while she was cleaning the refrigerator its inside light turned on — we had water and electricity barely six hours after Betsy had ripped through town. The gods were beginning to smile on us again.

We *were* lucky; the storm had crippled Baton Rouge. Initial damage estimates for the city were around 50 million dollars while the state suffered losses of somewhere between 500 million and 1 billion dollars. Worse, the New York *Times* reported that Betsy had killed at least 63 people in Louisiana and the New Orleans coroner had in his vaults another 15 bodies he suspected were also storm victims. Most of the deaths occurred south of New Orleans where raging tides and high winds had stranded many folks who had not fled before the storm. As the winds subsided "an armada of tiny boats" began searching the state's lowlands for stranded people. The Coast Guard promised, "We're using anything that'll float — pirogues, Coast Guard boats, any kind of civilian boat."

Within twenty-four hours the "armada" had rescued 30,000 people and the Coast Guard estimated another 10,000 were still stranded.[19]

The morning after the hurricane, Baton Rouge's Mayor-President W.W. (Woody) Dumas "huddled" at the governor's mansion with Governor John McKeithen, Senator Russell Long, Representative Jimmy Morrison, and U.S. Corps of Engineers' representatives to make plans to put the city back together. President Lyndon Johnson flew to New Orleans to inspect the damage and was scheduled to come to Baton Rouge, but "lighting that was not functioning properly" at the city's Ryan Field canceled his stop. The mayor-president did talk to the president on the telephone; Johnson promised immediate financial help and that he would "do everything possible to cut red tape."[20]

The city did not wait for federal help, however. The storm had knocked out electricity except to one neighborhood, half of its stop lights were inoperative, sewer pumping stations were without power, the water company's pumps were also still, there were "lakes" beneath all the underpasses that relied on pumps to clear the water, catch basins were clogged with debris, 190 of the city's 683 long distance phone lines were knocked out (it was two days before we could inform our families that we were safe), 386 phone poles were down, and one-third of the city's phones were inoperative.[21]

All this was only an inconvenience, however; the condition of LSU's football stadium seemed the most pressing question in the city because the university's first home game was only eight days away. That contest marked the opening of the town's social season. In humid 90-plus degree heat, women in fur coats and men in suits and ties came to see and to be seen and to sweatily cheer their Tigers to victory. The local newspapers, even as Betsy's winds were still howling, sent reporters to check the 67,000 seat stadium. They found it had suffered some damage and LSU's athletic director, James Corbett, predicted "we will have a major job getting [it] in shape to play the ... game next Saturday." Translation: if nothing else gets repaired in the city, the stadium will be ready by game time.

The story about damage to LSU's stadium was nine and one-half inches long and was separated by a box in the *State-Times'* hurricane-day coverage. Across town the damage at Southern University was much worse. Winds toppled a light pole at the field and the pole "collapsed

57

about 1,000 seats [in] the stadium's new addition." Worse, the storm blew down a forty foot section of the student union's brick wall; nobody was hurt, however. Black Southern University's much more extensive damage rated just three and one-half inches buried towards the end of a long article.

While we hunkered down, put Phoebe in the garage, and moved our meager possessions into our apartment, out in the streets city and utilities workers moved with practiced speed to put the city back together. Gulf States Utilities brought in 550 men from adjacent states to attack the power outages; 30 hours after the worst of Betsy's wind, the company had restored power to about 45 percent of Baton Rouge's homes, including ours. Bell telephone called in 100 linemen from out of town to reconnect the 50,000 phones that were out of order.

Baton Rouge's department of public works put all its employees on 12 hour days and sent 150 of them with 42 garbage trucks out in the streets to pick up anything homeowners left at their curbs. Another 400 public works men fanned out to cut up the trees that had fallen over the streets and push them to the sides of the roads. Another 15 men were delegated to repair, straighten, and reset the traffic lights that had been knocked out. All the city's street sweepers were out cleaning the detritus off the roads.

One hundred National Guard troops guarded the downtown retail areas and the shopping centers to prevent looting. The sheriff's department dispatched its squad cars and paddy wagon to rescue stranded families in the city's low-lying, flooded areas and take them to storm shelters that had been opened throughout the city. The fire department answered 200 calls, most of which were complaints about downed power lines sparking and smoking. Some electrical lines under the streets had also shorted out and "a large amount of smoke" was billowing from under one of the city's busiest streets.

The city was returning to normal, however, even before Betsy said good-bye. The weather reverted to its norm, with highs in the upper 80s, lows in the mid to upper 70s, and debilitating humidity all the time. LSU's sorority rush, one of the school's most important social activities, was in full blast only 36 hours after Betsy departed. The next day the local sports pages even managed a bit of humor with the leader, "Roosevelt Falls Victim to New Deal"; it seems that New Deal, Texas, defeated rival Roosevelt, Texas, in their annual football match. The big sports news after the storm, however, was that the Kansas City Athletics bought Leroy "Satchel" Paige, who admitted to being "just a little" over 50 but who was probably closer to 59. When Satch was asked how he could win at his advanced age, he quipped, "I'll just keep my fast ball off the fat of the bat." The Athletics had nothing to lose by sending the geriatric to the mound; they were buried in last place, 37 games off the pace.[22]

Betsy saved one last surprise, though. She had played havoc with Mississippi River shipping and the Corps of Engineers reported that 200 barges and tugs had been sunk or blown aground; the debris closed the river to shipping from Baton Rouge to Plaquemine Parish at its mouth. The corps brought in 500 "specialists" with "boats, aircraft, helicopters, and specialized equipment" to clear up the wrecks and reopen the waterway.[23]

Four days later the newspapers announced that one of the missing barges "was loaded with deadly chlorine gas" that was en route from the Pittsburgh Plate Glass Chemical Division at Lake Charles to the Goodrich Chemical Company's vinyl chloride plant at Calvert, Kentucky. The corps could not find it, but mayor-president Dumas assured Baton Rouge residents there was "no immediate danger" and the U.S. Public Health Service reported that water samples taken between Carville and Baton Rouge showed no traces of chlorine.[24]

A day later, on September 14, the barge suddenly appeared a great deal more dangerous. The press explained it contained 600 tons of the chlorine which it described as "a poison gas of the type often used in World War I" and added that that tonnage could, "by Government estimates, kill 40,000 people." Dumas averred he was "concerned," but "not alarmed." The local newspaper took it more seriously. The *States-Times* revealed that a high-ranking army officer said "partial evacuation of Baton Rouge may be considered" if the missing barge was found. Another military man explained that since none of the 116,000 gas masks stored in Baton Rouge would fit children, a partial evacuation was being considered.[25]

The immediate problem was that the corps could not find the barge. It searched from Baton Rouge 150 miles south with 36 army and navy divers in water that was "so laden with silt" that they had to "grope and feel their way." The flotsam rushing down the river further threatened the divers and the barge. Finally, nine days after Betsy, divers found the barge lying under 60 feet of water right off LSU's campus.[26]

LSU's football stadium, one of Huey Long's more controversial legacies, was located close to the river, but it would have taken more than 600 tons of chlorine to ruin the season's opening football party. Despite the 90 degree temperature, 68,000 fans turned out in their fall finery to yell, cheer, cuss, and throw their empty beer and whisky bottles from the upper seats. Downtown, things were less festive; hotels and motels evicted emergency personnel who were in town to help with the cleanup to make room for visiting fans. Dumas publicly decried the practice but a few who were evicted took it philosophically. One told a reporter "we're all football fans.... We understand and there's no hard feelings." Everyone left the game happy. LSU's Tigers, under Charles McClendon, beat first-year Texas A & M coach Gene Stallings 10–0.[27]

It took much longer to beat the barge. Engineers decided it was safe so long as it was under water and they worked throughout September and October to build a huge lift frame that resembled a bridge truss. They announced they would raise the barge on November 1, but then postponed the attempt, citing the need for more preparation because the gas, should it leak out, could kill 300,000 people.[28]

A new lift date was scheduled for Friday, November 12, after a long wrangle between Baton Rouge merchants who wanted it raised on a Sunday when their stores were closed and local ministers who did not want their services interrupted. On lift day, the city was deserted; authorities had warned everyone within five miles of the barge's location, which was almost all of the city, to be ready to evacuate. Thousands left, the highways were choked, and one evacuee complained it took him four hours to make the usual ninety minute drive to New Orleans. We and Phoebe stayed at home with all the closed schools, stores, and gas stations. A giant crane began the "delicate lift job" at exactly 8 a.m. and it went without incident. After workers washed the barge with pressure hoses, inspectors found the tanks still sealed. The only damage was a dent in the barge's stern.[29]

Two days earlier, everyone within a mile of the site had been evacuated, including about "230 elderly and infirm hospital patients, many of them with heart conditions ... taken to a hospital at Pineville, La., on two special trains." There "two elderly Negro women died of heart attacks in their hospital-train bunks... as the train stood on a spur track at the hospital." They were Betsy's last fatalities — the storm was finally over. Phoebe had been baptized.[30]

PART II

The Seething Sixties

3

Steamy Red Stick

Moving to Baton Rouge in the late summer, even one without a hurricane, is not recommended for anyone whose blood is thicker than vodka. Its oppressive heat and humidity, especially noticeable inside unairconditioned Phoebe, were only the most obvious manifestations of the sub-tropical city; south Louisiana was like a foreign country to us. Everything about it was more lush, liquid, languid, odoriferous, and alive than anyplace else we had ever seen. And I had spent seven years of my life during the Korean War and after growing up on the Louisiana Ordnance Plant located in the middle of nowhere, eleven miles west of Minden and twenty-nine miles east of Shreveport. But that was scrubby, piney woods country in Anglo Louisiana. It was brutally hot there half the year but the humidity levels were much lower than in Baton Rouge and I don't remember that it rained almost every day.

Not far beneath the torpid biological swill that engulfed the state capital bubbled a cauldron of potential violence that threatened to overturn the sixty-seven year old state-wide racial segregation laws that dated back to Louisiana's infamous "grandfather clause" that prohibited anybody whose grandfather could not vote from casting a ballot. Back in the 1950s we had moved to the ordnance plant from Scarsdale, New York, where I do not recall having ever seen an African-American. Being only ten years old at the time, I assumed that racial segregation was a perfectly normal, adult arrangement. Looking back from the perspective of over a half a century I do not recall sensing any of the tensions that must have underlain that peculiar social structure. But in rural north Louisiana before the Brown decision, local racial problems were addressed quickly, often through extra-legal or illegal means.

When we arrived in the middle 1960s, even after a decade of southern racial strife, we did not immediately recognize the tensions in Baton

Rouge that threatened to destroy what was left of the Old South. Initially we were fascinated more by the area's strangeness. It was as far removed from the Hoosier heartland, upstate New York, and even the northern part of Louisiana as, say, Bhutan. We could barely understand many Baton Rouge natives whose English was as unintelligible to us as their Cajun French was to visitors from Provence. The first time I called roll in a huge class at LSU, I had the kids rolling in the aisles as I mangled the likes of Hebert, Arceneaux, Thibideaux, and Fontenot. A telephone call to Breaux Bridge, for example, when all long distance calls went through switchboards, was a hoot as the operators spoke a French patois and as far as we could tell absolutely nothing else. Roberta once answered the phone only to discover that someone named Alamo was calling from Breaux Bridge. After much confusion she finally had him spell his name — Oddla Meaux — Alamo!

Baton Rouge's culture revolved around food. Its chefs could work miracles with biological specimens yanked from bayous, ponds, gulf waters, and mud. The locals spent inordinate amounts of time eating, talking about food, rating restaurants, planning their next meal, swapping recipes, and pondering in front of seafood cases; the gustatory preoccupations of blacks, whites, and Cajuns may have helped keep racial and social storms so long at bay. It is hard to protest anything with a belly full of hot boudin.

We fell in love with south Louisiana cuisine and even though we were always broke we ate exceedingly well when $1.50 bought three dozen huge, shucked oysters. We also discovered the joys of driving Phoebe down the River Road, the back way to New Orleans, that meandered along the Mississippi River past a dozen stunning antebellum mansions separated by clusters of chemical plants. Several small-town eateries, renowned for serving some of the best seafood around, were interspersed among both types of despoilers. They turned crab and crawfish into delicacies and heaped their tables with piles of both. None of them stooped to use table cloths; one just stacked layers of newspapers under the plates and when the guests finished the waiters tore off the wet strata to prepare for the next gourmands. Juices, oil, herbs, spices, and hot water dripped everywhere.

We quickly learned that we were conspicuous when we failed to present a visage of pure ecstasy as we sucked crawfish brains out of their shells. Our first mound of heads was off-putting but we soon discovered that boiled crawfish brains, cooked in the chef's secret recipe of God knows what, probably local hanging moss and pelicans' feet, were quite tasty indeed. In our early days there we barely noticed that only white people jostled cheek to cheek around the common tables in such joints.

Not surprisingly in a state with "rice parishes," Louisianians loved anything prepared with rice. The little grain was much respected, indeed revered, while a boiled potato was as rare as an Ohioan who could pronounce LaFourche. On Roberta's regular Thursday visits to the laundromat, she struck up a friendship with the owners, a Mr. and Mrs. Dubois, who evidently spent most of their waking hours there checking on their customers' cleanliness. Mr. Dubois looked as if he had slipped off the pages of whatever magazine passed for *GQ* in Baton Rouge. Always outfitted in a white suit, white hat, and white shoes, he had made his fortune in partnership with Dudley LeBlanc, the "Hadacol King," who had sold an enormously popular patent medicine laced with twenty-five percent alcohol, a particular favorite of upstanding yet slightly ill types who needed a pick-me-up early in the morning.

The Duboises took it upon themselves to adjust our attitudes, not on race, which was never discussed with strangers, but on the much more important Louisiana culinary traditions. They cooked a memorable run of crawfish etouffe dishes for us, which they delivered in their white Cadillac to Roberta and Phoebe at their laundry. Everything they fixed was a seafood concoction built around rice, delicious beyond imagining, and much appreciated because we could stretch their dishes for two or three days' dinners, an important consideration for hungry students.

Louisianians ate so many oysters that the state ballasted its roads with the crustaceans' shells. In their lush world, full of swamps and bayous, they built their roads up high to lift them out of the muck and allow the water from the torrential, almost monsoon-like rains to drain. Huey Long had built most of Louisiana's roads and bridges in the 1930s and the state had not added many after Doctor Carl Weiss riddled him with bullets in 1935. The department of transportation used shells for roadbed substructures because they were cheaper and more readily available than gravel.

Thirty-five years after meeting the Duboises, Phoebe enjoys the cool breezes on Lake Superior, where she shows off her capacious trunk that often brought home as much Cajun cooking as it did clean laundry from the laundromat.

The perpetual dampness and stifling humidity bred a miasma of fragrant odors all year round. Camellias bloomed at Christmas, Magnolia blossoms the size of dinner plates bent the trees' limbs down, bougainvillea erupted from every crevice, and water oaks clung to their leaves throughout the winter. Seasons meant little except that a damp cold overlaid with incessant rain chilled everyone to the bone after football season. Everything seemed to grow, swell, bloom, and entwine all year round. This fact had somehow escaped my ken when I agreed to mow the lawn in return for a discount on our rent. Little did I realize that the damned grass grew all year; I never mowed so much in my life. To beat the worst of the heat and humidity I attacked the perpetually shaggy lawn as close to dark as possible and often finished unable to see where I was going.

Anything built close to the ground was prone to instantaneous decay. Structures, roads, houses, outbuildings, and graves were all raised

Baton Rouge is a long way from the snow belt but on February 23, 1968, an inch or so fell, the first there since 1961. Roberta could not resist going out to build a snowman on Phoebe's trunk.

to avoid termites, snakes, worms, caterpillars, spiders, and alligators. Primarily, however, the disconcerting elevation of everything lifted everyone, dead and alive, out of the ever-present ground water. The "wet season," as near as we could divine, lasted all year. In the winter of 1965 it rained for 92 days, not just a daily drizzle or a shower — the water pelted down. There was often six inches of water covering everything. LSU's campus was designed to use its sidewalks as storm water conduits. Everything molded; we filled our shoes and suitcases periodically with formaldehyde to kill the green fuzz that had an affinity for leather. One day it rained 12 inches in fewer than 12 hours and Baton

69

Rouge's pumps that lifted its storm water over the levees could not keep up. By noon the roads were under three feet of water. As I drove Phoebe home in the afternoon I hung my arm out of her window and rippled the surface of the water with my fingers. We did well until we were blocked by stalled cars at an intersection and had to detour down a side street to a friend's house, where I parked her on the highest part of his yard, unfortunately his flower bed. At dusk, our mailman, garbed in waders, sloshed up our driveway and apologized for being late.

His eagerness to apologize when none was necessary marked an odd south Louisiana cultural trait that always left us a bit uncomfortable. Normal discourse of the kind we were used to, marked by frequent exchanges of quips and insults, are an integral part of meeting and connecting with people. Delivered with smiles, arched eyebrows, or a pat on the back, they are inflicted equally on friends and strangers. In the sea level South a hundred years earlier, however, such sharp and often insulting palaver would have drawn a challenge to a duel. Perhaps to avoid such affairs of honor or the violence that was apt to accompany such perceived insults, folks in the lower South honed a verbal affectation that was the opposite from what we considered normal; blacks and whites over praised, were too nice, often syrupy, almost obsequious. Initially it smacked to us of phoniness or insincerity, but in the violence-prone South, on the verge of losing the last vestiges of its legal segregation, such linguistic habits helped maintain a superficial social calm.

When the civil rights movement turned more confrontational in the mid–1960s its spokesmen were increasingly unwilling to adhere to conventional southern rhetorical norms. Black leaders such as H. Rap Brown, who hailed from West Baton Rouge, Stokely Carmichael, and Malcolm X dropped the superficial soft, fuzzy nature of southern discourse and talked like Yankees. They defied, insulted, shouted, posed, and confronted to threaten the long-defined relationships between the separated races and cultures in Baton Rouge. Their language and posture frightened whites, many of whom, although quite moderate on racial questions, tolerated the KKK, bombastic local sheriffs, and thuggish cops. Most southerners refrained from publicly lowering themselves to such confrontational levels of discourse. From that posture they could with straight faces maintain that racial discord was the work of "agitators" of both races, many of them "outsiders" who did not understand the softer, kinder, more paternal nature of southern society so manifest in its speech patterns. The rabid segregationists, symbolized nationally by Alabama Governor George C. Wallace, were the shock troops dispatched to preserve the fraying social, linguistic, and economic fabric of the Deep South.

Our New York and Hoosier accents marked us as suspicious characters, especially after "Yankee freedom riders" had for years threatened to turn the southern social structures inside out. Phoebe did nothing to help us to blend into the foliage either. Her New York license plates on front and back were billboards that advertised she and her owners were outlanders. Even after we got rid of her New York plates she still sported a prominent "C. Weaver, Utica, New York" decal on her trunk that we never did figure out how to remove. Driving around in Phoebe was akin to walking down a Baton Rouge sidewalk lustily whistling "The Battle Hymn of the Republic."

We soon understood that we had moved into a small, unique racial configuration. Only a few miles to the east, near St. Francisville and to the north above Alexandria, Cajun influence gave way to Anglo-Louisiana, with which I was familiar and which was more like the rest of the South. There the dividing lines between whites and African-Americans were narrowly drawn; the races rubbed against each other without the buffers of other ethnic and religious groups that competed for political power, social advantage, and cultural superiority. The ugly underside of race relations in the WASPish parishes was much more open and frequently shaped by tacitly sanctioned violence.

Not that the state's capital was a model of racial harmony. When we arrived, eleven years after the U.S. Supreme Court's admonition to desegregate with "deliberate speed," there were still a few "colored" signs posted over doors to private businesses. As far as we could tell, however, nobody paid much attention to them. Like many river cities, Baton Rouge had grown away from the water in a series of concentric circles, like tree rings, which alternated between black and white. A black ghetto with unpaved, dusty streets lay north of town tucked up against the chemical plants, but elsewhere the well-defined residential and commercial rings forced both races to live in a proximity that fostered social and economic intercourse. We lived just east of a black neighborhood and occasionally frequented restaurants there that attracted both a black and white crowd. We did not find that the differences in food, dress, language, music, and accents among adjacent rings to be great. It was awhile, however, before we noticed that blacks did not frequent white eating establishments; integration in mid-decade was a one-way affair.

There was virtually none of it, however, in the state's institutions of higher learning. LSU was almost all white while just to the north, Southern University was virtually all African-American. The two never met, certainly not on the football field or the basketball court, where most university matters of importance in the South are settled. Soon after we arrived we drove Phoebe out to look at Southern; we were the only whites we saw on campus that day. A cursory drive through illustrated that "separate but equal" had not applied to funding the two schools. Southern's physical plant was much shabbier than LSU's, its buildings looking as if they were relics of an underfunded teacher-training college while LSU's exuded an Old South atmosphere draped with the tropical overtones manifest in its stuccoed buildings, arches, and columns. Everywhere clinging vines drooped and festooned its arcades and structures, all redolent of tropical fecundity.

Southern University might as well have been located in Lithuania as far as pedagogical matters were concerned. As a graduate student I saw no intellectual cross-fertilization between the two institutions, no attempt to share equipment, skills, books, anything. Local newspapers rarely mentioned Southern, except when it played football against Grambling College, then the sports sections of both cheered for the local blacks.

Baton Rouge and its neighboring Cajun parishes harbored not only the two races that symbolized the entire South but an additional distinct ethnic group, the Cajuns. Moreover, the large number of Catholics in the city blurred the dangerous chasms that separated the three clusters. Each party flavored this social roux with its unique religion, culture, language, and approach to life. WASPs dominated the city politically; they controlled its newspapers, both very conservative and committed to the racial status quo. Unlike Nashville or Birmingham or Richmond, however, the WASPs' power was tempered by the Cajuns, their Catholic faith, and their church. The Arcadians gloried in a more easygoing lifestyle that mocked many of the centuries-old

Protestant-Puritan prescriptions for the good, Godly life that held sway in the rest of the South. In Cajun country, where the common, unifying French language and culture partially overrode traditional black-white differences, folks reveled in the pleasures of food, music, dancing, drinking, and public display. They enjoyed living for the present and took themselves less seriously than did WASPs.

Cajuns too recognized skin color but their French heritage, which historically had featured less racial sensitivity, and their own minority status in Anglo-Protestant Louisiana, made them more prone to promote at least a racial accommodation if not equality. Cajun and black Catholics forged common links that set them at odds with the WASPs. While the Catholic Church did little to alter legally mandated racial separation, it did at the very least buffer the harsher WASP proclivities. Blacks and whites attended mass together in the same, albeit segregated, churches. They might be buried in separate sections of Catholic cemeteries, but on All Souls Day relatives of both flocked to them to lavishly decorate their ancestors' graves.

The Wards and a few others constituted a fourth element in the mix, White, Anglo, non–French, Catholic, and Yankees — WANCYs maybe. We fell between the social seams, fit nowhere perfectly but at the same time everywhere. We could pass for WASPs, speak the language of Catholics, participate in church rituals and festivities, and win some acceptance amongst more moderate blacks; our accents announced we did not drag the historical freight most white southerners brought to race relations.

Initially we had only the haziest notion of the cross-currents that were reshaping Baton Rouge society. We had little first-hand experience with the intense racial, economic, and social storms that began blowing after I had moved back to New York from northern Louisiana. We were young, in the first blush of our marriage, fortunate to have Phoebe, and ambitious to succeed in graduate school — we were neophytes, naïfs, green as the local mold. We were about to learn fast about the elemental forces that were tearing the deep South apart, thanks to Phoebe, as we stood in a muddy cow pasture watching the local Ku Klux Klan engage in its century-old rituals designed to enfold white supremacy in the cloak of Christian morality and threaten those who would dare disagree with its racial dictates.

4

The Dairy Queen Klan

In the years I lived in North Louisiana I don't recall that anyone ever mentioned race or segregation directly except to explain to me what a white boy could and could not do. Most white southerners accepted the racial world they were born into and saw racial segregation as a means to maintain discipline and order in Louisiana's multiracial and multi-ethnic society. On the ordnance plant security forces were all white, as were all the plant's salaried employees. Blacks were relegated to the lower paying, more menial tasks. In the summer of 1961 when I worked for the Louisiana state police all the force's sworn officers, at least all those I met, were white. Trustees from the state prison at Angola, both blacks and whites, performed routine chores at headquarters and lived in dormitories on the grounds behind the main building.

Segregationists spanned the spectrum from those who abhorred the institution but saw no way to abolish it without inviting social chaos to those who hated "niggers" and fervently believed the state should remain, by force and intimidation if necessary, a white province. Many of those enamored of their pale skin and the advantages it conferred joined racially exclusive fraternities such as the Ku Klux Klan. Later they supported more respectable middle class offshoots, such as the White Citizens Councils, organized to resist court-ordered integration.

Barely a month after our arrival in Baton Rouge, Roberta drove Phoebe to the grocery store on Government Street. When she returned to the car she discovered a broadside slipped under Phoebe's windshield wiper that announced a Klan meeting that night in nearby Denham Springs. In a wink Phoebe had made contact with an extremist organization whose roots went back to Christmas Eve 1865 when a half dozen ex–Confederate veterans in Pulaski, Tennessee, formed "a club to relieve their postwar boredom." According to the accepted lore, they named their organization Ku Klux, a corruption of the Greek word *kuklos,* meaning circle. Because, like many southerners, they were of Scots-Irish ancestry, they added Klan to their club's title to honor the clans of their beloved Scottish borderlands from where most of their ancestors hailed.[1]

The original six founders modeled their new creation after other organizations, especially the freemasons, kept their rituals complex and secret, devised odd and sometimes corny names for their officers, and cobbled up a "uniform" of sorts to separate themselves from outsiders who were not authorized to wear such garments — even in secret. The early Klansmen were unusually gifted at conjuring up titles to identify rank in their Invisible Empire and, with few exceptions, they preferred awkward homemade words that began with the letter K such as Klaliff, Klokard, Kludd, Kligrapp, Klabee, Kladd, Klarogo, Klexter, and so on. The Klan met once a year in an Imperial Klonvokation, presided over by the Imperial Wizard, and attended by the Grand Dragons, leaders of the state Klaverns. They still retained some of their secret acronyms when they invited Phoebe to be their guest. To the initiated KIGY meant "Klansman, I Greet You." The less sonorous SAN BOG was a warning "Strangers Are Near, Be On Guard." If the Klan had not been so hateful, brutal, and divisive, its mumbo jumbo would have been funny.[2]

The Klan became less humorous and fun-loving when it came out of the closet in 1866. Initiates draped themselves and their horses in sheets and paraded through Pulaski where they frightened people, especially newly freed slaves, many of whom thought the Klan riders were ghosts of dead Confederates returned to haunt them. The KKK soon became violent as it spread across the war-torn, poverty-stricken South severely hobbled by Reconstruction politics, and scared blacks away from polling places or ensured that they and suspect whites voted "correctly." In 1867 General Nathan Bedford Forrest, only recently discharged from President Jefferson Davis' cavalry, was elected Grand Wizard and his KKK functioned as a police force as it assumed the judicial powers of enforcement and punishment. Radical Republican Reconstruction, in which civil governments were swept away across the South and replaced in many places by the U.S. Army's "colored troops," put the South under martial law in 1867; the political and racial tumult only served to increase the KKK's popularity. Other groups, such as the Pale Faces and the Knights of the White Camellia, joined the KKK on night rides and flogged, tortured, and occasionally killed both blacks and whites tainted with being radicals, carpetbaggers, scalawags, uppity freedmen, Unionists, or anything else that displeased them. They probably would not have liked Phoebe either; the name Chevrolet was foreign.[3]

Republican congressmen watched as the secret bands roamed the South, mostly at night, and threatened the Radicals' hopes for a new South that professed legal and social equality. Finally, in 1870 and 1871, Congress passed the Ku Klux Klan acts to uphold the recently passed 14th and 15th amendments. Forrest, who was dismayed at the turn his Klan had taken, formally disbanded the KKK in 1869, but it required the federal sanctions that outlawed masked riders and illegal nighttime activities to destroy it.[4]

Southern states then devised novel methods to disfranchise blacks and some poor whites who threatened to upset the post-Reconstruction social and political structure dominated by conservative white Democratic Bourbons. The Populist party threatened their patchwork system of racial repression in the late 1880s when it attempted to unite poor whites and blacks against their betters to win political control of the states. Starting in 1890 the ruling white Bourbons rewrote their state constitutions to legally disfranchise most blacks and many poor whites. It took eighteen years for the eight Deep South states to rework their legal codes to "purify" their electoral systems and to expand their Jim Crow laws to blanket their region with segregation.[5]

Against the backdrop of state-mandated racial segregation, a North Carolinian, Thomas Dixon, Jr., who attended Wake Forest College and later John Hopkins graduate school where he was a classmate of Thomas Woodrow Wilson, revived the Klan. Dixon had a checkered career and was at various times an actor, politician, Baptist preacher, lecturer, and writer. His book, *The Klansman, An Historic Romance of the Ku Klux Klan,* published in 1905 tells a syrupy story of an evil Reconstructionist Yankee congressman, very much like Thaddeus Stevens, bent on punishing the South by uplifting the black race.

The upshot of his efforts is that a black man, "gleaming apelike as he laughed" rapes a white girl who later kills herself. The KKK takes up her cause, gains revenge, and "in the end God's justice is done, Civilization is saved, and the South redeemed from shame."[6]

Dixon turned his book into a stage play and several touring companies took it on the road. D.W. Griffith bought the movie rights from Dixon for twenty-five percent of the profits. Griffith brilliantly put together a story that featured huge Civil War battles, lustful blacks, and hooded horsemen who rode to the girl's rescue, all with a score heavy on Wagnarian music; Dixon suggested the movie be retitled *The Birth of a Nation*.[7]

Many of the new century's political progressives hated the film and thought it "inflammatory." But former historian President Wilson, after a special White house screening, proclaimed, "It is like writing history with lightning" and added, "It is all so terribly true." The movie was scheduled to open in Atlanta in the fall of 1915 and Dixon, who had become a fraternal organizer, concocted a scheme to resurrect the Klan on opening night. He was more interested, however, in profits from initiation fees and selling Klansmen insurance than he was in enforcing American morals and racial stratification. On Thanksgiving night 1915, Dixon and his followers hauled a cross to the top of Stone Mountain, Georgia, erected a crude altar, performed some ritual mumbo jumbo, and set the cross ablaze. Its flames could be seen for miles; the Klan was back.[8]

The KKK was relatively impotent for several years until the end of World War I brought in its wake strikes, fear of immigrants, communists, socialists, labor unions, blacks who had worked in northern armaments factories, Jews, Catholics, all the moral changes that accompanied the popularity of the jazz age, and the automobile. Dixon hired Klan recruiters who spread out across the countryside and kept the organization's money machine well oiled. The KKK was also popular outside the South, especially in Midwestern states like Indiana where there were few blacks but numerous Catholics, Jews, flappers, foreigners, tipplers, and big city sinners.

Louisiana's large Catholic population dampened the Klan's popularity but it had widespread appeal in the Protestant northern part of the state. Klansmen so often resorted to violence, however, that they often defeated their purposes, while scandals on the national level in the 1920s injured their reputation for upholding Christian morality. In 1919 two of the Klan's recruiters, a man and a woman, were arrested in Atlanta "somewhat less than fully clad and sober" in a speakeasy raid that made the national news. A half a dozen years later, Indiana's Grand Dragon, David C. Stephenson, was convicted of second degree murder for the kidnap, torture, rape, and death of his secretary. At its zenith in the 1920s the Klan claimed about five million members, but the recurring exposés drove nationwide Klan membership down to only about 9,000 by 1930.[9]

While these developments all had only an indirect effect on Phoebe, they had a much more significant one on Huey Long. He made his first run for governor of Louisiana in 1924, and although he did not like what the Klan stood for, he waffled while his two opponents publicly opposed it; Huey came in third. He learned fast, however, and two years later when a wet Catholic senator he supported ran for reelection, Huey rallied his Protestant allies against the Klan to return the senator to Washington, D.C.[10]

The KKK remained relatively impotent during the depression. Its sporadic alignment with the German-American Bund, a crypto–Nazi outfit, did little to endear it to the public after Pearl Harbor was bombed. In 1944 the Internal Revenue Service struck hard at the Invisible Empire and placed a lien on its assets for over $685,000 to pay taxes due on the profits it made during the 1920s; the Klan disbanded for the war's duration. It was reborn in Atlanta in 1946 and the following year New York and California banned it and U.S. Attorney General Tom Clark put it on his list of subversive organizations. Small Klaverns sprang up across the South but the Klan organization was anything but monolithic.[11]

The *Brown v. Board of Education of Topeka* decision in May 1954 that ordered desegregation, the 1955 Montgomery Bus boycott that brought Martin Luther King Jr., to prominence, and the 1957 integration by bayonet of Central High School in Little Rock breathed new life into the southern Klans. In the four years after the *Brown* decision some 530 acts of racial violence, although not all Klan inspired, blazed across the South. Klans favored clandestine bombings, especially of black churches and homes. Louisiana suffered relatively few such cowardly activities; although in 1962 Shreveport's Klan bombed both homes of a prominent local black leader and wrecked a black Masonic lodge. A year later a solo bomb exploded on LSU's campus.[12]

Even with all the 1950s racial turmoil, the Klans did not achieve the popularity or size they had enjoyed thirty years earlier. By 1965 when we and Phoebe were invited to burn crosses, the Klan was already in decline across the lower South as more moderate local politicians, prodded by the federal government and the changing national mood, often withheld their support or publicly attacked the KKK. The Anti-Defamation League estimated that the "provable" nationwide Klan membership in 1965 was about 10,000 and guessed that another 25,000 to 30,000 southerners were affiliated with other racist groups. The Klans were organizationally splintered and often spent as much time opposing each other as they did trying to hold the line against "color mixing." Louisiana was not a hotbed of Klan activity in the 1960s; its biggest hate organization was the Original Knights of the Ku Klux Klan with perhaps a thousand statewide members.[13]

By the mid–1960s the Klan had become an urban phenomenon, drawing its members from "rednecks" and factory workers who had recently moved into towns from the surrounding countrysides. A sociological study done in 1959 found that the KKK "could best be understood more as a status than a resistance movement." Those who donned the robes occupied ambiguous and insecure social positions, somewhere between the middle and working classes, the same anxious types that had flocked to Adolph Hitler's Brown Shirts thirty-five years before. Klansmen had a "middle-class identification but without its prestige occupations and status." They were "still partially uprooted and only partly assimilated." Their attempts to gain self-prestige centered around their emphasis on their differences with blacks, the very people with whom they were often in direct economic competition. Sociologists found the typical Klansman "was usually a day laborer, a mechanic, or an industrial worker." His leader in the Invisible Empire, they asserted, "probably owned a one-pump gas station and general store, or was a deputy sheriff, an unemployed lightning rod salesman, or sold storm windows." Ironically, the KKK opposed integration most forcefully in areas of the South that had the fewest blacks. It was weakest in the traditional black belt areas, those counties with African-American populations as high as ninety percent.[14]

This was the world that created Phoebe and these were the people who invited her to their Klavern's public meeting in Denham Springs. We wondered why anyone would leave such a flyer on a car with New York license plates on both its front and back, unless the white robed contingent was bent on conducting a ritual human sacrifice. We were most curious, however, and jumped at the chance to observe a gathering that we expected to become an historical rarity.

We did not like the idea of driving Phoebe into the middle of nowhere at night with her orange and blue plates flashing like neon signs to announce, long before our accents did, that the outsiders who had brought all these troubles to the heart of the southland had arrived. Quite honestly we were a bit afraid of people who lurked incognito under cover of costumes and darkness in out-of-the-way back roads so isolated they were almost imperceptible gray lines on the map. We needed our own cover and called a new-found graduate-student couple to give us a ride and speak for us once we got there — we intended to act like mutes. The husband, George Walker, the proud possessor of a very fine north Louisiana accent, hailed from Monroe, where his

Roberta and Phoebe still look good forty years after the KKK invited both to attend their rally in Denham Springs.

80

father was president of what was then Northeast Louisiana University. More important, he had a car with Louisiana license plates.

It rained all that day — it often rains all day in Baton Rouge — and by nightfall it was darker than the inside of a cow. Denham Springs was a small town fourteen miles east of the capital, sitting on the edge of the strawberry parishes, a Protestant domain demographically similar to North Louisiana. The town long had a reputation for harboring the Klan. One of the first things we had heard after we arrived in Baton Rouge was to stay away from Denham Springs, because many of its 6,000 souls were rabid racists. It was rumored that the KKK was headquartered at the local Dairy Queen; I always thought it quaint that the man who pulled soft ice cream for long lines of waiting children might in his other life be the local Kleagle, Great Titan, Grand Dragon, or something equally sinister.

The gathering was scheduled to be held outside town and our invitation included a crude map marking a cow pasture. There was little need for written directions, however, for when we neared Denham Springs a fully gowned and hooded Klansman suddenly stepped out of the blackness waving his flashlight. A ghostly apparition, he was the only object visible in the utter darkness. He motioned us onward where we were picked up by another, also in full regalia, who indicated we should turn right on a road so narrow that it looked as if it had been lifted from the west of Ireland and plunked down in rural Louisiana. It was a paved two-lane but only wide enough for one and a quarter cars to pass. We were signaled on by a procession of flashlight wielding "knights" who parked us in the mud on the side of the road at the end of a long line of cars. We knew at once that we had been right to leave Phoebe at home.

On my immediate right a sharecropper's shack stood starkly outlined on a treeless rise in the middle of its fields. An automobile that appeared driveable was parked directly in front of it, suggesting that the family was at home or not far away. Yet not a single light burned in the house. Odds were the family was black and did not want to draw attention to itself. I soon stopped worrying about the sharecropper as I was almost blown down by a blast of amplified welcoming music that came from over a rise somewhere ahead. Played loud enough to shake the sharecropper's windows and to be heard all the way to the Denham Springs Dairy Queen, its chorus announced the night's theme:

Ship them niggers north boys,
Ship them niggers north.
If they don't like our southern way of life,
Ship them niggers north.

We knew we had found the place. We joined the other guests, or whatever Klan hangers-on are called, and walked slowly up the wet road towards the music's source. At the top of the hill we found ourselves face to face with a pickup truck that had a huge speaker mounted on top, while to our left about thirty Klansmen, who sometimes called themselves ghouls, and for good reason on a night that dark, were spread out across the wet pasture in front of three unlighted crosses, one rather tall and the others shorter. None of the Klanspeople seemed to be doing anything other than chatting; it resembled a typical suburban outdoor cookout, except that all the guests were dressed in outlandish costumes. Most of the visitors were still straggling up the road or gathered around a small souvenir stand that hawked right-wing racist literature and the record that was still playing. The *Ship Them Niggers North* song cost a dollar and would have been useful in my history classes but we hated to give the Klan any money and decided to forego possession.

The audience was a motley collection of maybe fifty damp, hot, white people, most of whom, judging from their vigorous applause, were enthusiastic supporters of the Klan's principles and in tune with the Invisible Empire's musical tastes. For some reason, as I look back on it decades later, I picture the people there as physically smaller than average; perhaps I was standing on a hillock. Or, more likely, I was so stunned to see that people like that *really* existed that they shrank as I looked at them in wonder.

I was surprised to see so many robed women and children there. Apparently this Klan was family-friendly, to appropriate a trite phrase popular a quarter of a century later. The admixture of ages and gender, however, made the occult practitioners appear less threatening; instead they looked decidedly ludicrous. The children, even the very young ones, costumed in full regalia that included pointed wizard hats and face masks, cavorted all over the field as normal kids are wont to do. And as in every backyard in America, their parents, also fully robed, yelled at them to "calm down," "come back here," and "straighten up." It was a bizarre sight.

The self-professed ghouls had brought along their lawn chairs, the ubiquitous aluminum ones with cross-hatched nylon webbing. They gave the scene its only touch of color; everything else stood in a stark black and white contrast, their white robes silhouetted against the night's pitch blackness. Most Klansmen and women remained seated the whole time, perhaps to claim their chairs or because they were tired from working all day, or maybe sitting was a part of their Klankraft, their official rules and rites. Seated and sprawled about awaiting the start of the ceremonies, the Klanfamilies appeared tired or lazy, not angry and threatening.

The scene was lighted with enough flaming torches to cast an eerie glow across the humid and hazy field. The flames pushed the darkness to the outer fringes around us and brought us all together. It is a scene that every summer camp counselor knows by heart. I could not help but be struck, however, by the torches — oil cans attached to the top of what appeared to be broomsticks or hoe handles. Inside rolls of toilet paper that had been soaked in gasoline or kerosene burned, very effective devices that put out a good deal of light and stayed lighted through the whole affair. I was struck, however, by the fact that every torch used Quaker State Oil cans, which seemed a most inappropriate corporate and religious choice. I doubt many Friends were ever tempted by the Klan's enthusiasms and, while the KKK had prospered in Pennsylvania in the 1920s, it was quite moribund in the Keystone state by the 1960s. On the other hand, it should have been quite easy to find the gas station owner in Denham Springs who was a Klansman, for Quaker State oil was not that common.

I had always pictured Klansmen as grubby, unwashed characters who oozed out of the social peripheries for their night time revels and disappeared at dawn's first light. The Denham Springs denizens, however, kept their robes quite neat and clean; they obviously took great pride in their appearance. Their Klan regalia may have been the best clothes they owned. They were soiled only where their hems had dragged on the muddy ground. A high percentage of the Klanspeople were smokers and they puffed away throughout the proceedings. To do so they had to raise their masks, which compromised their anonymity, especially since they had to continue to hold their masks up to exhale. Had we hailed from around Denham Springs we would have had no trouble recognizing who was hiding beneath those carefully ironed robes.

The Klavern's leader warmed us up to set the mood for the evening's featured speaker. I don't remember much of what he specifically said, but his general theme was that he was angry at America's loss of morality as its society became racially intermixed; the "niggers," one of his favorite words, were of course responsible for all the nation's ills and the cure was simple — the white race had to take its nation back. Somehow whites had "lost" the country, just like America had "lost" China in 1949, and it had to be found and whitened. As I listened to his simple but loud — for he used the sound truck to amplify his speech lest anyone miss a single charming detail — speech, I kept wishing I could resurrect Charles Darwin; he would have been appalled at how his well-meaning disciples, in this case those who had never read a word he had written and would bristle at being labeled evolutionists, espoused an extended and mangled version of his theory.

The local Klansman finally introduced the night's speaker, "all the way from New Orleans," a man whose name I had never heard, but who, it transpired, was the head of Louisiana's draft board. Much later I looked up the state's draft board and discovered it was headquartered in Jackson Barracks in the Crescent City. Its head that year is listed as one General Erbon Wise, who appears elsewhere in Phoebe's story. If he gave the keynote address that night, he was not in uniform. A draft official's participation, however, may explain why Louisiana and other states sent a disproportionately high percentage of blacks to fight and die in Viet Nam, a war that was becoming an explosive national issue as I listened to this state worthy.

The draft-man was much more sophisticated than the local speaker as he railed against members of the state's Washington, D.C., delegation for their softness on racial issues. He particularly singled out Thomas Hale Boggs, his own New Orleans' congressman, who he claimed was one of the principal culprits behind the mongrelization of the United States. Boggs, who served split terms in the House, first from 1940 to 1942 and later from 1946 until his disappearance in an Alaskan plane crash in October 1972, was hardly progressive on racial or social matters. He joined other southern congressmen to vote against the 1964 Civil Rights Act; to have done otherwise would have been political suicide. The congressman did, however, vote for the 1965 voting rights bill that President Lyndon Johnson signed on August 6, 1965, just a few weeks before the Denham Springs gathering. That act outlawed literacy and other voters' tests and authorized the federal government to oversee elections wherever fewer than one-half of voting-age residents were registered or voted. That may not have been enough to raise the speaker's hackles; perhaps he just hated anyone like Boggs who was a Phi Beta Kappa.

His other whipping boy was James Hobson Morrison, better known to his Sixth Congressional District voters as "Jimmy." Hailing from Hammond, Louisiana, Morrison was elected to Congress in 1942 and he was still there twenty-three years later. He belonged to that hardy band of perpetually reelected southern Democrats who wielded power in Congress and brought home cartloads of pork. Like Boggs, Morrison did not support the 1964 Civil Rights Act but he did vote for the Voting Rights Act. That decision may have cost him his seat; a year later, John Rarick, a right-wing upstart with Klan support, ousted Morrison by dint of paying the fees to list an obscure Jimmy Morrison with a different middle initial on the Democratic primary ballot. The two Morrisons split the Morrison vote and Rarick slipped into a run-off, one of the nastiest in the state's often tempestuous political history, and defeated the real Morrison.[15]

The gist of the state draft official's overly long speech was that he did not like anything and everything was going to hell; his comfortable and somehow biblical world in which the two races knew their places was crumbling and local politicians who ought to have known better openly abetted the changes that violated God's natural laws. After he finally wound down to enthusiastic applause, the Klansmen gathered near the crosses for the lighting. They extinguished their torches and the night they had held at bay instantly enveloped us; in their white robes they suddenly did appear ghoulish. They lighted the crosses and stepped back, better to see the blazing Christian symbols that they hoped would make the world safe for the white race. Nothing happened. They again closed ranks around the crosses and relighted them. Once more they backed away and watched as the little flames flickered out. I could only conclude that God had heard something in that cow pasture that displeased him. My theory gained substance as an unseen hand extinguished the flames in each of several further attempts. It was almost fun. Finally an enterprising Dairy Queen ghoul brought up a bucket of some flammable liquid and slopped it over the burlap-wrapped crosses. This time they blazed and licked high into the night sky and brought to mind all the old photographs I had seen of menacing Klansmen standing around *their* fiery crosses and here I was with them.

We remained until the fires began to die down and then walked back down the pitch-black road. Only then did we speak; Roberta and I had been absolutely silent during the whole rally. I noticed the share-cropper's car was still parked outside his shack, which was still cloaked in total darkness. I wondered if people were hiding inside, and if so, what they thought when they saw the blazing crosses. I hoped they understood that the country was moving away from the racial princi-ples those crosses up on the hill symbolized.

Phoebe's connection with the Invisible Empire, however tenuous, did not end with that night, however. The Klan soon came to visit us. In October 1965, a month after the Denham Springs Konvokation, the U.S. House Un-American Activities Committee began public hearings on the KKK. HUAC paraded 187 witnesses, examined thousands of documents, and interrogated the leaders of seven major Klans. Most Klansmen took the fifth amendment and two of them who refused to surrender subpoenaed documents were fined and sentenced to a year in jail for contempt. The committee discovered that the Klans hid behind innocuous fronts such as "hunting clubs, rescue squads, or even ladies' sewing circles." It was common knowledge all over the South that gun clubs were frequently KKK fronts. The negative publicity angered some Klan members but its long-run effect was to convince many to drop out of the organization. By the end of the decade the Klans across the South were in rapid decline.[16]

They were still active around Denham Springs and Baton Rouge, however. One night, not long after our visit with the torches and drag-ons, we heard noises in our front yard. We did not get out of bed because we would have had to go downstairs and outside to see what was going on. We had taped tinfoil over all our west windows to enable our two air conditioners to keep our apartment tolerably cool and thus we could not see the street.

The next morning we found a burned cross lying in our front yard. It was not a large one, probably not over six feet high. It had been jammed into the lawn and set afire; sometime later it fell over. We couldn't quite believe it was real and meant for us. Mr. and Mrs. B were staunchly southern and although perfectly satisfied with their segregated world, were much too bright to truck with the Klan. The sociologist who lived in front of us did suffer from the stigma of being a professor and an outsider but she was a Canadian and as politically oblivious as anyone we had ever met. That left us and more particularly Phoebe. Our garage, which had no door, was directly at the end of the driveway in full view of the road. We guessed that someone spotted Phoebe's license plate, assumed we were outsiders related however tenuously to those responsible for destroying everything southerners held dear, and decided to frighten us.

The explanation we wanted to believe was that some kids had been out fooling around with crosses and matches, but somehow it appeared less random than that to us. I mentioned it to an old family friend, Colonel Murphy Roden, who was superintendent of the state police, and his advice was succinct, something like "boy, get those plates off that car." I sped down to the license office where the waiting room was integrated and my recollection is that I was the only white person there. A woman I could not see sitting in a cubicle down the hall called people back to fill out their forms and pay. Every few minutes she would yell "auntie so-and-so" or "uncle so-and-so" and a black would walk back to her. My initial thought was that this woman had more damned relatives than most people and all their licenses came due on the same day. I couldn't have been more naive; when she finally called Mr. Ward, her first non-relative, I found that she was white; my presumptive world crumbled as I realized that in southern Louisiana whites commonly called older blacks "auntie" and "uncle," addresses they thought endearing; I did not recall ever hearing those terms used in the north Louisiana of my youth. Switching plates was no great hardship though; Louisiana's were good for two years and cost all of six bucks, a small enough tax to pay to keep the Kluxers out of my front yard before they did something worse.

The license bureau was a microcosm of evolving Baton Rouge race relations. It was integrated; we all came in through the same front door, waited to take our turns irrespective of color, filled out the same forms, paid the same fees, and left by that same door. Doors were still important in semi-segregated Baton Rouge — they were everywhere. Public buildings had extra doors, doors hard to find, doors in the back, doors upon more doors for washrooms, all labeled. The door a person used defined him and his place in that society. Everyone was careful about the portals they entered. Roberta's employer, for example, had a medical practice in an office that had one waiting room in the front and another in the back. Soon after we arrived he integrated both rooms but was stuck with a physical layout with public doors located on opposite sides of his building. After I shinnied up an electrical conduit to unbolt the colored entrance sign for him, blacks continued to use the back door and whites the front. Even though the back door opened directly onto his parking lot, whites continued to walk all the way around the building to sit in their accustomed waiting room out of habit and fear. It would have been interesting to see how long it would have been before some brave soul ventured to test the previously "wrong" door, but the doctor soon moved to a new office with only a front door and a single waiting room.

Those robed folks hanging around the Denham Springs Dairy Queen probably still called older blacks "auntie" and "uncle" in all public places and were livid at the idea of mixed waiting rooms and the disappearance of designated doors. The disappearing doors were proof-positive that the separatist racial society the KKK championed was crumbling even faster than the Klan. The ghouls could invite Phoebe to wet pastures to sing racist songs, burn crosses, applaud incendiary speakers, and even fire up a cross or two in private yards, but the reality was that the private and public faces of racism were slowly changing. By the mid–1960s racial hatred still lurked in many hearts but not in as many of Baton Rouge's doorways.

5

Long Hot March

The assassinations of Robert F. Kennedy and Martin Luther King in 1968 ignited one hundred and twenty-five race riots in twenty-nine states across the country. That year's report of the National Advisory Commission on Civil Disorders, headed by Governor Otto Kerner of Illinois, blamed the riots on white racism, the Tet offensive in Viet Nam gave the lie to President Lyndon Johnson's propaganda that America was winning the war, and the election of Richard M. Nixon to the presidency promised to solve none of America's wracking problems. The year was unforgettable.

What was forgotten in all the tumult was that the nation had been practicing civil disorder for several years, public debate was already rancorous, the races had further divided, the young had flocked to activist politics, and United States' political leaders appeared helpless to muster the courage to get out of the war and enforce the equal provisions of the laws that were already on the books.

A year earlier we drove Phoebe to what threatened to be yet another example of public racial chaos, the concluding rally of a violence-prone civil rights march from Bogalusa to Baton Rouge. The capital's newspapers, national news magazines, and television news had all been saturated with stories chronicling the breakdown of civil order that year, first with the six-day Newark riot in mid–July 1967, and then the unforgettable and frightening destruction of Detroit from July 23rd to the 30th which left the Motor City looking like Hamburg, Germany, after the allies had bombed it into rubble during World War II. By the time the rioters were spent, Detroit counted 40 people dead, 2,000 injured, and 5,000 homeless. It would have been worse had not President Johnson ordered 4,700 paratroopers to help local authorities squelch the rampage. Thirty years later the great swath of damage was still evident along Woodward Avenue; once the city's central artery, it was flanked with blocks of empty lots.

When racial disorders erupted in Louisiana and Baton Rouge the following month the whole nation, and indeed the world, was polarized and edgy. In Africa, Biafra had broken away from Nigeria that May, instigating a bloody conflict that raged for years. Some whites in the United States pointed to the African civil war as proof that blacks were incapable of self-government and required the protection and stability segregation offered. Some American blacks, however, applauded Africans who fought for their own destinies rather than waiting passively for change.[1]

The Viet Nam war reinforced blacks' resentment; on the television news programs they watched a disproportionate number of black soldiers suffer and die. Johnson assured the nation that U.S. troops

It was still a white corporate world in the mid–1960s as this cover illustration on Phoebe's owner's guide indicates. The enthusiastic white family behind the Impala convertible sport healthy suntans befitting a prosperous couple with the leisure to frolic in the sun with their top down.

were giving their lives to make South Viet Nam democratic and free, while those same liberties were denied blacks at home. Moreover, after American black soldiers served their thirteen-month tours in Viet Nam they were often immediately mustered out only to find that they were once again second-class citizens in their own homeland.

Louisiana's political and racial problems provided a fertile seedbed for violence on the 1967 Bogalusa civil rights march; even Baton Rouge's first line of defense was on the verge of revolt. Mayor-President W.W. Dumas, who had just returned from an appraisal of "riot-torn Detroit" had, at the behest of a city-parish bi-racial committee, proposed to integrate the capital city's police department. It had 271 sworn officers, fourteen of whom were black. They were not assigned to traffic divisions, however, and Dumas proposed to put them in integrated two-man patrol cars. The department's white officers were adamant that was not going to happen and formed the Baton Rouge Police Association on August 12 which announced that every officer would walk out if Dumas ordered blacks into patrol cars. The cops claimed they had the support of other local police departments and the general public. They also implied that they were backed by Congressman Rarick, who had addressed their organization behind closed doors. The Bogalusa march, fraught with portents for violence, was on its way to the capital while Baton Rouge's police department threatened to join it in the streets.[2]

On the state level, Governor John McKeithen, a racial moderate, was seeking reelection and the public interpreted his every move during the march in light of the forthcoming Democratic primary. The winner of that tally was certain to claim the governor's chair because the Republicans had no chance to carry the general election. McKeithen faced four primary opponents, but Rarick, "a former state district judge and the state's newest congressman," was his only serious competition. In her forty years Phoebe has had only two political stickers affixed to her bumper. The first was for McKeithen in his race against Rarick, a contest we won. We put the sticker on Phoebe not because McKeithen was a liberal energetically supporting civil rights, but because he was less il-liberal than anyone else in the race. The governor understood that times were changing and it was folly to buck them. He pushed for court-ordered integration as fast as possible as long as he could avoid conflict and violence. Like Lyndon Johnson, McKeithen believed reasonable people could always sit down together to achieve reasonable goals. Phoebe's other bumper sticker supported Albert Gore, Senior, three years later when William Brock challenged for his Tennessee Senate seat; we lost that contest.[3]

McKeithen's plan to prevent violence in 1967 was to play "good cop, bad cop" with the Bogalusa marchers and the public. In the media he belittled and threatened the demonstrators with jail if they broke the law while at the same time he took all possible steps to ensure that they would not be assaulted along the route. He wanted to prevent another Detroit and keep federal troops out of his state, but at the same time he did not want to alienate his relatively moderate white, Protestant constituents. He was on a political tightrope as the election approached.

The threat to the governor's political aspirations and the capital's calm arose from racial conditions in Bogalusa, a city of 21,423 in 1960, situated on the Pearl River on Louisiana's "toe," right across from Crossroads, Mississippi. A tough paper-mill town in Rarick's congressional district, Bogalusa had a history of racial unrest and Klan activity. Two years earlier James Farmer, head of the Congress of Racial Equality, had launched a drive to promote voter registration, integration, and better job opportunities there. The town exploded. Blacks were beaten and their houses burned, nightly marches were held, rabble rousers such as J.B Stoner addressed thousands of whites to stir the hate and violence, the Klan patrolled Bogalusa's streets at night, and blacks organized the Deacons for Defense to protect themselves.[4]

In 1965 the Bogalusa Klan publicly dissolved — to circumvent court injunctions and what it termed FBI harassment — and reformed as the Anti-Communist Christian Association under whose banner it continued to stir up racial conflict in the divided city for two more years. White resistance to black demands was encouraged in the summer of 1967 when the state legislature's Joint Legislative Committee on Un-American Activities gave the state's Klan a "clean bill of health" and declared it a "political action group" with "a certain Halloween spirit." The committee, which had held its only hearing on June 16, "without public notice," declared the Klan "was no more secret than Masonic groups or the Knights of Columbus" and "found no illegal activities in connection with the group." The committee concluded that the KKK, which it said claimed between 18,000 and 19,000 members in the state, "fills the need for citizens to express 'frustration with the current national administration.'"[5]

With political support on the state level, the Klan remained active in Bogalusa and helped thwart black aspirations. A. Z. Young, head of the city's Civic and Voters League, decided to escalate the struggle for black equality by taking the fight statewide. He announced league members would march one hundred and six miles to Baton Rouge to conduct a voter registration drive and present their demands to Governor McKeithen. The announcement of Young's march appeared in the New York *Times* a day before it did in the Baton Rouge newspapers.[6]

McKeithen feared violence might ensue, for the league planned to walk through some of the state's most staunchly racist areas. The governor's initial response was to assume the mantle of a "bad cop." He proclaimed the whole thing "absolutely silly and ridiculous" and promised he would not meet with the blacks because he planned to "be in church" where "they should be." He was tough with both sides, though. He warned that the "color blind" state police "would arrest anyone who stirs up trouble." McKeithen also assumed a wounded air, claiming that if asked he would have been happy to go to Bogalusa, as he had in the past, to discuss black demands. He reminded everyone that Young and his aide Robert Hicks "had been flown to Baton Rouge in the past to discuss Negro grievances" and that "every Negro, every person in the state knows that all he has to do is call up the governor's office for an appointment and I'll be glad to see them [*sic*]." In light of his openness, he believed "these two men are leading the march just to bring themselves publicity with the hope they can create an incident [to] cause chaos and anarchy."[7]

Young and Hicks were seeking publicity, but their subsequent actions over the march's eleven days indicated they bent every effort to keep their demonstration peaceful. They started out on a muggy, ninety-plus degree Thursday, August 10, about a hundred strong, chanting and singing down highway 21 towards Covington. Hard rains overnight lowered the temperature into the seventies the following day when about seventy-five marchers gathered in front of the Money Hill tung oil tree plantation (whose manager had parked his car across the plantation's entrance to keep them out) to continue their walk to Covington.[8]

The marchers reached there by nightfall. The next morning 115 blacks gathered to walk twelve miles along route 190 to the village of Robert. About forty-five of them stopped at Covington's city limits while the remaining 70 "plodded steadily ... through southeast Louisiana forest lands," escorted by "helmeted state police on horseback" to Hammond. During the day Young vowed that the marchers would "squat" on the capitol's steps until McKeithen agreed to meet them.[9]

At nightfall, the league held a rally while seven miles away at Ken's Riverside Service Station, several carloads of blacks approached a knot of white men standing outside and asked for beer. Eyewitness accounts varied, but the whites claimed the blacks fired at them with shotguns, rifles, and pistols. Several whites "grabbed guns from the bar-service station" and returned fire. Five whites were wounded and the police arrested ten blacks, including two women. The news hit Baton Rouge like a thunderbolt, for this was exactly what McKeithen had feared, the first blood had been drawn. The superintendent of state police, Thomas Burbank, Murphy Roden's successor, hastened to the governor's mansion and then rushed out to take personal command of his troopers at the scene.[10]

The following morning McKeithen declared that "the backers of the civil rights march had accomplished one of their purposes: 'To get somebody shot and get a lot of publicity.'" He promised "there's going to be a considerable group go [*sic*] to the penitentiary." Young "denied that any of his followers took part in the shooting," while the local sheriff, trying to keep the lid on an explosive situation, claimed that several of the arrested blacks were only "curiosity marchers," not members of the regular "walking force."[11]

On Monday, Young, clad in his uniform of blue overalls and wearing a straw hat, led his marchers out to route 190 again. As they walked through the hamlet of Baptist a crowd of about a hundred whites stood around a filling station and grocery store watching them. One shouted, "Why don't you let them march at night?" At dark the march stopped near Albany, just inside Livingston Parish, a noted Klan area, where the New York *Times* announced that "fiery crosses, a symbol of the Klan, were burned" while the marchers were in town. The next day as the league members walked towards the little hamlet of Holden the first violence directly associated with the march erupted when about twenty white men appeared alongside the road. The state police stopped the marchers and walked up to the whites when suddenly they bolted through police lines and "engaged in a brief but fierce fist fight with Negro marchers."[12]

Livingston Parish, home of the Dairy Queen Klan that had invited Phoebe two years earlier to attend its rituals, lived up to its racial billing on the following day. As the marchers, protected by 150 state troopers, plodded along on the left side of the highway towards Satsuma, only a couple of miles outside Denham Springs, they saw about 100 white men, three abreast, marching down the right side of the road towards them. As the two groups passed each other, the whites rushed the police lines to attack the blacks. The police fought them back with billy clubs and rifle butts, leaving several whites bloodied, and arrested nine of them for disturbing the peace. Unlike the other acts of violence, this one appeared to have been well planned.[13]

The march's leaders decided to take Thursday off. Burbank tried to convince Young to skip the rest of his march through Livingston Parish to avoid Denham Springs and restart it in East Baton Rouge Parish where the marchers would find a less hostile reception. Young must have intimated his assent, for when he announced late Thursday that his marchers would walk all the way, including through Denham Springs, he caught Burbank by surprise.[14]

To prepare for the influx of black "outsiders" Denham Springs whites turned their fury on local blacks. Shots were fired around town, shotgun blasts tore through a black-owned hardware store and a black family's house, and someone even fired at a sleeping sheriff's deputy and his wife. There were also rumors "of several Ku Klux Klan meetings in Livingston Parish" to which Phoebe was not invited.[15]

McKeithen went on a statewide television hookup with a "completely non-political" address in which he called the march "silly, ridiculous, and absurd." He asked Louisianans to "'stand strong and tall' amid racial tension and show the world the state deserves a position of leadership." He promised that if a riot started it "would be stopped at once ... even if a few people have to be killed." To show he was serious, the governor issued a call for another 1,000 National Guardsmen to protect Baton Rouge over the weekend. He explained that one of the reasons for the Detroit riot was that the National Guard there had been ordered to stand at parade rest when the destruction began. That was not going to happen on his turf. He warned that Louisiana's units might carry live ammunition and have their bayonets fixed. He promised the state police will be armed "with Tommy guns and everything else." And McKeithen warned the local fiery radical, H. Rap Brown, the scheduled speaker at the league's Baton Rouge rally, that if he "advocated burning draft cards or talked of desecrating the flag" he would be jailed.[16]

A scant hour after McKeithen's state-wide message he ordered 650 National Guardsmen and 175 state police to meet in Livingston Parish to escort the blacks the rest of the way to the capital. Young told a press conference in New Orleans that the marchers did not need that protection nor would they fight back if provoked. He promised, "We'll be watched by the same one who has been protecting us all these years — God Almighty." The governor had other reasons for activating the guard, however. The Bogalusa blacks were due to arrive in Baton Rouge and demonstrate on Saturday and the Klan was scheduled the same evening to burn a cross on the city's south side. The National Knights of the Ku Klux Klan, headquartered at Stone Mountain, Georgia, had requested a permit to parade to the capitol on Sunday when the Bogalusa marchers planned to rally there. Both sides were granted permits for their parades and rallies but their times and routes were staggered so that they would not overlap.[17]

East of the capital the marchers, state police, and National Guardsmen all stepped off from the appropriately named Walker, Louisiana, at eleven o'clock on Friday morning and reached Denham Springs an hour later. The locals were waiting. Whites had sprinkled tacks and roofing nails in the streets and when the town's police chief tried to sweep them up he was booed. Whites in the crowd twice threw eggs at the guardsmen and troopers, someone tossed a cherry bomb into their midst, another heckler threw a bottle, and some dimwit heaved a brick. A few whites turned their attention to local blacks watching the parade and chased them down a side street trailed by state police and national guardsmen. The most popular word in Denham Springs that Friday was "nigger" spit at the marchers, "nigger lovers" directed at their protectors, and "one well-dressed young white girl" put a Christian variant on the epithet calling the guardsmen "Goddamned nigger lovers." An elderly woman screamed at them to "leave the niggers here just five minutes." She then paused thoughtfully, "naw, naw, just two minutes — that'll be enough." Later, Gail Jenkins, secretary of the Bogalusa league, uttered the understatement of the day when she told a New York *Times* reporter "these people are uncivilized."[18]

After the group crossed the appropriately named Amity River and reached the relative safety of East Baton Rouge Parish, Young told reporters, "I think the protection was fine today.... . That place would have been a slaughter pen without the National Guard." Protecting the blacks was a huge and complicated task. Four helicopters flew overhead checking the roadside for potential trouble, troops inspected every bridge for explosives after they found a fake bomb under one, the governor checked on the march from the air, and the superintendent of state police was on the ground directing operations.[19]

An editorial in Baton Rouge's *Morning-Advocate* suggested that the "best thing for all of us to do is to follow our usual weekend routines of lawn mowing, going fishing, doing handy-man work around the house ... and loafing." The editor assured his readers that he offered this advice "without any discrimination whatsoever as to race, religion, nationality, age, or sex." He believed "most of us regard [the marchers] as trouble-makers and publicity seekers bent on disturbing the peace of the community and undoing years of good work by people of both races who are far more public-spirited." He opined that the march was "dying on its feet" until the violence along the way gave it a new life. His final bit of advice was for his readers to go to the LSU stadium on Saturday night and watch the Saints play the Steelers.[20]

On another page the Bogalusa Voter League inserted a small notice advertising that H. Rap Brown would address the demonstrators on Sunday at two o'clock on the capitol steps. Brown's proposed topic was a bit puzzling: "the East-West runways in black America." And it remained a mystery because McKeithen received the best news of his whole hectic week when he heard that Brown had been arrested in New York City early Saturday morning for "illegally transporting a firearm while under indictment." Brown had a 30-caliber "automatic carbine" in his possession and was jailed in lieu of a $25,000 bail bond, which he could not raise. William Kunstler, Brown's attorney, charged that his client was a political prisoner. McKeithen didn't care what kind of a prisoner he was so long as he stayed out of Baton Rouge.[21]

The Bogalusa veterans sang civil rights songs as they marched in the rain into Baton Rouge and followed a tightly proscribed route to the Capital Junior High School. The following night they held a rally featuring Lincoln Lynch, the associate national director of the Congress of Racial Equality. Just about the time the Saints kicked off to the Steelers, Lynch denounced the governor and President Johnson to the crowd of around 400 people and promised that "if it takes a Newark or Plainfield or a Detroit then that's how it has to be." He continued that "white feet on black necks have been there too long." In the middle of his speech a "rally official" interrupted to whisper something in Lynch's ear. Lynch continued, "I am told there is a new philosophy now that I didn't know about. Don't say Negro ... this was a name given you by the white man." After that he talked only about blacks. Others in the audience already knew that; the man in charge of security, known only as Sam, explained to reporters he dropped his last name "because it was the one 'the white man gave me.'" Young took over the podium and swore he would overthrow Louisiana's government through voter registration. He promised that he was not there "to incite a riot or create a disturbance, but to get jobs for black folks."[22]

Seven miles south of the city the Klan gathered at its rallying ground and preached quite a different message to its 400 attendees. Jack Helm, the head of the Universal Klans of America, praised McKeithen for the job he had done and revealed that he had called the governor to congratulate him for his state-wide speech. McKeithen must have taken the opportunity to convince Helm that the Klan's presence at the capitol on Sunday would be counterproductive because Helm announced that his Klan would not march with the Georgia Klan to the capitol steps. "We don't want agitation," he claimed, "we just want the niggers to get out of town and leave us alone."[23]

Ferrall McCormick, the grand dragon of the Old Original Knights of the Ku Klux Klan, followed him to the podium. He avowed that "we are no different because we are members of the Klan. We are not a murderous organization" and as proof introduced his wife, Dimple, the grand dragonette. Helm returned to remind the Klansmen that "there is only one minority race in the country today, and that is the white race." The klansmen then burned a forty foot high cross and a Vietcong flag.[24]

The stage was set for Sunday's grand confrontation on the capitol's steps. The weather could not have been more oppressive with sunny skies, temperatures in the low nineties, and humidity ranging up to almost eighty percent during the afternoon. It was much too uncomfortable to take the *Morning-Advocate*'s advice to mow the lawn, cook-out, or do handy-man work outside. We decided to ignore the newspaper editor's advice and to go downtown to the capitol to watch the proceedings. Everyone we mentioned this to told us that we were nuts. We could not believe, however, that with over 2,200 National Guardsmen, state troopers, city police, and parish sheriff's deputies that Baton Rouge could become another Detroit. And besides, as Roberta always says, "We don't want to miss a hanging."[25]

We drove Phoebe as close to the capitol as we could get, which was about two blocks away, and parked her in a residential neighborhood where we hoped she would be safe. We walked over to Huey's edifice, one of the biggest state capitols in the United States, and were stunned at the tight security measures; there were even armed men positioned on the roof of the capitol's wings. We had hoped to stand on the lawn that falls away from the building's front steps where we could find a bit of shade. Guardsmen, all holding their rifles with fixed bayonets at the ready, ringed the entire capitol grounds to keep out all spectators and marchers, whether black or white, robed or not, even those wearing khakis and button down shirts.

We retreated to the two story pre–Civil War building across the street that gave us a view of the proceedings and some shade. The closest the troops would allow us to stand to the capitol's front door was perhaps 300 yards while our vantage point was a couple hundred yards farther away. We were surprised that so few people turned out. The newspapers later estimated 1,200 to 1,500 curious onlookers, but we guessed it was about half of that number.

The 250 Bogalusa marchers stepped off from their junior high school headquarters at exactly noon and began their 3.1 mile parade to

Louisiana National Guardsmen protected the Bogalusa marchers on the state capitol's steps on August 21, 1967. Phoebe was parked about two blocks behind the capitol in the center of the picture.

the capitol. Heavily guarded by motorcycle police, their ranks swelled to some 900 folks by the time they reached the state capitol at about 1:30 p.m. As the demonstrators climbed the steps they passed a black National Guardsmen, one of twenty in the entire state contingent. One marcher shouted, "Stupid nigger! You should be out here fighting with us." The league's vice president tried to bring the meeting to order but a fracas broke out between the Bogalusa group and black power advocates from

100

Baton Rouge led by a hulking fellow who called himself "big, black Billy Brooks." There was scuffling as Brooks attempted to wrest the microphone away from league spokesmen.[26]

Even the opening prayer was disputatious. When Zelma Wyche, president of the Madison Parish Voters League, asked for God's mercy on Governor McKeithen, she was met with derision as some blacks yelled Wyche was an "Uncle Tom" and told her to "pray for him yourself!" Everyone finally quieted down to listen to R.T. Young, the league's treasurer and brother of leader A.Z. Young, read a petition to the absent governor. It called for state employment of a "fair proportion" of blacks in all agencies, noting that there were no blacks in any state offices in Bogalusa or Washington Parish except in "traditional slave jobs, pushing a mop or broom."[27]

Lincoln Lynch from CORE, who had addressed the crowd the night before, delivered the principal speech, warning that unless things changed the movement was going to become increasingly confrontational and violent. He reminded his listeners that the governor had given the state police orders to shoot to kill and "many black people are talking about dying." He advised them that "when you go, take somebody with you." He quoted John F. Kennedy that "change can come peacefully or it can come violently" and averred that "if peaceful change is not forthcoming, violent change is inevitable. There is going to be change." To prepare for it, he recommended that blacks improve their education, send their children to school, register to vote, and fight for "decent housing and the right to walk in the state without having National Guardsmen and police" protect them.[28]

A.Z. Young followed Lynch to the microphone and denounced the Viet Nam War. "Your war," he proclaimed, "is in this state of Louisiana and in these United States." He told the crowd that he had fought in World War II and "stayed 186 days on the frontline fighting for freedom, a freedom that does not exist." Pointing out that the black movement was anything but monolithic, "he warned his people to beware of middle-class type Negroes and any Negroes appointed by President Johnson or Gov. McKeithen." Those blacks, he contended, were "not working for us." The only solution was to register blacks who "will knock him [the governor] down because he doesn't mean no good."[29]

The rally was over by 2:20 and it took "another 15 minutes for the Negroes to drift away." The Klan was due at 3 o'clock and during the transition the afternoon's only altercation took place. Whites moving towards the capitol began harassing some blacks who were leaving. The scuffle brought guardsmen "rushing down the hill to prevent the disturbance from flaring up further" and they arrested one white man.[30]

While the league was gathered on the steps a steady stream of cars full of whites, most flying the Confederate flag and some showing the stars and stripes as well, passed us slowly and circled the capitol under the watchful eye of police and guardsmen. As they went by us we heard them shouting epithets and cursing the "niggers." They were the vanguard of the second gathering, which turned out to be an embarrassment for the KKK, as it publicized that the Klans were more badly split than the civil rights movement.

According to the *Morning-Advocate,* about fifty robed Klansmen appeared, none of whom were masked because Baton Rouge's police

National Guardsmen ringed the entire capitol complex to prevent the Klan and its sympathizers, shown here driving past waving the American and Confederate flags, from initiating violence.

chief had issued a "no mask order." Before they started their meeting, however, United Klans' state officers arrived and ordered their members to go home. The Kleagle Koordinator for the United Klans in Southwest Louisiana told the press that his organization "formally disowned" the rally because "we feel that there are enough law enforcement officers here to keep everything under control." He promised, however, that "when and if law enforcement breaks down, we stand ready to assist in any way they see fit." After the United Klansmen left, only eight robed men remained on the capitol steps surrounded by perhaps 300 white sympathizers.[31]

The Rev. William Fowler, who called himself a "non-denominational Christian minister," announced that he was "the acting chief-of-staff" and the rally's principal speaker. The reverend just "happened" to be driving through Louisiana on his way to a Klan gathering at Stone Mountain, Georgia, when he heard about "the alleged violence committed by the Bogalusa Negro marchers against whites in Hammond" and headed to Louisiana instead to lend his assistance.[32]

Clad in the "full robes of his Kludship" he lashed out at the Bogalusa marchers, claiming they were inspired by the communists. He excoriated McKeithen, who, he claimed, had hit the "panic button" when he called out 2,500 troopers and guardsmen to protect "a handful of niggers" and Jews who, along with H. Rap Brown and Stokely Carmichael and the communists, were the real civil rights instigators. He concluded his oration by declaring how wonderful it was to be in the South where he was allowed to express himself publicly.[33]

Fowler relinquished the podium to Baton Rouge's own Virginia Harris, who was a candidate for the Democratic State Central Committee. Harris closed the rally by reciting "an original patriotic poem entitled 'Forget Hell!'" which a reporter remembered "had been received enthusiastically at a Klan rally held here Saturday night." On that bright note, the Klansmen and their followers walked off the capitol grounds.[34]

McKeithen, who was reportedly in the nearby governor's mansion throughout the afternoon keeping in touch with Burbank, had with his overwhelming show of force kept the two groups apart and restrained onlookers from provoking violence. He had also made it impossible for either group to communicate its message from the steps to anyone except the press representatives and heavily-armed guards.

The rest of us had to await the morning newspapers to find out exactly what had been said. Loss of freedoms of speech and congregation were two of the sad prices paid for the maintenance of a peaceful segregated society.

The rally petered out, participants went home, the guardsmen and cops left, and we walked sweatily across the capitol's lawn and down the street to Phoebe. We initially had qualms about parking so close to the action, fearing that if the demonstrations got out of hand, rowdies might range down the nearby streets bashing automobiles. We needn't have worried, for the afternoon had been so tightly structured and enforced it had been almost dull.

The long hot march was not over, however. The league's members returned to Bogalusa, McKeithen dispersed National Guard units to their armories immediately after Harris finished her poetry recital, and Superintendent Burbank released his state policemen to return to their barracks. Some local blacks, however, energized by what they had seen on the steps or because they saw a chance to work off their frustrations by creating mayhem, went on a rampage that night in Baton Rouge's black areas.

Starting at sundown, small bands of black youths set fires around black sections of the city. Police reported that the disturbances were caused by "only five or six carloads of people" that kept on the move to thwart attempts to arrest them. Mayor-President Dumas activated all the city's officers and sent them out to patrol the most affected areas. With an all-white police force on the street, Dumas took no chances. His cops drove "four to a car with riot guns protruding out open windows." To calm tensions they tried to herd everyone, especially young black males, off the streets. If they resisted, the police arrested them and hauled them downtown.[35]

One of the first detained was "big, black Billy Brooks," who was held on charges of "battery on a police officer, intimidation of a police officer, and inciting aggravated arson," although he claimed he had only attempted to stop a black city juvenile officer from making a call during the disturbance. His arresting officer was a ringleader of the cops who had threatened to resign if they had to share their cars with black police. "The husky militant" was held on $15,000 bond. The police discovered his real name was Walter Leon Jenkins and officers tried to discover whether he was the same Jenkins, a Houston, Texas, Congress of Racial Equality worker, who had been arrested in Baton Rouge two years earlier after he demanded that the city open and integrate its swimming pools.[36]

At ten o'clock that night Dumas asked for the National Guard's help, as his police and fire departments were stretched thin. McKeithen refused but did order some state police units back into Baton Rouge to patrol the streets. Dumas publicly disagreed with the governor's decision, saying, "When there's rats in the cellar and rats in the sewers, we've still got problems." Throughout the night roving youths set ten fires and called in uncounted false alarms, but with the fire trucks out on patrol the blazes were quickly extinguished; they only did $1,500 worth of damage. Other rebellious kids tossed Molotov cocktails into and on top of buildings but they were untutored bomb makers; almost all of their bombs failed to ignite and many of their bottles did not even break. Some rowdies stood on overpasses and dropped cocktails down on passing cars, but all failed to hit their targets. Roving carloads of blacks tossed rocks and bottles through store windows and quickly sped away only to repeat their mischief somewhere else. The police arrested ten blacks and herded hundreds more off the streets that night.[37]

Numerous well-armed white civilians prowled the disaffected areas and compounded police problems. When possible the officers stopped them and confiscated their arms. The sheriff reported that his men took guns from fifteen carloads of whites; they arrested one man who had "an M-16 semiautomatic rife, several pistols, and nine boxes of ammunition in his car."[38]

With the police ordered to shoot to kill and numerous whites driving mobile arsenals, it was a miracle nobody was killed. By early morning the city had calmed down. During the lull the local and state police coordinated their plans for the coming evening and devised a "beehive" patrol pattern for the troublesome areas. But no violence erupted and by midnight many police officers were sent home for a well-earned rest. The march's after-effects were over; Baton Rouge was not going to be another Detroit.[39]

The capital's morning newspaper's editor patted himself on the back and congratulated citizens for following his advice to ignore the demonstrations. He pointed out that only one half of one percent of the town bothered to go over to the capitol, only "one-fifteenth as many people who attended the football game between the Saints and the Steelers." Of those who did go to the capitol, the editor noted "a significant number were from out of town and out of state, one operating out of New York and the other out of California." At least he did not call us communists.[40]

The breakdown of segregation and racial strife was late coming to Baton Rouge, a city never on the social or political cutting edge. The delay enabled citizens to see what such unrest had done to other population centers. The massive race riots that had already visited the Northeast, Los Angeles, and Chicago in 1966 and Detroit and Newark early in 1967 served to convince many southerners that their region had superior racial arrangements that kept the peace. But that argument was breaking down by the time of the long hot march. Supporters of the segregated order could still prate that all the South's troubles were brought on by Yankees and communists, but increasingly those who marched, preached, and shouted were home-grown men and women, black and white. The only identified outsider on the capitol steps on that Sunday was the Reverend Klansman from California.

The Bogalusa to Baton Rouge march did not immediately accomplish anything. It did indicate, however, that Phoebe's world was changing. The civil rights movement was becoming increasingly radical as black power advocates gained influence and portended more violent clashes to come if the pace of change were not stepped up. "Big, black Billy Brooks," a crude variant of Malcolm X, was the movement's future, not Bogalusa's Young brothers who still sought to work through the system to peacefully achieve their goals of equality. The march also showed just how splintered and ineffective was the Klan. Their hooded members were scary only on their shrinking home turf and then only at night. They railed at the marchers and threw bricks and eggs more in a rage at their own powerlessness than in any real belief that they could sweep back the national tides of racial change.

Governor McKeithen, who went on to beat racist John Rarick in the Democratic primary and to win overwhelming reelection in 1968, and Mayor-President W. W. Dumas were examples of the new breed of more moderate, pragmatic southern politicians. McKeithen was no devotee of futile gestures as was George Wallace, but he was never going to move out far ahead of his constituents on racial matters. He understood that as segregation was dismantled it freed up social and economic opportunities for blacks. His piney woods heritage of fiercely independent Protestant individualism had conditioned McKeithen to accept that perhaps rights should be extended to all, but he was determined that they be accorded at a speed he could sustain politically. The Bogalusa march demonstrated that Louisiana and Baton Rouge would continue to change but not burn.

PART III

Literary Connections

6

Sugar-Boy

Sugar-Boy is an unforgettable character in Robert Penn Warren's thinly veiled classic look at Louisiana's Huey Long, called Willie Stark in the novel *All The King's Men.* Sugar-Boy is Huey's driver, body-guard, and gofer, always at the Kingfisher's beck and call. We meet Sugar-Boy early in the book driving Stark's Cadillac at his usual break-neck speed, passing a slow-moving hay wagon close enough to "wipe the snot off a mule's nose," as the Boss egged him to go even faster. Warren's Sugar-Boy suffers from a terminal stutter and when he tried to talk "he'd spray the inside of the windshield." Warren gives us a hint of Sugar-Boy's future role in the story when he tells us he "wouldn't win any debating contests ... but then nobody would ever want to debate with Sugar-Boy," whom Stark had seen "do tricks with the .38 Special which rode under his left armpit like a tumor."[1]

Warren's Sugar-Boy stands only about five-feet two, is balding and young, perhaps in his mid to upper twenties. "He is Irish, from the wrong side of the tracks" and always wears a red tie. Under his clothes, Sugar-Boy has "a little Papist medal on a chain" that the book's protagonist, Jack Burden, who also rides with Willie in the car when Sugar-Boy drives Louisiana's back roads at maniacal speeds, hopes "to God ... was St. Christopher and that St. Christopher was on the job." Sugar-Boy, whose given name is not revealed but whose surname is O'Sheean, is so tagged because everywhere Huey stops to eat Sugar-Boy steals all the sugar cubes from the table and sucks on them. [2]

Sugar-Boy's main role in the story plays out when a Dr. Stanton comes to the state capitol and pumps two shots into Willie. Burden, who is standing nearby, says his gunshots "were lost and merged with other more positive staccato series of reports" that sent Stanton reeling backwards and falling to the floor. Burden rushed to Stanton, who was "bleeding heavily ... stitched across the chest" and dead. Only then did Burden look up "to see Sugar-Boy standing there with the smoking automatic in his hand, and off to the right, near the elevator, a highway patrolman with a pistol in his hand."[3]

Just then Sugar-Boy "dropped his automatic clattering to the marble and uttering some strangled, animal-like sound, rushed back beyond the statue of Governor Moffat" where the Boss was sitting on the floor "staring straight ahead," blood pouring out of his chest. "Sugar-Boy leaned over him, weeping and sputtering, trying to speak. He finally managed to get out the words: "D-d-d-d-does it hur-hur-hur-hurt much, Boss — does it hur-hur-hur-hurt?"[4]

"Sugar-Boy," a caricature of Long's real bodyguard, Murphy Roden, taught me how to drive on the highway, although not in Phoebe, whom he would meet later. In 1955 he took me to Shreveport to buy a car for me. It was an unforgettable, nerve-wracking trip both ways. Sugar-

Murphy Roden taught me highway driving techniques in this ex–Army 1942 Ford V-8, four-door sedan. The Army must have painted its cars weekly; this one had about ten coats of olive-drab paint on it.

Boy sat next to me in my olive-drab 1942 Ford we intended to use as a trade-in and ordered me to drop the right wheels off the road and practice getting back on without swerving into the oncoming lane. We were on highway 80, then the main thoroughfare across North Louisiana, heavily trafficked in the mid–fifties. He ordered me to go faster, practice swerving the car, slam on its brakes, and drive on the tarred welts to feel them throw the wheels. After each trial he gave me hell, explained what I had done wrong and demanded I do it over, correctly. He was a tough taskmaster, but to this day whenever Phoebe's wheels slip off a road and I ease them back on, I always hear echoes of Sugar-Boy sitting there critiquing my performance. It seemed as if it took two days to drive those sixty miles.

We visited every used car lot in the town and when Sugar-Boy found a car that might be suitable, he'd take off his jacket and slide under it on his back. We were not going to buy what he called "a country car"

We traded the 1942 Ford for this 1950 V-8, two door sedan. I had it repainted light yellow and black and its nose leaded. After only one winter in upstate New York both its rocker panels rusted completely through.

because he had worn out several Cadillacs and Packards driving madly around Louisiana's unpaved back roads with Huey. Used car dealers were not adept enough to fool him and we did not find a city car that met his high standards. I must have passed his driving test, however, for soon after I was issued an illegal Louisiana driver's license with my correct birthdate that plainly showed I was underage. Sugar-Boy still had connections even though Huey had been dead twenty years.

Roden was "Colonel" to most who knew him. Obviously Warren did not because his fictional portrait of Murphy was most flawed. The colonel *was* a little man, probably taller than five feet two inches but not much more and he *was* quite bald when I knew him. But the physical resemblance stopped there. Murphy certainly did not stutter, although he was no voluble individual. He spoke clearly and always straight to the point. He was Irish, but the most Protestant of the species — he could hardly have been otherwise coming from piney woods country in North Louisiana — although I do not think he went to church. I never remember him mentioning religion. I also have no recollection of a red tie Warren claimed he always wore, but one weekend morning I rode my bicycle up to Murphy's house, three doors up from ours, and found him puttering around outside. He asked me to guess how much the clothes he had on were worth. After I missed several times, he proudly announced that he had spent ninety-five cents for everything he had on.

Warren was dead right that "nobody would ever want to debate with Sugar-Boy," but it was not because he was packing a rod. Murphy had a manner of looking right at his interlocutor with steely eyes that penetrated straight into his thought processes. He must have been the world's most frightening interrogator; I never could muster up the courage to try to lie to him. And he seemed to know everything. One afternoon, I and two of my school chums, one whose father was the local judge, figured out a foolproof way to play hooky. We skipped out after lunch and drove far out of town on back roads to some woods where we climbed a fence and walked back into the middle of nowhere to a small pond. We sat on the bank for some time tossing pebbles into the water and congratulating ourselves on our cleverness at escaping an institution that might have taught us something. Suddenly, without having made a sound, Murphy stepped out of the trees and asked,

We celebrated our wedding rehearsal dinner August 27, 1965. Murphy Roden, Huey Long's bodyguard, who shot Dr. Weiss after he shot Huey, is on the left wearing glasses. My father, James Ward, is behind him against the wall.

"Son, shouldn't you be in school?" To this day I am not sure how he found us, although it must have been through our cars, which we had left on the backwoods road. Sugar-Boy just knew things.[5]

I met Murphy in 1951 or 1952 after my father had been sent from Scarsdale, New York, to the Louisiana Ordnance Plant to straighten out its production snafus during the Korean War. We lived on the ordnance plant complex, which had twenty-five houses on a seven-eighths of a mile circle. Father was given carte blanche to bring in his own management team and he had a strange and wonderful ability to spot the most unlikely folks, burden them with heavy responsibilities, pay them well, and get results. He spent the better part of one week on the phone trying to locate one Harry Guenzler, a man he had known in earlier life, and finally found him working the cherry harvest in Michigan. Father wanted him to run a land mine loading line and Guenzler and his family, which included a very attractive daughter exactly my age, showed up in a twenty year old car with everything they owned tied all over it. It was as if Steinbeck had scripted their arrival.

Another old friend whom Father indelicately called "my little Jew," who was indeed very little and Jewish, he located selling musical ceramic windmills in California. He joined the nation's defense efforts forthwith. I do not know where Father found Murphy, for I don't think he had ever stepped foot in Louisiana before, but he was one of Father's most perceptive hires. Murphy was still closely identified with the "Long machine" and when it controlled the governor's mansion Murphy was superintendent of the state police. The Longs were out of power in 1951 and Father hired Murphy to head plant protection and to oversee security on a 16,000 acre patch of scrub land in the middle of nowhere, but not far from Arcadia, Murphy's home.

Murphy understood the labyrinth that passed for Louisiana politics, knew everybody who mattered in the state, held the keys to closets full of skeletons, and was as closed-lipped as a Vatican diplomat. Loyalty was his most impressive character trait. I never heard him denigrate anyone in the Long family or "machine" which he served until his death; those folks had made him, lifted him out of Arcadian obscurity. He owed them and he always repaid his debts.

In 1959, after we had moved to Utica, New York, Murphy called Father from Louisiana in the middle of the night because Uncle Earl Long, the Pelican State's governor, had just been arrested in New York City along with several prostitutes and the cops had tossed Uncle Earl into the drunk tank. The governor had exhibited increasingly erratic behavior for several years. After divorcing his wife in 1958, he had been in numerous well-publicized escapades with a New Orleans stripper, Blaze Starr. He had even been incarcerated in his own state's mental institution. While there he used his authority as governor to fire the institution's director and replaced him with a man who signed Uncle Earl out. When Longs got in trouble, Murphy was often called upon to bail them out. He phoned Father to find a first-rate New York lawyer to spring Uncle Earl so Murphy could get him back into friendlier judicial territory, which is what happened.

Murphy had similar loyalty towards my family, although he never had to bail any of us out of jail. He connected Father with people in the state who mattered and solved political problems for a manufacturer who employed 7,000 citizens. He gave me a job at the Louisiana State Police for two summers when he was superintendent and I was in college. More important, he kept a wary eye on a teenage boy who had an innate ability to do dumb things while growing up in Louisiana.

The colonel met Phoebe twice. He and his wife, Aulene, drove up to Logansport to attend our wedding, to meet my wife-to-be, and to visit with my mother and father. Roberta has never forgotten that as Aulene got out of their car, she looked at me and said "Jimmy, whatahver happened to your hayair?" The rest of it had fallen out since I had last seen her. They must have pined for a good North Louisiana Baptist praise meeting as they sat through an hour and a half high mass in Latin the following day, but they appeared to enjoy our reception and joined the crowd that waved to us as we drove away in brand-new Phoebe. They knew we would be in Baton Rouge in a few weeks, and I suspect Murphy tucked away the thought that he ought to watch out for us; he always had and he did.

The following year I needed a summer job and Murphy hired me to work in the identification department, where I was assigned the most menial tasks, principally filing cards on everyone in the state who had had a legal infraction, from serial murderers to parking violators. I staved off terminal boredom by haunting the dead cases property room, where I searched in vain for the evidence from Huey's assassination. The state police, as far as I could tell, never threw anything away, even from the 1920s and 1930s, but there was not a whit of evidence that Huey had ever been in Louisiana — or had died there. His records were gone, or perhaps stored somewhere else under lock and key, although if they were, nobody at headquarters knew about them. I also spent a lot of time hanging around the fingerprint bureau and learned to read and classify prints, a skill for which I have found absolutely no subsequent use.

Two years later we drove Phoebe from Baton Rouge up to North Louisiana to poke around in my old haunts and stopped in Arcadia to have lunch with the Rodens. We discussed for the last time that fateful 1935 September day in the marble-lined state capitol hallway. I also tried to talk him into writing his memoirs, but he just gave me a wry grin and said he couldn't, "There are too many people still alive."

The man who was born in Brushy Valley in Bienville Parish in 1905 but lived most of his life in the little nearby North Louisiana town of Arcadia, and who probably never graduated from high school, had started his career as a motorcycle cop for the Louisiana state police. It was his good fortune to be assigned to guard Huey Long, who was every bit as astute as Murphy in judging people. He soon became the governor's permanent bodyguard-chauffeur. From the late 1920s until the shooting, Murphy accompanied the Kingfish everywhere and even lived with him when he went to Washington as senator.

My major professor, T. Harry Williams, talked to the colonel when he was researching his biography of Huey that won Harry his Pulitzer. Williams later told me Huey's former bodyguard was tightlipped but he did pry some interesting information from Roden and other bodyguards. It seems Huey was always surrounded by armed men, all employees of Louisiana's Highway Patrol or its Bureau of Criminal Identification and by 1930 Williams noted that Roden "had become one of the favorite guards."[6]

Huey lived with his protectors in D.C. hotels because his wife, Rose, stayed in Louisiana. Three were always with him, two sat outside his door and admitted visitors while the other "stood behind Huey until the callers left." They even went with Huey to the Senate and sat in the gallery while he was on the floor; everywhere, "they went armed, carrying plainly bulging pistols under their coats," but they had to check their pistols in the Senate. Once, when they forgot, they had to flee the gallery and dash to Huey's office to get rid of their hardware. At least one of three, although usually not Murphy, carried a sawed off shotgun wrapped in a paper package with one end cut out to expose the revolver-like butt and trigger. While some thought Long a bit paranoid with all that firepower following him around, events proved that he was not; the irony was that his three bodyguards with all their guns were unable to prevent his murder.[7]

Sugar-Boy had a big, glass-fronted gun cabinet in his living room that he always kept locked. On several occasions he opened it to show me the wristwatch whose face Dr. Weiss' bullet had mangled. It must have left a terrific bruise on Murphy's wrist, for the face of the watch was horribly contorted. He also let me hold the pistol he used to shoot Weiss, which was, if I remember correctly, a revolver rather than an automatic as Warren claimed. Murphy had a fascination for firearms, his cabinet was crowded with them. Most were rifles and perhaps a few were shotguns but I don't think Murphy hunted. Perhaps the guns were a legacy from his days with the state police; maybe they were the reason he went into law enforcement in the first place.

He liked to tell me the story about a large diamond ring he habit-ually wore with a stone that was so big and cut in such a way that if he held his hand up he could use it as a mirror to see what was back of him. He claimed that he could use the diamond to accurately fire a pistol at a target behind him. By contrast, the Ward household was almost unarmed. My father, however, had been a captain in the National Guard's horse artillery in the 1930s, in which his prime responsibility, to hear him tell it, was to brew the beer in the stables at Fort Drum on summer maneuvers. He had been issued a .45 auto-matic pistol, a relic from World War I, which he kept unloaded in a bedroom drawer. In February 1958, a few months before we left Louisiana, Father showed it to Murphy, who said it was valuable because it had a very low serial number, 177,367, which has always seemed high to me. Murphy cleaned the pistol, coated it with Cosmoline, wrapped it in oilcloth, covered that with butcher paper, taped it all up, and signed and dated it. Father never unwrapped it and he passed it down to me; it is the only autograph I have of the man who shot Dr. Weiss.

What Murphy told me that day we took Phoebe to lunch with him about that fateful evening, September 8, 1935, when Huey Long was in Baton Rouge ramrodding a special session of the state legisla-ture, accords closely with what he and others told T. Harry. Rumors swirled through the capitol that an attempt would be made on Huey's life at the session and the superintendent of state police delegated ten state cops to help protect the Kingfish. It was almost impossible to guard Long, however; he walked at a run and darted into offices and hallways at will, leaving his protectors strung out behind him, puffing to catch up. That's what happened about nine twenty that evening; Huey was in a crowd outside the governor's office making certain that his legislative henchmen knew about a meeting scheduled for the next morning to discuss pending legislation.[8]

While Huey was talking, a man in a white suit approached him from the opposite side of the corridor and, as Murphy told T. Harry, "he brushed through" the throng and walked up close to Huey. He raised his right hand that clutched a small pistol; another bodyguard saw it and struck at his arm. Just as he did so, however, Dr. Weiss pulled the trigger. Huey yelled "I'm shot" and turned and ran for the door that led to the capitol's cellar. Simultaneously, Murphy jumped on Weiss and the two men hit the floor with Weiss on top. As they wrestled Weiss fired at Murphy, smashing his wristwatch. Then Weiss got up off Murphy and backed away in a crouch. Murphy pulled his pistol as he got off the floor and he and another bodyguard, Elliott Coleman, fired at the same time, hitting Weiss. T. Harry sifted through the evidence and concluded that Coleman's bullet hit Weiss first; Murphy was certain that his did. It doesn't really matter for as soon as they fired, numerous other guards and state police reacted and pumped more bullets into the doctor, who had collapsed face down on the marble floor. When he was examined, the final count was thirty bullet holes in his back, twenty-nine in his front, and two more in his head. Many of the bullet holes in the front of Weiss' body were made by exiting bullets fired from behind. The man's corpse was in tatters. Murphy later told me that when they lifted the body bullets fell out and as they hit the marble floor they sounded like hail.[9]

Carl Austin Weiss was a young ear, nose, and throat specialist in Baton Rouge who, as far as everybody knew, was apolitical. Certainly Huey, who knew virtually everyone in the state, did not know him and after he was shot kept asking who that man was. When finally told, he wanted to know why he had shot him, a question that has never been satisfactorily answered. Huey had many known enemies who wanted him dead and yet he was shot by a total stranger.[10]

One of Huey's cronies found him staggering around in the cellar and helped him into his car and sped him to the nearby Our Lady of the Lake hospital. Preliminary examination showed a small entrance wound on Huey's right side, under his ribs. The bullet had exited near his spine. The wound did not appear bad, but Huey's blood pressure was dropping and his pulse kept climbing, a sure indication that he was bleeding internally. Huey asked specifically for several doctors to attend him but they lived all over the state and it took hours for them to get there.

The Kingfish needed immediate attention and Dr. Arthur Vidrine, the superintendent of Charity Hospital in New Orleans, who had been at the legislative session, operated on him although he only had minimal surgical training. Vidrine found two perforations in Huey's colon, which he stitched up, and no damage to any other internal organs. He closed Huey up. Several hours later the Boss was again in trouble and his requested physicians catheterized his bladder and found a large amount of blood which indicated a renal duct to his kidney had been hit. By then Huey was too weak to withstand another operation. Thirty hours after Weiss shot him, the Kingfish was dead.[11]

Huey died the way he lived, in the public glare. His operating room was full of doctors and politicians standing around talking. His hospital room was crowded with family, friends, political cronies, and anyone who cared to squeeze in to see how the Boss was doing. One of his henchmen, Seymour Weiss, no relation to Doctor Weiss, was the manager of the Roosevelt Hotel in New Orleans, which was often Huey's home away from home. This Weiss had been in charge of the infamous "deduct box," sometimes called "the black box," in which all the cash Huey raised from contractors who did business with the state, state employees, and political supporters was kept. The day before he was shot, the senator had played golf with Weiss and told him that he had enough money to finance his run for the presidency in 1936 and to support Long candidates in state races. Weiss assumed Huey had the deduct box in the Riggs National Bank in Washington, D.C. After they returned to Weiss' office in the Roosevelt Hotel, however, Huey mentioned that he had moved the box. Before he could tell Weiss where, the phone rang calling Huey back to the fateful legislative session in Baton Rouge.[12]

As Huey lay dying, drifting in and out of consciousness, Weiss pushed his way up to his bed and shook him, saying, "You've got to tell me. Where is the deduct box?" Huey roused himself and whispered, "Later, Seymour, later." Shortly Weiss tried again but received the same reply, "Later, Seymour, later." The box, stuffed with millions of dollars in cash, was never reported found. In a footnote, T. Harry mentioned that Huey's wife, who had a legal claim on the box and its contents, hired agents who scoured locations in the United States and Canada but failed to find it. Some "Long associates" who asked T. Harry not to identify them thought that a "Long leader" or "leaders" took the box and the booty.[13]

Thirty-three years later at our lunch I asked Murphy about the deduct box. He told me that right after Huey died someone sent him down to the Roosevelt Hotel to get the box, but it was not there and he did not know what happened to it. A few sentences later, however, with a thin-lipped half grin, he said that very soon thereafter he bought 144,000 acres of prime Louisiana delta bottom land.

If Murphy had taken the box — and since he never left the Kingfish's side, he had to have known where it was — he wouldn't have told me. At that remove, however, he was indirectly confessing that he knew what had happened to it and that he had shared in its contents. He left me with the strong impression that someone close to the Long family had sent him for the money. He was the obvious man to delegate with the touchy task; he was a loyal insider, knew the details of how the Long machine had raised the cash, and was always discreet. I suspect he picked it up, delivered it, and was suitably rewarded for his years of faithful service and perhaps for his future silence. T. Harry's confidential sources, some of whom may have shared in the booty, intimated the same thing. On his own, Murphy would have never, even after the Boss was dead, grabbed the millions for himself— he was too loyal. Moreover, in Louisiana's politically charged atmosphere in which nothing could be kept quiet for very long, he never would have gotten away with it — and he knew it.

Murphy certainly did not live as if he had shared in the Long loot to the tune of whatever 144,000 prime acres were worth. He had no surviving children, his twins had died very young, and his house in Arcadia, a typical 1950s ranch was, while well-appointed and trim, not outstanding even in his own neighborhood. If you are what you drive, Murphy had a penchant for Dodges, especially the bottom of the line model, a two-door sedan, but with a V-8 engine; he still liked to drive powerful cars, but without Huey sitting beside him to urge him to go faster, he had slowed considerably. When I worked for him at the state police he drove a Buick, but I was never certain whether it was his car or a state vehicle.

To the end he was a careful man, more so than his early career would have indicated. He remains the only man I know who bolted a fire extinguisher to the transmission hump in the front seat of his new car, anecdotal evidence that indicated the care he took with all aspects of his life. As we prepared to leave after lunch, Murphy told us he had left his money to the local nursing home in return for its promise to take care of him and Aulene as long as they needed it. My last glimpse of Murphy was in Phoebe's rear view mirror as we drove away. He died soon thereafter and took all his secrets to the grave. Aulene followed him three months later.

7

Road Writings

"The American really loves nothing but his automobile." — William Faulkner, quoted in *Automobile Quarterly* (Executive Planner, 2005, p. 160).

I have spent a goodly number of hours observing America through Phoebe's windshield. She has accumulated 200,000 miles and at an average speed of say 30 miles per hour I have been behind her wheel for almost seven thousand hours, 292 twenty-four hour days. Through her glass I have seen monstrous stupidities, wrecks, fires, floods, hail, fog, sleet, and snow. I've glanced at passenger trains long forgotten now, Fenway Park in Boston, the brooding Adirondacks, enticing taverns, mini-skirted lovelies prancing along boulevards, derelicts diving in dumpsters, ambulances on their errands of mercy, geese honking in formation, fabulous sunsets, and towns with hitching posts on their squares.

Since the internal combustion engine has been mated to wheels, America's writers have felt a compelling need to write of their motoring experiences. They sought to put their changing world into a new perspective to reveal fundamental truths about themselves. The motorcar gave everyone a chance to become an observant world-wanderer and maybe even a literary lion. Automobile travel literature, now a genre of its own, arose from auto aficionados' attempts to describe the thrills of motoring in gas buggies, the sensation of the road rushing past just beneath their feet, the wind rustling their hair and clothes, the taste of bugs on their teeth, and the exhilarating smells of exhaust and burning oil as driver and passengers dashed toward new thrills.

Speed was an essential ingredient in the earliest literature, a swiftness wholly under the drivers' control that introduced an element of

Check out the *Tennessee Alumnus*
on the Internet via the World Wide Web
http://loki.ur.utk.edu./default.html

PRINTED IN U.S.A.

Phoebe had her one moment of literary fame when she was featured on the back cover of the *Tennessee Alumnus* magazine in the winter of 1996. The theme of the piece was that I had started teaching at the University of Tennessee at Chattanooga on September 1, 1969, and have driven Phoebe to class every day since.

excitement and risk into their otherwise circumscribed, sober lives attuned to moving at the pace of animals. Many of the early automotive literary adventures told of efforts to drive somewhere in "record" time. The very best of such recitations provided insights into human nature and the cultures the writers espied on their mad dashes aboard rickety, explosive vehicles. The Long Island Vanderbilt races in the new century's first decade fascinated writers amazed that the human body could tolerate open-air velocities of up to thirty miles an hour. Speed record attempts on Daytona Beach's sands evoked similar breathless prose as motorcars approached the magic mark of one mile in one minute.

Early promoters devised wicked competitions to see who could drive the fastest between distant points, preferably located across inhospitable, trackless terrain. An Italian journalist, Luigi Barzini, penned a travel classic, *Peking to Paris: Prince Borghese's Journey across two Continents in 1907,* describing just such an ordeal. His book is entrancing because he recounts more than simply the pratfalls of crossing Asia and Europe in a huge, raw machine. He draws his reader into the tight little social grouping that developed, one that threw together an Italian prince related to popes and everyone else who mattered in Italy, a self-made journalist-adventurer, and a mechanical genius who in his spare time laid under the car and memorized every nut and bolt. The most creative novelist could not have conjured an odder trio. Barzini stirs into his compelling account descriptions of the passing geography and the people they met. No reader could forget the illiterate Siberian peasant who made them a new wooden-spoked wheel using only his thumb to measure and a hatchet to craft it, or the lonely telegraph agent in the Gobi desert who had been on the job for six years but had never sent a telegram. It is a lovely piece of writing that takes the reader along for a ride on the winning Itala as it roars across two continents with its exhaust cutout wide open, sometimes hitting a breathtaking forty miles per hour.[1]

Driving across only one-third of the earth whetted others' appetites to attempt something longer and more strenuous. In 1908 the New York *Times* sponsored a race almost around the globe, from New York west to Paris. The race was won, as the *Times* had hoped, by an American car, a huge Thomas Flyer that bested six other entrants; automobiles had already become nationalist symbols. The race spawned a number of histories, including Dermot Cole's *The 1908 Auto Race from New York to Paris,* which chronicles carloads of men proudly flying their nations' flags, braving unimaginable elements in their push to reach the Eiffel Tower in the shortest period of time.[2]

All over America men and some women set out to test their machines' durability and their mettle by driving across the United States, something Phoebe has never done. After the first couple failed, Dr. Horatio Nelson Jackson and Sewall K. Crocker drove their two-cylinder Winton in 1903 from San Francisco to New York City in 63 days, 12 hours, and 30 minutes. Jackson, a non-practicing physician whose wife was a patent medicine heiress, bet friends at the University

Club in San Francisco fifty dollars that he could do it. In less than a week he purchased his car and impedimenta, and teamed up with Crocker. Practically everything on his Winton broke at least once, including its springs, axle, and motor. Jackson's journey was more an endurance feat than a speed run. His success, however, proved that the new invention, when driven by tireless, mechanically minded, stubborn daredevils with deep pockets, was capable of almost anything.[3]

The duo averaged a little over twelve miles an hour when the Winton was running, setting a record for others to best. Soon afterwards, dozens of people chugged and roared across the continent going in both directions in ever shorter times. The literature poured forth, mostly in pamphlet form and written in purple prose, relating madcap auto escapades featuring men caked alternately with dust and mud who endured hunger, thirst, and every known discomfort. In every trip the men and women became at one with their automobile; the people and scenery along the way were something to get past and through in the shortest time.

And there is something cheerfully superfluous about all these forays. Drivers and riders could have purchased railway tickets and crossed the continent more quickly, safely, and in much greater comfort. Long-distance driving feats were expensive and time consuming and still are even in more modern cars such as Phoebe. Many of the transcontinental auto pioneers were well-to-do Americans who were fearless and overactive. Their penchant for publicizing their fun drew ever more automobilists out to crowd the nation's wretched roads and trails.[4]

Such motorcar literature often says more about the authors than what they did; travel is always personal. Despite our postcards home saying we "wish you were here," we rarely mean it. More often we leave to get away from them. Harriet White Fisher, however, took some of them with her and wrote it all up in *A Woman's World Tour in a Motor*. White was a formidable, buxom widow who owned and managed an anvil factory in New Jersey. Well off, she had a summer home on Lake Como in northern Italy to which she repaired each summer to hobnob with European royalty who whiled away those long pre–World War I summer days in the temperate mountain climes. Usually she took a steamship over in the spring and returned in the fall, but in 1909 she decided to take her car and drive home the long way around the world.

She purchased a huge Locomobile, bigger than Phoebe, and took her chauffeur, English cook, Italian maid, and bulldog "Honk." For thirteen months, her rolling menagerie, which soon included an ape and birds, motored across the globe in style. Fisher describes what it was like to sit high in her expansive car and look down at all those non-royals she habitually referred to as "peasants," people who would later drive Biscaynes. She complained mightily of high prices, poor accommodations, bad roads, dust, heat, and dirt. Although her Victorian attitudes were a throwback to the previous century, she was at the same time an adventuresome, twentieth-century capitalist who dared to break through the boundaries that limited women. She was also an early "Ugly American"; in Japan she had to literally drive her car through the walls of a house to make a sharp turn in the road.[5]

By the end of the automobile's first decade, travel was becoming so ordinary that even families drove around the world; William Hall, for example, made his fortune as the first pulpwood paper manufacturer in New England and then took to the road, spending summers in Europe. Automobiles intrigued him and in 1902 he took his wife and son, Melvin, to Europe where he hired a two-cylinder Panhard and a chauffeur for a grand motor tour. By 1911 the Halls were accomplished automobilists and decided to drive to King George V's Durbar in India and then back home around the rest of the world. They shipped their 1911 Packard to Europe and set off. Years later Melvin, who eventually drove around the globe four times, set down the wonders of the family's 1911 trek in his *Journey to the End of an Era*. It's a classic piece of travel literature; his description of the Durbar, full of egregious pomp, says more about British colonization in India than shelves of formal histories.

Underlying all the trip's colorful characters and experiences, however, is the sense that it was a bit of an indolent ramble as was ours in Phoebe exactly ninety years later. Melvin and his mother (his father returned to the United States after the Durbar) wandered about peering at the world. They pursued nothing, they went where the roads took them, just to see what was there. The important thing was just to be on the road — somewhere, it didn't matter so much where. The following summer they again went to Europe and drove to road's end in Lapland.[6]

Not all such early automotive exploration was so relaxed and personal, however. As the world's premier industrial power, the United States was assembling the rudiments of an empire in the Roosevelt and Taft years to carve new markets for the nation's expanding production. Hundreds of American automobile companies were eyeing the profits from foreign sales. Abetted by the state department, many companies sent salesmen abroad touting the wonders of American technology. Robert C. Hupp, the prime mover behind a new Detroit auto corporation, concocted a promotional scheme in 1910 to send a Hupmobile around the world on a demonstration drive to sign up foreign dealers. Three men drove west out of Detroit on November 4, 1910, in a brand-new 1911 Hupp touring car and circled the earth, driving 47,000 miles in fifteen months through twenty-seven countries and colonies on one of the world's longest business trips. They were rolling embodiment of President William Howard Taft's "Dollar Diplomacy."[7]

After the trio toured the Philippines the company published a profusely illustrated pamphlet recounting the first half of their journey. It showed the Hupmobile in front of famous or exotic places, shrines, and mountains. Hupmobile's corporate prose was not beguiling but it surely whetted some Americans' appetites to take to the road, to experience the world's wonders, at least those only a few miles away. Implicitly it leagued all automotive journeys with the enduring national notions of freedom and individualism. Everybody with a few dollars could be freer, see new things, meet interesting people, control their own destinies, prowl the world, and make their nation stronger and more prosperous. The magical aspects of the new vehicles lingered on into Phoebe's era.

While Hupmobile's public relations writers tried hard to convince the world that everything looked better with a Hupmobile in front of it, others of different ideological persuasions emphasized how the motorcar threatened to destroy that same world. The Russian author Ilya Ehrenburg wrote his "non-fiction" novel *The Life of the Automobile* in 1929 from the perspective of the Soviet experiment that showed that freedom means different things depending upon one's presuppositions. The Soviet experiment created a society in which people did not worship at the altar of individual rights and freedom. From Ehrenburg's perspective the automobile symbolized capitalistic exploitation and corporations' greedy search for profits at any cost, usually by driving down their workers' wages to near subsistence levels. To make a profit, he wrote, companies like General Motors had to cheapen their product so much that it became unsafe.

In his "novel," however, Ehrenburg prophetically explains the need for more gasoline, caused later in some small measure by Phoebe's anemic in-town fourteen miles per gallon, that will guarantee future wars. He even attacks the Soviet Union, arguing that it is driven by some of the same capitalist imperatives to compete. His is a dreary book, yet it contains a kernel of truth throughout; his open roads lead to death and impoverishment — the antithesis of the usual travel literature, a tale that makes the reader consider crushing Phoebe and taking the bus.[8]

Sixteen years later the novelist Henry Miller, long an expatriate, used the automobile as a symbol to bash his native land. In *The Air-Conditioned Nightmare,* Miller takes an ostensible automobile tour of the United States. As his book progresses, however, his excursion

If Miller's automobile was air conditioned it was one of the earliest; Packard made the first air conditioning available in 1940. Phoebe's slim-line unit installed in 2001, shown here, puts out a gale of freezing air regardless of the outside temperature. It also makes a handy bracket upon which to hang my small radio.

becomes increasing internal, a jaunt through his memories and personal prejudices; only one chapter talks about his trip. In the others he compares America unfavorably with war-torn Europe. Like many authors of his depression generation, and Steinbeck immediately comes to mind, Miller is fascinated by society's losers, those down and out, the poor, the lumpen proletariat. He is so exasperated with his native land he writes that he's sorry the South lost the Civil War because it destroyed its culture.[9]

Miller cares nothing about automobiles. The only thing he notes about the one he is driving is that it overheats all the time. His musings on why show that he knows nothing about automobiles. When he anthropomorphizes his car, however, he is an artist, a man with a profound understanding of the human dimensions of automotive machinery. He views the motorcar, the very thing he does not understand, as the salvation of humankind. Miller thinks "the automobile was invented in order for us to learn how to be patient and gentle with one another," certainly true for anyone who drives a car as slow a Phoebe. He wrote this, of course, long before "road rage" became a common reaction to the frustrations of crowded roads and highway gridlock.[10]

Miller characterizes autos as women. "It doesn't matter about the parts," he writes, "nor what model or what year it is, so long as you treat *her* right." Without changing a word Miller's admonition neatly fits into the typical marriage guide of his day. "What a car appreciates is responsiveness.... It's the way you handle her, the pleasant little word now and then, the spirit of forbearance and forgiveness," he advises in his motorcar sex manual. But like many men, Miller has a mean streak and proffers advice on how to end an affair with an auto. There is "just one thing to remember about driving any automotive apparatus," he reminds his readers, "when the car begins to act as though it had the blind staggers it's time to get out and put a bullet through its head."[11]

There's a bit of Ehrenburg in Miller that undoubtedly was the result of his Paris carousing and his native land's censorship of his sexually explicit *Tropic of Cancer* and *Tropic of Capricorn*, books that presaged Kerouac and the beat movement. Kerouac, in New York City, was busting to break free of the sterility of middle-class mores that drew their inspiration from the American Puritanical strain that later

Only someone with puritanical aesthetic tastes could have styled an automobile this big in the gaudy 1960s and hung so little decoration on it. Even Phoebe's hubcaps are understated.

prompted automen to design a car as severe as Phoebe. Kerouac had seen too much of traditional America, he wanted to find truth and freedom by breaking away and wallowing in new experiences in booze, drugs, sex, talk, music, especially jazz and blues, and the cultures of those who were outside the nation's mainstream.

For three years Kerouac criss-crossed the country in a delirium to sample life in the raw and draw from his encounters fundamental truths about his own existence. The upshot of his exhausting pursuit of the unpursuable is his classic *On the Road,* published in 1955, in which he looks for essential truths among Americans who lived in another dimension, one as far from Puritan discipline as possible. On a trip to Mexico, for example, he and Neal Cassady spend a memorable afternoon getting high on the world's largest marijuana cigar and then engage in a series of seemingly impossible physical romps in a bordello.[12]

On the Road is a blur, a kaleidoscope of instant snapshots of life along highways in a country that has just won another great war but is unsure of what it has won. The nation wallows in Cold War fears shaken by great paroxysms of faux-patriotism. In the 1950s those self-anointed national saviors destroy the beat generation and end its quest for what the New York *Times* reviewer called "excesses to serve a spiritual purpose with a still unfocused affirmation."[13]

Kerouac, however, had already discovered his truth before Senator Joseph McCarthy spewed his malevolent poison across the political and cultural landscape. Kerouac's nugget was small, but for him profound; the central truth of existence, he writes, is that "nobody knows what's going to happen to anybody besides the forlorn rags of growing old." That's all there is, but it is a helluva ride to get there.[14]

Fifty years later we ventured out at a much more sedate pace in Phoebe visiting and appreciating the more "traditional" cultures that Kerouac, Miller, and others so despised. And like the 1950s, the countryside we motored through in 2001 was in transition. America had won the Cold War but was uncertain about the fruits of its victory and citizens were wondering whether the cost had been worth it. Even in that pre–9/11 time, national politics were becoming nasty; only a few months before the U. S. Supreme Court had chosen the country's new president. While the national scene was all very upsetting, in the nation's nooks and crannies Americans still queued for ice cream on warm summer evenings, proudly flew flags on their houses, and mowed the verges where their tilled fields abutted the blue roads; there are comforting essential human traits in such activities. To us, one of the most basic is simply that there exists a cultural momentum that shakes off cataclysmic news and events and strengthens folks' addictions to their usual routines. We and Phoebe, for example, kept plodding along, albeit at a snail's pace, on Steinbeck's and Kerouac's quests. For us, slowness is the familiar pace.

John Steinbeck, although no beat writer, shared many of Miller's and Kerouac's interests. In books such as *Cannery Row, Tortilla Flats* and *The Grapes of Wrath,* Steinbeck delves into the plight of the agricultural underclass in his native California. His books try to arouse the nation's consciousness to recognize those left behind, especially in the Great Depression. A couple of years before he won his Nobel, and with his literary reputation on the wane, Steinbeck decided to explore America. Like most travelers he wanted to take an accomplice and chose his aged French poodle, Charley. *Travels with Charley: In Search of America* is disappointing because it does not come close to fulfilling its subtitle's promise. Like most travel writers, Steinbeck wanted to get out into America's heartland and talk to "normal" people to see what his country is all about. He does that admirably; he picks up a wonderful cross-section of the North American continent, but makes little attempt to distill meaning, any meaning, from his palaver.

He can be funny though. His story about driving to the Canadian border at Niagara Falls only to be told that he ought not to enter Canada because the U.S. customs officials will not allow him to bring Charley back into his native country is a howler. Steinbeck turns back to American customs where he is told he cannot bring Charley back into the U.S. because he has been out, even if he has not been in another country. The American customs men finally relent and let poor Charley come home but Steinbeck misses a wonderful chance to expand upon this small bureaucratic, canine vignette.[15]

Like Steinbeck we have discovered unintended and interesting things in Phoebe. We often stop at local cemeteries, for example, for

With her huge trunk, Phoebe would have been the perfect car for a funeral director to use to carry caskets. The Very Old Barton box contains antifreeze, oil, brake fluid, tools, fire extinguisher, rags, and the indispensable duct tape. Note the instructions for using the jack are still pasted to the underside of the trunk lid. The jack has never been taken out of its clips.

they are the quickest way to take a town's pulse (no pun intended) and to discover what kind of people settled there. We once stopped in Constableville, New York, a little village located away from a blue road, that never claimed more than 600 souls. There we identified six graves of men who had died far away in the Civil War. They were a moving testament to the widespread sorrow that civil conflict caused and we left certain that there were probably more casualties of that war interred there who lay in less well-marked graves.

In 2002 when Tennessee faced bankruptcy and was hacking my university's appropriations in lieu of raising taxes, we found ourselves hopelessly lost in Grundy County, one of the state's poorest, not 75 miles from home. We passed a dilapidated single-wide house trailer with a yard full of thoroughly dead automobiles and piles of colorful, broken, plastic toys. Roberta commented that those folks probably would not support a campaign to increase taxes to restore the university's library budget — an obvious blue-road political truth driven home in Phoebe.

Steinbeck's truth gleaned from the road was in a line which I allude to later, wherein he asks "Who has not known a journey to be over and dead before the traveler returns?" That happens to Steinbeck when he reaches Abingdon, Virginia, where he tucks tail and speeds back to Long Island. Moreover, he notes that sometimes "the reverse is also true; many a trip continues long after movement in time and space have ceased." "My own journey started long before I left," he remembered, "and was over before I returned" — just like our 2001 ramble with Phoebe. After driving from Maine to the Mojave, Steinbeck becomes thoroughly lost in New York City, only a few miles from his home. Unfortunately his book does too.[16]

In 1963, three years after Steinbeck lost interest in being on the road, another noted American writer whose reputation was on the wane, William Saroyan, with his cousin, jumped into a 1941 Lincoln Limousine and set off across the country to talk about himself as they sped through the wide-open American spaces. Despite the fact that their journey started in New York City, the book begins in Ontario, South Dakota, the first clue that this is not a traditional travel account. Rather, it's a series of rambling disquisitions on the meaning of life and death, family history, accidents as moral and personal failings, other writers, especially Ernest Hemingway, and being an Armenian in America.

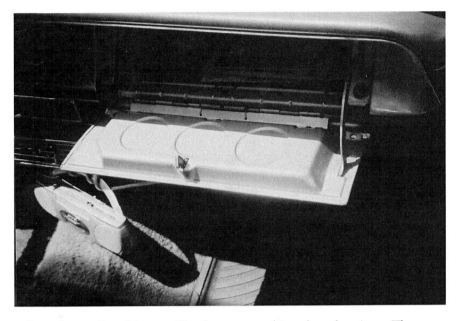

Even the smallest things on Phoebe say something about her times. These cup holders were designed to be used at drive-ins while the car was parked. Had Saroyan placed his coffee here at seventy miles per hour, his cousin would have been scalded.

The twenty-two year old Lincoln is almost as intriguing as Saroyan's ruminations. The writer bought it from an estate sale specifically for his cross-country trip and it has only 5,000 miles on its odometer. It has a leather chauffeur's seat and the original owner's initials painted on both front doors. Saroyan likes driving the car at seventy miles an hour, which may be why it burns a quart of oil every 100 miles. Fortified with ice cream and coffee, he drives far into the wee morning hours talking at his poor cousin who sits next to him much like Steinbeck's Charley. Saroyan refuses to allow his cousin to spell him at the wheel, for he believes that he is at one with the machine and any other driver would be dangerous. He could have just as well have written the book at a table in the back of a New York cafe.[17]

If the nation's foremost literary figures could not wrap their minds around America's vastness and complexities as they motored across it, others concluded to dwell on specific aspects of automotive travel to find their own verities. Phil Patton took this approach in his book *Open Road: A Celebration of the American Highway*. He believes that what we drive *on* helps define us. Where we locate our roads and their architectural contours determine what we see and experience. Sadly, engineers captured control of United States highway planning and made its roads increasingly functional at the expense of aesthetics; everything became more efficient — and more sterile. Patton is also interested in the roadside clutter along the more "scientific" roadways, most of which were built after Phoebe's first foray south in 1965, especially the rise of the much-copied Howard Johnsons with their distinctive orange roofs and the death of ma and pa roadside auto courts and attractions.[18]

Patton does not neglect the importance of the automobile. He argues that "the automobile from its beginnings was not associated so much with a vision of some modernistic future, but with the restoration of old values." He thinks the auto renews "the values that the railroads and big business had destroyed, the values of the frontier and the individual." To Patton the motorcar is "a way to return to lost freedoms and a lost sense of discovery of America." In other words, we are what we drive and what we drive upon.[19]

Two years later in 1988 Susan Kelly narrowed her purview even further and took a close look at *Route 66: The Highway and Its People*. Starting in Grant Park, Chicago, the famous highway ended at a small park on the Pacific in Santa Monica. Route 66 became a shorthand notation for adventure, freedom, youthfulness, speed, and a fresh start; it was the most famous trail to the newly motorized wild West, a route Phoebe would enjoy following some day. Kelly follows its construction from the mid–1920s through its completion in 1938. Like America, it was never finished and was choked with traffic before the builders poured the last concrete; they started widening it before it was completed. And like the American West, it was dangerous. Thousands of tourists on it were maimed or killed in frequent wrecks.[20]

Michael Witzel picks up on Kelly's interest in roadside attractions in his *The American Gas Station* which looks at how oil companies altered the nation's roads, architectural face, and driving habits. Witzel chronicles the evolution of buying gas in tins and from huge bulk tanks to the beginning of streetside pumps in 1908. Particularly interesting is his story about solving the problem of how to measure the number of gallons that flowed into each gas tank. Until World War I most gas stations were shanties with their pumps at the curb that ensured that cars waiting to fill up blocked traffic. Around the Great War oil companies began to upgrade and standardize their outlets. ARCO built stations that featured a Greek classical design while Pure Oil erected hundreds with a cottage theme. By the mid twenties most gas pumps had been set back from the curbs and during the Great Depression oil companies standardized their attendants' attire. Gas jockeys appeared in clean hats, bow ties, and jodhpurs, uniforms with a distinct military appearance.

Oil companies lured the motoring public in with gifts, especially free road maps starting in the 1930s, Christmas displays, pretty girls, clowns, grand openings, all kinds of hoopla. Gas stations also discovered that they were affording relief as well as services and promoted clean "restrooms." Phillips Petroleum hired registered nurses to check its sanitation standards while Texaco used mobile inspectors to assure the public that its restrooms sparkled.

The "modern" world intruded in 1947 when Gas-A-Terias introduced the novel concept of self-service in Los Angeles. Interstate highways sped up the revolution in roadside service because they bypassed almost all of the older stations. The 1973 oil shortage alone drove five percent of all gas stations, 10,900 of them to be exact, out of business as the big oil companies cut their fuel allocations. Witzel ably chronicles the steady march towards mini-marts clumped around interstate interchanges, where it is possible to purchase gas, pay at the pump, buy sodas and munchies from a machine, and enjoy relief without talking to a soul, the ultimate in travel loneliness and anonymity.[21]

Richard Gutman, in an equally narrow investigation of the connection between the automobile and the American essence, looked for enlightenment in the changes and evolution of roadside eating establishments in his *American Diner: Then and Now.* Gutman (a wonderful name for a diner historian) who implicitly believes that Americans are to a great extent what they eat and where and how they choose to eat it, concludes that for over a century the diner has characterized national culinary proclivities.

He dates the first diner to 1872 in Providence, Rhode Island, and they soon became male bastions and remained so until the first war because women refused to sit on stools, at least in public. In the 1920s a few enterprising diner owners installed booths in their lunch wagons to attract women. In the following decade diner architecture changed radically from unkempt wagons into the streamlined art-deco buildings we think of as the classical diner. They were not only more eye-catching but much easier to keep clean. Owners also hired waitresses to replace the often overweight, unshaven men in stained aprons who had traditionally toiled over the hot grills and served their customers. The eateries became larger and by Phoebe's birth had turned into small restaurants complete with picture windows, stone facades, brocade-vinyl booths, and wagon-wheel light fixtures.

Diners' prosperity was tied to the traffic density on the roads that fronted their businesses. Often located near factories or in busy downtown areas, they suffered from the flight to the suburbs, the new interstate highways that funneled traffic around towns, and motel restaurants. They were hurt most by the rise of franchised fast-food outlets that catered to the eating habits diners, ironically, had introduced. Diners had acclimated Americans to expect large portions of quickly prepared basic foods that they could eat standing up, seated on stools, or sitting in their cars. McDonald's, Burger King, and White Castle are really the old diners in disguise, but located alongside the new busy highways and strip malls, that have adapted modern business practices to training, advertising, purchasing, food preparation, and service.[22]

In all our 2001 perambulations in Phoebe we did not find a single old-fashioned diner, largely because we avoided big cities. There are numerous such places still open, however, and the "classic" 1930s diners with their fluted, stainless steel exteriors are once again popular, as the Steak 'N Shake outlets indicate. One of the unintended consequences of the country's driving habits, food preferences, and highway design and location is that Americans have become fat; obesity is one of the nation's leading causes of death.

William Least Heat-Moon brought many of these changes together in his 1982 classic book *Blue Highways: A Journey into America,* the work that more than any other prompted us to take Phoebe out for one more, perhaps her last, ramble around the country. Heat-Moon records his reactions to people, ideas, smells, loneliness, topography, weather, rock strata, hair styles, everything. He rates cafes and diners by the number of calendars they have hanging on their walls, from a low of one for an interstate fast food joint up to five in an establishment he suggests a traveler keep "under your hat or they'll franchise." A teacher at the University Missouri, he took to the road after his wife left him, observing that "a man who couldn't make things go right could at least go," and go he does, across the nation twice.[23]

Like the best travel writers, Heat-Moon is always introspective. In the Nevada desert he ruminates that "a mirror may not reflect mind, but man's response to landscapes, faces, events, does." He concludes that "a man [is] looking at himself by looking at what he looks at." A fuller knowledge of himself can only be had by seeing ever more places. A hundred and forty pages later he quotes Henry Miller, saying, "Our destination is never a place but rather a new way of looking at things," including, he could have added, ourselves.[24]

Heat-Moon seems unsure of all this, however. As he approaches the end of his journey he claims about 8,000 miles of blue roads have given him "an opportunity to poke at the unseen and hoping the unseen will poke back." It did. His often funny and poignant reflections on America tells us as much about him as they do about the people and countryside he pokes. The author, who is part Native American, is as complex as the nation into which he journeys. In drawing his self-portrait he illuminates many of our collective idiosyncrasies; like all good travel writers, he tells his readers something about himself as well.[25]

Lesley Hazelton certainly does in her *Driving to Detroit: An Automotive Odyssey.* In the mid–1990s the Ford Motor Company loans Hazelton, who lives on a houseboat in Seattle, an SUV for her trip to the Motor City. The automotive reporter combines a working trip with her rather eccentric personal interests to produce an equally quirky travel account. She stops to see Craig Breedlove try to set a new world land speed record in his jet-propelled speedster, the *Bluebird,* and attends the famous Pebble Beach Concours d'Elegance, where she sniffs at all the moneyed folks showing cars that they never drive. She laughs at a reporter who is amazed to see his reflection in a Duesenberg, but admits when she looks at the car's perfectly detailed engine "I saw a reflection of the human body," and wonders whether cars have souls; I suspect Phoebe does.[26]

Phoebe's straight six cylinder motor may not be a "reflection of the human body," but it is perfect for those who prefer slowness to "connect." The final inspector's crayon marks are still on the firewall, just to the left of the master cylinder. It was too bad Phoebe did not come with a notation on just what "52K" meant.

Hazelton was not looking for some central truth about the nation; instead she sought thoughtful, illustrative vignettes. A self-confessed "car-freak" who loves to drive fast, she concludes that "slowness connects, speed disconnects. The one makes you see the world, the other makes you enter the world." If that is true, Phoebe is the perfect touring car, for she cannot go fast enough to disconnect from anything. The reporter continues, "Only when you go slow can you think and absorb. Only when you go slow do you have time to see." Most Americans speed up whenever possible even on the blue roads.[27]

Larry McMurtry, a screenwriter and author of *Lonesome Dove,* is one who prefers speed with its disconnects to the vulnerability of going slowly. In his *Roads: Driving America's Great Highways,* McMurtry drives only America's interstates. He doesn't want to stop and talk to anyone; he frequently drives 800 miles a day with stops only to refuel, eat, and relieve himself. He often passes fewer than twenty words a day with anyone and loves every minute of it. He looks beyond the architectural sameness of highway interchanges and professes that such commonplace stops can never homogenize America on his beloved Great Plains.

McMurtry has three main interests — books, women, and the road. He talks about books all the time, looks for women along the highways where he never stops anywhere for long, and claims no interest in the blue roads, where women and books are found, because other authors have covered them. *Roads* is a sad book written by a loner who wants to connect emotionally but refuses to do so. He would not like Phoebe.[28]

Much travel literature was written by people who set out on long, sometimes arduous journeys seeking solitude and enlightenment. And almost every one of them at some point in their trip encounters an overwhelming sense of loneliness, a feeling of being divorced from everything else in the world. They often describe blue periods enveloping them late at night in their motel rooms after they have spent all day cooped up in their cars alone, with their pet, or a hapless traveling companion upon whom they heap compound sentences for ten or twelve hours. The road is a lonesome place, even in crowded fast food outlets or a line to buy gas. The culture of the road is not fed by human warmth or human discourse; it is a sub-civilization that exists strictly on the cash nexus — an archetypal example of American capitalism with all its benefits and faults. We pay, we receive, we go away. There are no intimations of future contact or greater intimacies. It's a cold, profit-centered world along the nation's busiest highways.

I think most travel writers and wanderers along America's byways understand that to sojourn among strangers in the privacy of their own motorcar may be the last way to achieve aloneness. Automobile explorers, however, do not really want to be totally alone, that's why they often take passengers with whom they can feel alone during long periods of comfortable silence. An old historian driving his old Phoebe takes his wife and best friend, Roberta, for that very reason. Kerouac travels with groups of hell-raisers who act so egregiously that they create private spaces for themselves far removed from the more traditional locals they encounter.

The road's solitude allows the thoughtful traveler time for intro-spection to look at himself against new backdrops and to judge his reactions to unexpected experiences, the ones that "poke back" at him. A New York *Times* journalist, writing about the benefits of hitting the road, characterizes highways as "sacred space." She contends that the byways are "a place of romance, solitude and self-discovery" which, with their "healing and redemptive power," have spawned a genre of literature. Worthy road authors, she contends, such as Steinbeck and Least Heat-Moon have searched for themselves along lonely roads while for others, getting away in their autos "has been an act of self-transformation, the highway haven for renegades and nonconformists from Bonnie and Clyde to Thelma and Louise."[29]

Going on the road can also be an escape which can lead to self-transformation. Steinbeck and Saroyan took off as their literary reputations faded, the Hall family fled the smelly world their pulp and paper mills created. Kerouac fled his middle-class upbringing with its limitations and expectations and Henry Miller used his automobile as a pulpit to distance himself from everyday concerns and to amplify his criticisms of America. McMurtry fled notoriety for the anonymity of the interstates and Least Heat-Moon escaped a failed marriage and college teaching career to poke at things outside his narrow little worlds. The Wards meandered across the country in Phoebe to escape southern summer heat, rediscover long-forgotten worlds, and to prove to ourselves that we and Phoebe were not as decrepit as we feared. Discoveries we made along the road reminded us of the youthful world of wonderment that we had once enjoyed long before we were corrupted by experiences and cynicism.

The popular assumption among writers is that solitude is the price paid for freedom. Serious commentators on the automobile's social and cultural effects have emphasized that the motorcar enables its occupants to avoid the restricted schedules and routes of trains, buses, and airplanes, all with their public social spaces, and replace them with unmatched license to wander. Motorcars freed farmers from their isolation and released women from the confines of their homes. They allowed teenagers to escape the tyranny of their family's front porch swing for the all-weather privacy of the front or rear seats in cars.

More adventuresome motorists quickly tested their new freedom by wandering far afield. Hundreds of drivers chugged out to the old American frontier to see for themselves what so fascinated Teddy Roosevelt. The West was thought to be a place where everybody could start over, seek renewal, or escape his troubles. It was the perfect place to find solitude by getting lost. Motorists invaded areas that only a couple of decades earlier had been Indian territory. They did not wear Tom Mix hats and sit astride white horses, but rather bent over the steering wheels of their Coles, Hayes-Appersons, Northerns, and Wintons as they bumped across the trackless wastes. In doing so they irrevocably altered the West by demythologizing it. Auto pioneers, tired of bogging down in sand, streams, gullies, mud, and ruts, demanded that roads be built in places as remote and mysterious as Wyoming and Utah. By the Great Depression travel across what had once been thought the Great American Desert was as comfortable as in any other part of the country.

The American West and the country's back roads have always attracted restless people more interested in how to get somewhere than in their destinations. They are more apt to allow their impulses to select routes, which is probably why in so much of the good travel literature the drivers compare their new experiences with similar places, books, movies, and people they have long known. Thoughtful backroads travelers are foreigners in their own land. They bring a childlike curiosity and freshness to even the most mundane experiences. They leave us with novel perceptions that bring the promise of renewal. They help us to define and understand ourselves; they make life more interesting — and fun.

PART IV

Back Roads

8

Out on the Blue
Roads Again

By 2001 we were free, our cat was dead, and our daughter had graduated from college and married. We were almost as footloose as we had been that hot summer of 1965 when we drove Phoebe to Baton Rouge to greet Betsy. As we mulled over where we would go that early summer of the new century, we talked about this book, still in its planning stages, and decided to combine "research" with some fun in the upper Midwest driving Phoebe across the country. We were no strangers to that region; every year we had visited Roberta's parents and family in northern Indiana at least once. During those mandatory family get-togethers, however, we were always on a tight schedule and took the interstates so many times that we had them memorized and drove them unconsciously.

We opted to drive Phoebe on a month-long exploration of middle America's "blue roads" made famous by William Least Heat-Moon, to wend our way back to where we went to college, met, and married, the land of our youthful dreams. We wondered how much of our 1960s world remained in out-of-the-way places and whether we could find any of it. We harbored no illusions about divining the nation's essence, what it meant to be an American; others more talented than us had attempted that, always with disappointing results. Instead, we looked for signs of the recent past, places with slower tempos and small businesses that still served the traveling public. We wanted to talk to folks, to explore a world not yet wholly tamed and homogenized by forty years of franchised corporations. We sought Robert Frost's roads less traveled and hoped to find that they led us back in time. In some respects we wanted to turn back the clock, our timepieces at least, to rediscover something of those years before Viet Nam, political and racial assassinations, and the long, hot summers.

We drove a 1960s technological artifact in the half-hope that if we are what we drive, then we could once again be those kids we were in those heady days of the first half of that decade — or prove to be as ancient and fragile as Phoebe. I half-jokingly suggested we comb our attic for clothes that we kept from that era, but we settled for using a 1965 map that for decades had been imprisoned in Phoebe's glove compartment. The reality of this "adventure," as we called it, was much more prosaic than our stated grandiose and probably unrealistic expectations, however; simply being a middle-aged couple putting around back roads in an old car tinted a sepia brown some of our romantic illusions about recapturing the blush of our youth.

The author stands with Phoebe in Fort Wayne, Indiana, the day after his wedding. The author still has the suit, tie, shoes, car ... and wife. Two of the five went on the 2001 adventure into the upper Midwest.

Phoebe was not designed for twenty-first century interstates and we avoided them whenever possible. Early in her life she was well-suited to run the New York Thruway and the Ohio Turnpike, roads she traversed many times, with their strictly enforced fifty-five mile per hour speed limits. Thirty-six years later Tennessee allows 70 miles per hour on its interstates, which encourages people to

On our 2001 adventure with Phoebe we stayed at locally owned motels. This one, Martin's motel on Lake Huron, advertised "Lake view rooms, clean, cozy, coffee, HBO." It lived up to its billing.

drive ten to fifteen miles per hour above that; the fastest I have ever driven Phoebe is 76 miles per hour. Moreover, her stopping abilities are suspect and with only lap belts her willingness to stop fairly quickly is vital to our safety. Phoebe also has no air bags, crumple zones, shoulder harnesses, padded interior, or seat head rests; our lives depend on being obsessively observant and maintaining a "space" around her which is difficult on overcrowded interstates.

We also had aesthetic reasons to stick to the blue roads, which are now red on most maps. Years ago author John Stilgoe noted in his *Metropolitan Corridors* that railroads create a unique environment between their fences. Interstates do the same; they too are designed to keep the real, every-day world away from traveling strangers. Houses, animals, people, telephone poles, flowers, parks, lawn ornaments, cemeteries, and libraries are either hidden or so far away that they are a blur. Strangers everywhere are suspect; when we stopped for lunch at a pub on the courthouse square in Bowling Green, Missouri, two-dozen regulars stopped talking and stared at us until the waitress certified that we really wanted something to eat. Only then did the pub return to its noisome self. To protect locals from threatening people like us, the states fence in the interstates and provide few exits and entrances — like prison yards.[1]

Interstates are also fraught with violence. Slashing along at 70 miles an hour wreaks visual violence. Images are fired into the driver's brain in increments of maybe $\frac{1}{32}$nd of a second, too fast to focus or think about anything. The driver's perception becomes tunnel-like, trained on inanities such as the sign on the back of the truck trailer just ahead that asks "Is my driving OK?" and suggests calling an eleven digit phone number to report. Most who drive interstates admit they think of nothing at all; my mind just goes into overdrive; it hums along without connecting with anything. The visual violence is compounded by aural assaults. Noise bombards drivers and passengers in a perfect dissidence with visual images and embedded in the din are the ever-present signs of mechanical distress. Engines scream and clatter, gears grind, brakes squeal, tires thump over the tarred welts of freeway expansion joints and their carcasses along the roadsides testify to their beatings, air brakes release sudden hisses, and everywhere unnatural wind gusts buffet ears and car.

The sensory havoc between the fences is partially mitigated by rolling up windows, something we could not do driving across the country that summer of 1965 in an unairconditioned car. Technology from the 1960s has its limits; not everything from that era is desirable or even acceptable, so we decided to air condition Phoebe for our adventure. Adding an air conditioner to a thirty-six year old automobile, however, is not a simple matter, nor is it all that rational. Phoebe was not designed for it and her radiator capacity is several quarts lower than that of her cooled sisters. We compensated by raising her water pressure from 13 to 16 psi and using almost pure water, which cools more effectively than anti-freeze. I had her radiator boiled and cored, her heater core replaced, and a new thermostat installed to prepare her for the additional stress of keeping us cool.

The system we had installed is a marvel. The compressor draws only 4.7 horsepower so Phoebe does not stutter every time it clicks on. Moreover, it is very small, tucked under the alternator, with thin hoses running into the cabin's floor which go far to maintain Phoebe's physical

With the air conditioner compressor tucked under the alternator and the hoses attached to the fenders and firewall, Phoebe was not horribly violated by the addition of air.

integrity. The most worrisome aspect was the heat exchange unit that impedes flow to her radiator. The installer could not fit the usual two fans in front of the radiator because Phoebe has front-end bracing that blocks them. He mounted only one fan on one side and planned to compensate for the missing fan by concentrating the air flow with a radiator shroud. We might as well have decided to use a Faberge egg as a hood ornament; 1965 radiator shrouds are more rare than the eggs. They are not to be had anywhere, at any price.

We departed in a miasma of Tennessee heat and humidity without assurances we had enough cooling capacity. But we did have a surfeit of cold; never had we felt an auto air conditioner that poured out such frigid air. We rode in absolute comfort — while it worked. On the third day the compressor burned out with an intermittent, ear-piercing death screech. On our entire 3,820 mile adventure the only part on Phoebe that completely failed was her only new one. When we reached our daughter's house in Michigan we had a new compressor "overnighted" and installed. Phoebe had no overheating problems, not even around St. Louis on an unbearably hot, Baton Rouge–like, day when a local radio announcer comforted us with the news that the heat index was 108 degrees. That afternoon Phoebe's interior temperature remained close to frost inducing.

To maintain her aged mechanicals and enhance our comfort and safety I had her oil changed, her greedy fittings greased, her front wheel bearings lubricated, her brakes and brake hoses closely checked, and her tires replaced with four new radials. For added safety we brought along a fire extinguisher, a small, battery-powered radio to listen to NPR and books on tape, a vinyl center arm rest cum storage bin, and a set of wooden beaded seat covers to allow air flow across our backs and keep us from sliding across Phoebe's slick, vinyl-clad bench seat. Throughout the adventure she feasted on high-test gasoline to help her climb hills and atone for the lack of leaded fuel she was designed to ingest.

Most folks who light out on adventures over back roads take somebody or something to ward off loneliness and attract conversation. Steinbeck took Charley, others took friends, relatives, co-workers, and even an aged cat. In our case we took Phoebe. It took all of a couple of hours to discover that she was as adept as cats, dogs, and babies in attracting people. At our first stop in Smithville, Tennessee, people walked over to talk even before we got out of the car. As they did everywhere on the trip, they made initial comments about Phoebe that included a guess as to her birth year, most of which were wrong, applauded our bravery for driving her across the country, proffered advice on the best local diner, and suggested interesting things to see in the area. They often followed with a precis of their lives right up to the minute we met. One gentleman in Smithville detailed all his vacation trips since World War II. We also discovered there that women were as apt as men to stop for a chat; perhaps they believed that any man who bought a car that tame and ugly could not be a threat. He must be what he drives.

Phoebe attracted numerous memorable folks, many of whom appeared to have all the time in the world. In West Union, Iowa, on July fourth, we stayed at a motel plopped down in a residential neighborhood. An older couple next door relaxed in lawn chairs in front of their garage. The husband sauntered over to look at Phoebe and invited us to come and "sit a spell." He was a retired Armour hog buyer anxious to tell us about how meat packers' hog preferences had changed over his half-century career. After World War II, he explained, Armour bought hogs that averaged about 1,200 pounds each. Consumer tastes changed, however, and they demanded leaner meat. When he retired he was buying 550 pound hogs that, thanks to drugs, were only six months old. It was a week before we could face bacon with our eggs.

In Dewitt, Iowa, we stopped to ask directions to Roberta's ancestors' cemetery. The Catholic church we found was locked but next door a fellow was tending his flowers and watched us, with more than the usual interest, get out of Phoebe. After we explained who we were and what we wanted, he thought for a moment and then in a blink he ran Roberta's lineage through two generations and concluded that he was a shirt-tail relation of hers. Then we had to explain Phoebe. Only after he had placed us squarely in his firmament did he direct us to the nearby, out-of-town cemetery.

As we drove to the graveyard, located behind the now-closed church in Villa Nova, we were stuck behind an ancient farmer astride an equally old John Deere tractor whose maximum speed on the winding highway was in the low single digits. We followed him onto the road beside the church, where he stopped to inquire why folks who looked old enough to know better were following him in an old car. After we told him, the 93 year old ticked off Roberta's forebears back before World War I, pointed out the farms and farmhouses they had worked and owned, and directed us to where they lay among the jungle of tombstones. He had been a fixture in the area a half century before Phoebe was assembled. After he left we found his wife's grave, obviously carefully tended and covered with fresh flowers every day; she had died barely two years earlier.

Sometimes Phoebe attracted folks in the most surprising places. We stopped in Shipshewana, Indiana, where we ate lunch in an Amish cafe that was surrounded by horses and buggies. After lunch, as we prepared to get into Phoebe, an elderly Amish man ambled over, correctly guessed Phoebe's year of birth, admired her, and then told us that his wife had died recently and he was very lonely. As he was talking I saw three Amish boys come out and get in their buggy. As they turned it around I saw that they were towing a trailer carrying a fishing boat with a motor on it. We had wandered into a world that was struggling to maintain traditions it had established long before the invention of the Evinrude.

Not everyone who stopped could even remember 1965. In Bayfield, Wisconsin, we parked Phoebe on a side street and walked several blocks for lunch. When we returned a young girl, perhaps twenty years old, was sitting on the sidewalk, propped up against a streetlight across the street, with a big sketchbook across her lap. She explained that she was an art student and had walked all over town to find something interesting to draw. She was only three blocks from a national park of unimagined beauty, full of wilderness islands, quaint lighthouses, and miles of wooded shoreline, and was drawing Phoebe because, she said, it was a "cool" car. We liked her instantly but never saw her again to check the results of her exquisite taste.

We were struck that people everywhere were so inquisitive even as they were so ready to proffer details of their personal lives. Phoebe was an open invitation to ask questions about us and our car and a springboard for them to reminisce about their own cars and lives. Most people we talked to were more interested in people than abstractions and generalities. They thought small; we and Phoebe were a discreet bit they could affix to their personal worlds. Nobody was interested in national or state affairs or their new president. It was more important for them to know why we were wandering through their precincts; they found us a pleasant diversion from musing about the weather.

Frequently we struck up conversations at local cafes. Back in the dark ages of the 1960s, such establishments were where important local questions were debated and opinions on weighty matters were formed and solidified. Nearly forty years later the physical aspects of such gathering places have changed little. At mealtimes we cased small towns for a diner that seemed a local favorite and soon discovered that it was more likely to be located in the middle of a block than on a corner, although we have no idea why.

Holiday Inn advertisements promise no surprises for travelers; surprise is exactly what we sought and family restaurants are full of them. For example, they are often either overheated or cooled, but sometimes that had its compensations. On the hottest day Ely, Minnesota, had seen in a year we ate on a screened porch shaded by massive old trees that held just the barest hint of a cooling breeze; it was a wonderful ambiance, especially after having been cooped up and chilled in Phoebe all morning. Everywhere chairs and china were mismatched, tables rocked and swayed as we ate, floors tilted, handwritten menus had prices crossed out and changed, flies flitted with enthusiasm, and owners and guests alike cherished such foibles. Their decors were just as varied. Signs that read "Damned is not God's last name" competed with mounted fish, old maps, pictures of the biggest pumpkin ever grown in Grant County, and the ubiquitous framed first dollar slapped up helter-skelter on walls. At an old inn in Ashland, Wisconsin, every inch of the inside was festooned with Hollywood and Kennedy memorabilia. John Kennedy, Jr., had stayed there for several nights with his kayaking buddies and had charmed the entire staff. We ate there twice and never finished reading all the stuff.

One of the nicest things about eateries was that, as in the mid–1960s, their fares featured local items not delivered frozen on a Sysco truck. They often buy produce from local farmers, although our June jaunt was too early for the first vegetables. Strawberries were "in," however, and were everywhere. We ran out of grits and okra as we drove north and by Minnesota we discovered the joys of wild rice. As we followed the Great Lakes roads for a couple of weeks we ate what seemed like the yearly catch of whitefish. Almost every cafe featured homemade soups, just as they had almost forty years earlier, real ones made with a stock base and chock full of leftovers from what we fervently hoped was only the day before. In numerous cafes we were given a free rundown on the history of the building, its owner, and the town; diners' habitués like to talk.

We were surprised, however, that even in the most remote towns current trends have made inroads. Local beaneries offer such upscale and inedible items as tofu, bean sprouts, bean curds, and "lite" items. Pita bread has become popular in America's heartland and is sold stuffed with almost anything. Many cafes had newspapers scattered about and we found one in Owosso, Michigan, with computer terminals for its customers' use. We should have been forewarned when we noted its menu offered a meat sandwich topped with cherries. It was not as tasty as advertised.

Americans, even in the small town eateries that advertise home cooking, eat very few vegetables. French fries are the national vegetable and maybe the national fruit as well. And despite the menus' offerings of trendy, less fatty foods, the preferred method of cooking is still deep-fried. Americans will eat anything covered with a brown batter. Sometimes we could not find anything on the menu that was not fried and might come with a vegetable. Some folks heed nutritional advice, but preponderantly Americans stick with diets that were popular in 1965. And our absolutely unscientific sampling was done almost entirely in cafes and restaurants that offered wider selections than the more popular fast food franchises that sell mostly burgers, fries, and cokes.

The villages' downtowns, where most of our cafes were located, were an equally mixed lot. Our impression was that only towns with fewer than about 2,000 citizens lack strip malls out on their fringes, but even a few of the tiny ones surprised us with their homemade versions of concentrated commercial clutter. Despite the fact that Wal-Mart has devastated mercantile businesses that were commonly located on Main Streets in the 1960s, we found that there is a reverse migration all over the Midwest in which smaller, more specialized, and trendier shops have taken advantage of lower downtown rents to replace the businesses that earlier closed or fled to the malls. Even the smallest towns feature antique shops, boutiques, candle emporiums, drug stores, taverns, newspaper offices, legal firms, and specialty clothing shoppes on their Main Streets. Some businesses such as hardware and appliance stores have also bucked the trend toward mega-stores. We did not see a downtown grocery store anywhere, however; families have to trek out to their local strip mall to buy food to cook at home.

Town fathers all along the back roads have abetted the return to the mercantile norms of Phoebe's youth. Small towns like Horse Cave, Kentucky, Paoli, Indiana, Marshall, Michigan, Hurley, Wisconsin, and Spillville, Iowa, have spruced up their core business districts. Antique light poles, hanging baskets of flowers, new curbs, brick streets, decorative trash containers, and manicured parks point to their newfound pride in local distinctiveness. Many villages have refurbished their old railroad freight and passenger depots. Albion, Michigan, boasts a nice Italian restaurant in its former freight warehouse; Logansport, Indiana, uses its depot as the headquarters for its yearly Iron Horse Festival; Two

Harbors, Minnesota, installed a logging railway display outside its former depot and uses the building as an information center and museum. The depot at Alexandria, Minnesota, stands at the head of a lake so that diners who choose to eat under the old train shed have a scenic vista that combines an industrial artifact and one of Minnesota's more than 10,000 bodies of water. More important, a nice breeze blew off the lake the hot day we ate there.

The roads that are the lifeblood of hundreds of such small towns were in better condition in the summer of 2001 than most of the interstates and certainly were better than we remembered them being in 1965. Most were newly paved and smooth, and some were even banked. It was obvious that they do not bear the destructive traffic of heavy eighteen wheelers that pound freeways to death. Only Michigan, where all roads are miserable, was an exception. In our week exploring the state we saw only one construction project — in the middle of nowhere on the Upper Peninsula. Signage everywhere was more than adequate; we probably did not get lost more than a dozen times and every one was our fault. If anything, there was a surfeit of highway signs; the following year we drove through British Columbia where Canadians believe that one small sign announcing anything up to the second coming is more than adequate. We never believed the first signs we spotted and waited for the next ones; there weren't any. We were perpetually lost.

On the negative side, the blue roads' curves were often tighter and some of them, particularly in the mountainous regions in East Tennessee and Kentucky, are still corkscrews. Most roads are laid on top of the natural topography without resort to cuts and fills that might have leveled them. Just as she had thirty-six years earlier, Phoebe balked at the ones that had long hills with sharp curves that cost her her momentum. Few blue roads had shoulders, probably because road builders assumed that flat tires are best changed in the middle of the driving lane. We drove through Iowa during a dry spell and a dusty haze hung over the whole northeastern part of the state. The airborne Iowa topsoil advertised that many of that state's farm-to-market roads are still unpaved, just as Indiana's were back in the 1960s.

We tried to keep Phoebe off unpaved roads; we did not drive into baseball's "field of dreams" for that reason. But we got caught just south of Spillville on route 150 when Roberta insisted we return to the world's smallest church that she had visited as a child. The turn-off was paved but once we got over the first hill we found ourselves driving on a road with the consistency of vacuum cleaner debris. As it was only a couple of miles to the church we continued and the detour was worth the trouble. We felt sorry, however, for the farm family just up the road that was having what looked like a family reunion; we billowed immense dust clouds over its picnic both times we went by. They had their revenge though; all of Phoebe's twelve lubrication joints are exposed and the dust and grit played havoc with them. She immediately began to squeak and even a grease job that night did not end her protestations. Three days later, when lost in Quincy, Illinois, we found

Phoebe visited the world's smallest church, located outside Spillville, Iowa. She ingested so much dust from the dirt road leading to it that her joints groaned for days.

a mechanic who doused her ball joints with WD-40 which finally eased her pain.

Driving the blue roads, whether paved or not, requires a different kind of concentration than when we batter along hour after hour on the interstates. We never had any idea of what lay over the next hill, for example; anything could be there: farm machinery, railroad crossings, strip mall entrances, narrow bridges, crows eating carrion, or a family's cocker spaniel scratching himself on the yellow line.

We had to hone our 1965 map reading skills again; road signs were smaller than those we were used to on interstates, intersections often were marked by a half a dozen route signs, all of them the same with black numbers on white backgrounds, and the clutter of billboards, business signs, and buildings, especially in towns, occasionally obscured vital signs. Every morning we planned our day's route to pass any place that appeared interesting, was generally in the direction we were headed, or was oddly named, such as Floyd's Knobs in Indiana. Because there were many fewer billboards in rural blue-roads areas and they tended to be local, we read all of them to learn that the Kiwanis met every Tuesday at noon, a village with fewer people than dogs checked its speed limit with radar, Bardstown, Kentucky, was holding its world famous Rolling Fork Iron Horse festival soon, and there was a Jehovah's Witness church just eleven miles ahead.

The paucity of billboards allowed us to survey the countryside almost without visual interruption, admiring barn sizes, dairy cows that clumped at their fences to watch us pass, and thousands of lawn ornaments, which are Roberta's particular expertise. She did not miss a cement deer, flamingo, flower-garden toilet, or bathtub Madonna for almost 4,000 miles. And she found the world's last cement black boy-holding-a-lantern statue, in Canada of all places, sitting on a spit of land that juts into Minnesota's Boundary Waters.

The concentration required to drive back roads was more invigorating than tiring. It was fun to search for local industries, for example, to divine what folks thereabouts did for a living. For thousands of miles we applauded Midwesterners who still mowed the verges in front of their fields along the highways across to their neighbors' lawns to lend the whole region a manicured look. People who take that care do not litter. Unlike Tennessee and the rest of the South, where littering is a skill taught in kindergarten, Midwesterners take their roadside environments personally. We could tell much about the people who lived along our roads by reading the names on their mailboxes and noting the largest churches. Regional denominational dominance told us a great deal about who settled there decades before Phoebe was built. In parts of Minnesota we could not throw a rock without breaking a Lutheran church's window and their sheer numbers were testimony to the magnitude of the Scandinavian immigration at the end of the nineteenth century.

From New Ulm, Minnesota, south to route 9 in north central Iowa, the Lutherans petered out and the many Catholic churches announced the beginning of German-American territory. Huge churches in some of the small villages around St. Ansgar and Cresco proudly standing on their town's highest point, nearer to God than everyone else, could be seen for miles. They reminded us of parts of Europe where steeples measure the distance between villages. Some rural Iowa churches are the size of cathedrals, seemingly far out of proportion to the local population density. We toured one in Dyersville, Iowa, where we were taken in hand by an enthusiastic guide. His church was a basilica, he carefully explained, an official residence for the Pope should he ever visit Dyersville, an occurrence I thought rather remote. The dome over the altar featured a wonderful mural of saints in which all but one wore a halo; he was a former pastor. The docent hastened to add that such a good man must be amongst the anointed.

Near route 31 in the center of Kentucky a grouping of villages, St. Catherine, Loretto, St. Francis, St. Mary, and Holy Cross, advertises the numerous Catholic settlers there. In the midst of them stands the nation's oldest order of Cistercian Monks, more commonly known as Trappists, at the Abbey of Gethsemani. They have been there since 1848 and came to national notice when one, Father Louis, better known to the public as Thomas Merton, became an international figure with his book, *The Seven Storey Mountain,* published in 1948. Merton became a household name in the 1960s when he railed publicly against racism, the Viet Nam war, and the probability of nuclear annihilation. When researching my biography of Ping Ferry I went through Merton's papers at Bellarmine College in Louisville. Ferry, a noted leftist, was vice president of the Center for the Study of Democratic Institutions in Santa Barbara, California, in the 1960s when he disseminated writings that the censored monk smuggled out from behind his monastic walls. I had to see where Merton spent his most productive years during Phoebe's youth and pay my graveside respects.[2]

Our visit was made more poignant because we spent the evening before in Bowling Green, Kentucky, where we toured the Corvette Museum that memorializes the sleek, powerful, low-slung, fiberglass sports car that is an icon representing America's mid-century material acquisitiveness. The museum has a copy of every 'vette ever built, including many one-off models. It is rather much for all but the most dedicated Corvette enthusiast, however, and we were overwhelmed. The museum's parking lot has special parking spaces reserved for visitors who drive their Corvettes to the marque's shrine. There were a couple of 'Vettes occupying the honored spots when we arrived and parked Phoebe among the plebeians. When we came out, however, there were a half a dozen people gathered around Phoebe, the plainest Jane of all Chevrolets ever, while not a soul was examining the pair of Corvettes still parked in their special places.

The following morning, before we drove up to Gethsemani, we toured the nearby Corvette factory. It was already blistering hot when we arrived at 8.45 a.m., but thankfully the part we toured was air conditioned. It was the cleanest plant we had ever seen. Surprisingly, the work force averaged over fifty years in age. We were told that the comfortable working conditions and the line's slow pace — it only builds a maximum of about seventy cars an hour — made assembly line work there plum jobs that require years of union seniority to get. Once there, workers rarely leave.

We departed the world of Corvettes and all they symbolized about the pace and aspirations of modern life to mosey north on back roads to Gethsemani, where the monks go about their appointed tasks in silence and where the fields and walls fall away in perfect neatness, a visual feast of the rural ideal. The whitewashed abbey sprawls across the top of a hill, its buildings embracing the church. There was not a car in the small parking lot when we arrived and as we walked towards the church we felt as if we had stepped out of the bustle of the industrial world straight into the Fourteenth Century; it was unnerving.

The young monk at the information center appeared determined to make up for all the hours he had been silent. The church was a surprise, for inside it was Twentieth Century modern. Ping Ferry had complained that he found it painful to kneel on its gravel floor; it may have been gravel in the 1960s but it is now pebbled concrete which looked hardly more comfortable. Merton's grave was easy to find. Although it was adorned with the same simple cross as all the other graves, it was swathed in fresh flowers. The chatty brother told us that admirers stopped every day and left the bouquets. We felt rather sorry for the other monks who had no one to remember them with mounds of colorful blooms.

We had no intention of turning our adventure into a pilgrimage to religious sites. But they loomed everywhere on the back roads, in stark contrast to the interstate highways devoid of anything that smacks of religion. On our way home, we left route 67 in Illinois to visit Nauvoo, whose odd name is a Hebrew word that means "beautiful location," the historic Mormon town founded by Joseph Smith in 1839. We arrived on a sweltering afternoon to a forest of no vacancy signs. We finally found a room in a Mormon family motel, I think that was the name on its roadside sign, that gave discounts to missionaries. Before we signed the register the owner quizzed us about how long we had been married, the number of children we had, where we had been and were going. He was very nice, but I suspect had we been on a sinful, unmarried adventure we may have been looking for another room. The motel was strangely shaped and was criss-crossed with exceptionally wide, long hallways. The miles of its walls were festooned with prints of Mormon dignitaries and historical scenes. I felt guilty as I fixed myself three fingers of single-malt for a pre-prandial libation and went out to the back parking lot to savor it and a smoke. Virtually every car and all the tour buses parked out there bore Utah license plates; the guests were on real pilgrimages, their own personal and spiritual adventures. When we went down for breakfast the next morning we found a dozen families already eating, but not a soul was talking. Their eyes were all glued to television sets that were showing a rerun of a NASCAR race. If the box has seduced the family-centered Mormons so easily we wondered if was there was any hope. We reminisced about how on our first trip south in Phoebe we were lucky if our motel room even had a TV.

After a pleasant dinner at the Hotel Nauvoo, an old inn that offered the largest buffet we had ever seen and bragged it served 1,500 dinners on a recent Mothers' Day, we took Phoebe on a tour of the modern town and drove out to "Old Nauvoo." The Church of Jesus Christ of the Latter Day Saints promotes "Old Nauvoo" as "the Williamsburg of the Midwest" and there is more than a grain of truth to that assertion. A driven and industrious people, the Mormons drained the swampy lowlands they had chosen, built numerous sturdy structures of brick and limestone, and their village was soon the 10th largest town in the nation. Their temple, which later burned and was afterwards flattened by a tornado, was for a time the largest building west of Philadelphia.[3]

Not all was harmonious in old Nauvoo, however. Neighbors, jealous of the Mormons' prosperity, became hostile while internal divisions ripped the sect apart. Violence ensued in 1844; after Smith ordered the Mormon presses that criticized his leadership burned, he was incarcerated in the nearby Carthage jail. A mob stormed the building and lynched Smith. That convinced most of Nauvoo's settlers that if they were ever to live in peace they would have to find a more isolated spot. Under Brigham Young's leadership, most began trekking out to the Great Salt Lake district to build their city on the hill. Those who remained formed the Reformed Church of the Latter Day Saints and the legacy of that split can be seen today in Nauvoo; there is an LDS welcome center that controls almost all of the site and a RLDS historic center that maintains Joseph Smith's home, his family cemetery, the Nauvoo mansion house, and a building that once was Smith's office.

There were practically no people walking about the evening that we visited and we wandered the streets peeking into the windows of the perhaps twenty-five buildings still standing. They are more scattered than at Williamsburg but all stand on their original plots; in many vacant lots we could see the depressed outlines where later buildings had once stood. At the end of our stroll we enjoyed a spectacular sunset over the Mississippi; it took forever for the brilliant sunburst to settle below the horizon. As we savored the spectacle, Mormons began arriving in their cars for a sundown service on the river bank. We were tempted, but opted for showers and an early night.

On our original peregrinations with Phoebe back in 1965 we did not have the money or time to investigate interesting places we espied along the roads. On this driveabout we often did not "make" a hundred miles a day. Intriguing possibilities lurked everywhere. For example, we were tempted to wander some miles outside of Logansport, Indiana, when we came upon a crossroads on highway 24 with signs pointing to Peru, Chile, and Mexico. After a few hours of cruising through miles of prosperous Indiana farmland, however, we decided we could not miss the Menno-Hof Mennonite-Amish museum in Shipshewana, tucked up against Michigan's border.

Both sects derived from the Anabaptist movement that originated in Switzerland in 1525. They were founded on the idea that only adult believers should be baptized and only after they made a confession of faith. The Anabaptists charged that infant baptism was a manifestation of corrupt state control over religion. Led initially by Jacob Hutter, who believed in communal living following the example of early Christians, the Anabaptists met with opposition everywhere they went. A Dutch priest, Menno Simons, believed that he and his followers should live and work in the secular world and organized the Mennonites in 1536. The roughly 750,000 Mennonites today drive cars, use electricity and telephones, and take advantage of labor-saving conveniences. Anabaptists, however, were prone to splits and in 1693 Jacob Ammann led his Swiss followers out of the Mennonite fold to found what became the Amish. Ammann accused the Mennonites of becoming too worldly and preached that his flock should remain apart from the sinful world and cling to its traditional ways.

Often crippled by severe political reprisals, especially because they called for a separation of church and state, the Mennonites accepted William Penn's invitation to settle in his New World tract. They began immigrating to the area around Germantown, Pennsylvania, in 1683. Like the Quakers already there who exercised political control over the admiral's wilderness, the Mennonites refused to swear oaths or participate in wars and five years later drew up the colonies' first protest against slavery. Like the Quakers, the Mennonites and the Amish were hard-working, purposeful, prosperous people with large families who soon became land hungry and joined the exodus to the west. In 1841 they arrived in Indiana and soon spread southward along the state's eastern boundary, where they remain today.

Mennonites in the United States have split into several sub-sects but four of them joined to create a non-profit "information center" in Shipshewana. Built to resemble an Amish barn, even to its post and beam construction, the museum was erected by believers, working communally, in only seven days — a biblically symbolic building. The center is part museum and part a proselytizing effort and is a great deal more sophisticated than such repositories were in the 1960s. Its exhibits draw visitors through Anabaptist history from Christ's era to the present. The proselytizing begins quietly midway through the tour when the displays become topical, emphasizing Anabaptists' sense of community, diversity, humor, music, simplicity, care, and peace. The tour ends with a visit to a reading room that includes materials explaining their religious beliefs and a computer terminal on which it is possible to locate the nearest Mennonite church to the visitor's home. The museum's pamphlet reinforces its religious message, listing Anabaptist tenets, most of which are couched well within the Christian mainstream.[4]

Our first reaction to the information center's proselytizing was unfavorable. Upon reconsideration, however, we agreed we had learned a great deal about the churches' history and gained a sense of the theological differences that set the Anabaptists apart from more traditional Christian organizations, those being the very elements that made them so unique and interesting in the first place. The buggies that were quietly passing the museum as we emerged reinforced our sense that we had spent a couple of hours wandering through a world that had preserved elements of its uniqueness well into the nuclear and electronics age. Had we driven Phoebe through Shipshewana in 1965, we suspect that it would have looked little different than it did in the new century.

Proselytizing comes in many guises, not all of which are religious. One of the big differences between traveling the back roads in 1965 and 36 years later is that communities, museums, local businesses, and cultural institutions have to struggle harder to attract the public's attention. It is now more important for them to do so because everywhere the tourist dollar has become so important. While religious centers such as Gethsemani, Nauvoo, and Menno-Hof advertise their dramatic differences from present norms, secular institutions more often resort to hyperbole, much like carnivals and Florida alligator farms of yore, to hawk their profferings.

9

Home Again, Lickety-Split

The remainder of our adventure was decidedly more secular. On our return trip, for example, we made a wide swing through western Minnesota to visit the Runestone Museum at Alexandria. In 1898 a nearby Swedish farmer had unearthed the stone upon which had been carved Scandinavian runes that described a Norse journey with thirty men to the area in 1362. It tells of how ten of them were killed and that the party had another ten "by the sea" two weeks' journey from the marker. The find created a furor, the farmer was accused of forgery, and he eventually gave the stone to a graduate student, Hjalmar Holand, who embarked on a one-man crusade to prove its authenticity.

In several books he spun a tale supported by circumstantial evidence that featured King Magnus of Norway, who had authorized an expedition in 1355 to find and return to Christianity Greenlanders who had disappeared from that island's Western Settlement. The ten men at the sea, said Holand, had built the tower at Newport, Rhode Island, itself long the center of controversy. Holand traced the exploration party's purported journey to Alexandria along a series of rivers bounded by what he argued were mooring holes the Norse had bored into rocks to tie up their boats. His theories drew hosts of skeptics and after Eric Walghren, a professor of Scandinavian literature at UCLA, wrote his book, *The Kensington Stone: A Mystery Solved,* in 1958 in which he argued that the runes used were inappropriate for 1362, most experts agreed the stone was a forgery. Only lately, since our adventure, have "experts" again advanced the case for the stone's authenticity. If it is a fraud, the enduring question is by whom and for what end.[1]

It is most likely a fraud, but we drove a good bit out of our way to see it anyway. We had no trouble finding the museum; as I drove

Phoebe down Alexandria's main street a thirty foot tall statue of a Viking erupted ahead from the yellow line, a good 1960s kind of understated advertisement for the museum's location. Fully bearded, the figure has a distinctly hostile demeanor. With his spear, sword, and shield he appears to be guarding the museum's front door. In an outsized manner

In her long years on the road Phoebe has met with some strange sights, but none more odd than this outsized Viking standing in the middle of the street in Alexandria, Minnesota, advertising its local museum that holds the controversial Kensington stone. "Big Ole" was originally constructed for Minnesota's state pavilion at the 1964–65 World's Fair in New York.

he announces that all non-believers in the stone's authenticity will have to deal with him. Curiously, his helmet sports Mercury-like wings where I might have expected the traditional, but historically incorrect, horns.

I was terribly disappointed to learn that the Kensington Stone had been shipped to Vienna, Austria, for display, one of the few times it has been out of the state, and had been replaced with a replica. It was interesting, however, to see how the museum treated the whole controversy over the stone; it studiously avoided stating that it was a genuine artifact. Instead, the curator presented a very good history of the events surrounding its discovery and early history and a display of other possible Norse artifacts found in the general area. All this was accompanied by "authoritative" statements that the stone was really what it purports to be. Additionally, the museum's visitors' pamphlet devotes a page to "endorsements" of the stone by such worthies as the Minnesota Historical Society Commission of 1910 and the Minneapolis Norwegian Society Commission of 1909 that "voted 2–1 that the stone was authentic." Despite all the hoopla about the stone, the museum is an intriguing depository with informative displays of local history and life. Without the Kensington Stone, of course, it would attract much less notoriety and traffic.[2]

Many back-road museums are hidden in out of the way places, do little in the way of self-promotion, and are easy to miss. We stumbled upon such a jewel in Spillville, Iowa. A German immigrant, Joseph Spielman, founded the town in 1854 and modestly named the place Spiellville, later anglicized. His settlement attracted Bohemians who gave it its unusual character. Antonín Dvořák brought the village notice when he spent the summer of 1893 there making "some final corrections" on his *New World* symphony and writing at least one quartet.

The house where Dvorak stayed contains some memorabilia upstairs while the downstairs is reserved for the Bily brothers' clock collection. The two men were born, raised, and died on a nearby farm. Neither married and starting in 1913 they spent their winters carving incredibly intricate clocks, many with animals, people, and scenes that spring into motion at appropriate times. They collected rare woods from around the world and cleverly worked them into their creations, some which tower almost to the museum's ceiling. Their artistry and

The Bily Clock Museum in Spillville, Iowa, is a superb example of a local museum tended with care by Spillvillians who believed their collection of hand-carved clocks merited wider attention.

mechanical sophistication gained them fame and they once turned down a million dollars for a particularly intricate creation. They kept their collection together and moved it to the old Dvorak house to make it available to the public. The clocks still work, erupting in a frenzy of motion on the hour, and the woman who showed us around treated them with a reverence usually reserved for religious relics. The brothers died just as Phoebe was born.

Not every blue roads attraction we visited was such a gem, however. We more or less followed the Great River Road down the Mississippi River and decided to stop in Mark Twain country to take a peek at the early influences on his life. As we approached Hannibal, Missouri, the tell-tale rise in heat and humidity warned us that we were nearing the river. As we crested a hill that overlooked the town we were shocked to see it teeming with cars and people; we could not figure out how they got there because the road we traveled was lightly trafficked, but after a glance at the map we concluded they must have snuck into Hannibal on interstate 36, a freeway that ends abruptly not far north of town. The city was gridlocked, but we nosed Phoebe into the traffic and let it jerk us along past Twain's boyhood home and Becky Thatcher's house, after which we fled as soon as we could escape the snarl.

In contrast, Columbus, Indiana, located on busy 1–65, is an architectural revelation and relatively free of tourists. We approached it coming north through Brown County, a beautiful, hilly, forested region of the state, taking highway 46 from Gnaw Bone, which we could not resist, into Columbus. Home of Cummins Engine Company, Columbus' private companies and governmental agencies hire the world's leading architects to design their new buildings with such success that the town promotes tours featuring about 65 stunning creations. Just ten years earlier when the Association of American Architects asked its members to rank the nation's most architecturally significant cities, Columbus was voted sixth, behind only Chicago, Washington, New York, Boston and San Francisco.

Buildings all over the city are striking. Columbus' fire halls, schools, jail, power house, senior center, post office, library, and city hall are outstanding edifices designed by the likes of Eliel Saarinen, I.M. Pei, Roche Dinkeloo, Skidmore, Owings & Merrill, and Harry Weese. Its private buildings — banks, churches, corporate headquarters and manufacturing complexes — are no less distinctive. Taking a cue from European cities, the little town boasts numerous public sculptures and takes pains to ensure its bridges on second street and over 1–65 are also architectural masterpieces. There is so much to see that the city's recommended "short driving tour" takes two hours.

We stopped on a threatening, overcast day and decided we needed lunch and the exercise of a downtown walking tour. In front of the Bartholomew County Courthouse we found the most moving war memorial, save Washington, D.C. 's Viet Nam shrine, that we had ever seen. It has about 20 pillars jutting perhaps 30 feet into the air. Each one contains the names of county war dead from all American wars with short excerpts from their letters home. Many are moving epistles, often their last ones. When the lights built into the floor are lighted on a pitch-dark night, the memorial must be a stirring, spiritual sight.

The monument held our attention longer than we had anticipated; the sky was turning inky black and the winds were starting to gust. No sooner had we torn ourselves away from the county's war dead than the heavens opened with such force that our umbrella was useless. We got soaked, but it felt good because the water and lashing wind cooled us down.

Towns and cities are becoming adept at packaging themselves to lure tourists off the interstates. While Columbus touts its cutting-edge, modern architecture, other places such as Galena, Illinois, glory in what they missed while they slept. Located in Illinois' northwest corner, Galena peaked in the decade before the Civil War as a lead mining, smelting, steam-boating port. In 1853 it bragged it had a population of 8,000 souls, almost four times more than Columbus had that year. Unfortunately the railway arrived the following year and negated the town's river advantage. Galena's claim to fame is Ulysses S. Grant, who resigned his army commission in 1854, tried his hand at farming and then moved there to clerk in his father's leather goods store. The town was a nursery for Union generals; eight other residents pinned stars on their uniforms and joined Grant.[3]

Galena's great fortune was that it declined as quickly as it boomed and became a backwater, quite literally, given the enormity of the floodgates that guard its downtown. Buildings dating to 1826 remained in use and when the town fathers awakened, about the time Phoebe hunkered down under Hurricane Betsy, they discovered they lived in a nineteenth century museum. Their 1839 courthouse and Grant's home were still used. When the Illinois Central Railroad ended passenger service, the town converted its 1857 depot into a visitors' center.

The nineteenth century's appeal worked; travelers detour from nearby freeways to poke about in the debris of the past. Citizens fixed up many downtown buildings and transformed them into restaurants and gift shops while retaining the town's vaguely Gilded Age look. We ate lunch in an old storefront on Main Street whose ceiling must have been fifteen feet high and still sported its silver-painted, pressed tin covering.

Mackinac Island, Michigan, has taken one long step farther back in time; it bans all motorized vehicles except for its fire trucks. We drove Phoebe to nearby St. Ignace across the five-mile-long Mackinac Bridge. I had been warned that its deck over the one and one-half miles that soar above the water was built with see-through grid plates. Being wary of heights I rather dreaded crossing it. I need not have worried, because the views are spectacular and distract drivers' attention from the fact that the road looks like Swiss cheese with more holes than substance. Instead, I kept thinking as we crawled across the span, at the mandatory reduced speed because of the dangers of violent crosswinds, that this would be a helluva place for Phoebe to give up the ghost.

We encamped in a St. Ignace room that was a scant twenty yards from Lake Huron and came replete with a bold seagull who patiently stood at our back door staring at us for two days in the expectation of a morsel. The following morning we caught the ferry to Mackinac on a perfect summer's day with acres of cloudless, azure sky soaring above us. The Vikings claimed they could smell sheep before they spotted land; we could smell horses, or at least their droppings, long before the boat docked. We arrived early when suppliers were making their deliveries to the stores and hotels. The island allows trucks on its docks to transfer their cargoes to horse-drawn drays. Teamsters expertly backed their two-horse wagons up to the trucks for the transfer. Just off the docks, polished carriages with matched teams attended by formally clad coachmen from the Grand Hotel, a most aptly named and priced sprawling hostelry, awaited their first guests of the day. Two and three horse hitches pulled tourist wagons up and down the steep hills on the island's southern end. In the afternoon we watched the UPS man, clad in his brown shorts, swing his legs off the edge of his horse-drawn wagon that was piled high with boxes, certainly the slowest express service in the nation.

Fort Mackinac, a state park, stands lookout over the island's tip and recreates life in the nineteenth century, although its history dates back to the American Revolution. A fellow dressed in nineteenth century baseball togs, tossing a "soft" hard ball from the era, proved immensely popular as he invited folks to play catch. We ate lunch on the south side of the fort, which overlooks the straits, in a cafe catered by the Grand Hotel. The view was memorable, mother nature resplendent, and the service obsequious. With only about 500 permanent island residents, businesses have to import workers for the tourist season. They recruit them from the Caribbean and people of color are heavily represented on Mackinac. The sing-song lilt of Caribbean accents are everywhere; I closed my eyes and almost believed I was down in the islands.

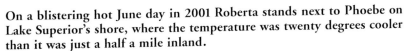

On a blistering hot June day in 2001 Roberta stands next to Phoebe on Lake Superior's shore, where the temperature was twenty degrees cooler than it was just a half a mile inland.

We left St. Ignace and drove Phoebe along the north shore of Lake Michigan as far as highway 2 followed its sandy beaches. It was an unnaturally hot day for anywhere, especially for the Upper Peninsula, but the temperature along the coast was a good ten to twenty degrees lower than inland. We stopped at a small rest area, rolled up our pants, waded into the water, and instantly understood how sailors shipwrecked in high summer could die from hypothermia. After we ran out of shoreline we turned north on route 77 through Germfask to highway 28 to Marquette and then shot inland across the rest of the peninsula on our way to Wisconsin's Apostle Islands. The countryside reminded us very much of northern New York state, scrubby, hard-scrabble land that yields its riches grudgingly. Both areas still look very much as they did when Phoebe was a spry youngster.

Our arrival at Bayfield, Wisconsin, brought us welcoming breezes off Lake Superior. The town is home to only about 800 people and not many of them were out and about; we had the village to ourselves. Just offshore lay the twenty-two Apostle Islands. We took a boat that threaded through the pristine isles to Raspberry Island, where we wandered through its lighthouse and small museum that recounted the lonely existence of lighthouse keepers and their often large families. The light guided oreboats through the islands down to Ashland to unload their cargoes. A young National Park employee, who spent his week alone on Raspberry, had been disturbed the night before by a bear who left its paw print on the old lighthouse keeper's back door. As no bears live on the island, the evidence was a bit of a surprise. This one, perhaps with her cub, swam over. The park service had brought out a bear trap just before we arrived to try to catch and relocate the animal to protect her and the tourists from unwanted encounters.

The backroads national and state parks, particularly on the cusp of tourist season, are wonderful places to see nature unchanged, not just from 1965 but from the eras of exploration and discovery. We drove Phoebe through Minnesota mining country around Hibbing, where tailing piles jutted out of the landscape, down to Grand Rapids, Minnesota, where we found a homey, 1960s diner across the street from a new strip mall. It was a coolish, drizzly day, and the view inside the diner, full of people, pots of steaming soup, and grill fumes, was obscured by its fogged windows, a sure signal it was a great place to eat. And it was; its homemade soup was among the best we tasted.

Fortified, we lit out southwards along three-digit numbered highways, on which we sometimes met no cars for miles through scrub country interspersed with ragged farms until we came to Lake Itasca, the headwaters of the Great Muddy. Henry Rowe Schoolcraft, guided by an Ojibwan named Ozaawindib, discovered the headwaters in 1832. His assertion that this was the Mississippi River's origins, however, was questioned by many who argued that other creeks and lakes are the river's "true" source. Exploring what is now a state park, we turned down Itasca's winding, forested road to its interpretative center, where we discovered a horde of people milling about. It was like stepping back into civilization. We walked a short distance down a woodlands trail, slapping at the flights of mosquitoes that apparently preferred us to all others, to the lake which has been much reshaped and redirected since its discovery. Like everyone else, we took the mandatory single step across the brook whose water would complete its 2,550 mile trip to the Gulf of Mexico months later.

Afterwards we realized it was getting late and we were in the middle of a motel lacuna. On a lark, we stopped at the park headquarters

A mile or so behind the author and Phoebe are the headwaters of the Mississippi River in Lake Itasca.

to inquire whether it had a room in its inn. Because it was July 3rd, we rather doubted it, but we lucked out. As we drove around to the back of our building we passed a dormitory where the park's youthful summer help lived. The kids were outside engaging in horseplay when Phoebe poked her long bonnet around the corner. They all turned and the looks in their eyes said, "Where did that come from?" and they gave us a host of friendly waves. Dinner in the rustic Douglas Lodge was memorable because its front porch, which was supported by tree trunks, was crammed with swallows' nests full of fledglings screeching for attention. After dinner we took a stroll and discovered a cottage the WPA had built out of huge boulders on the shore of the lake; we could not begin to guess how they moved, much less lifted them.

Part of the fun on routes less traveled was enjoying the little, often odd, parks that graced towns of every size. The smallest frequently favor a gazebo with enough space around it for the locals to gather on whatever night the local horn players choose to entertain. Two Harbors, Michigan, has a huge lawn in front of what is really a bandstand rather than a gazebo and we were lucky enough to be there to hear the local band perform. We flopped on the grass with the townspeople and enjoyed the music and camaraderie that ranged about us; village dogs seemed to enjoy these weekly get togethers as much as their owners did. When we found Protivin, Iowa, we had to stop at its gazebo because it had entered Roberta's family lore. Her father hailed from outside the town and when he took his kids back in the 1950s to show them where he grew up, he drove into Protivin as the oom-pah-pah band chuffed away. He took what he thought was the road to the family farm and a short time later they again circled the gazebo where the band was still playing the same march. Her father loudly proclaimed that he never got lost, but every road he took out of town brought him back to the bandstand. We only passed it once, however, and while I snapped a picture of Roberta standing in front of her family's monument to its genetic disposition to become lost, I could feel a host of eyeballs looking through the tavern window behind me wondering what we were doing.

Cairo, Illinois, an old river town that appears to have never reversed its decline, has a park right on the confluence of the Ohio and Mississippi rivers that proved a great disappointment. It was unkempt and filthy and every trash can overflowed, as did the porta-lets located around the grounds. Everywhere litter tumbled about. We arrived just four days after Independence Day and perhaps the town had not gotten around to cleaning the place up. The view, however, was spectacular.

It was a hot and muggy morning and as we stood among the debris looking at the map to see where we wanted to go next, John Steinbeck's prediction in his *Travels with Charley* that some trips "are over and dead before the traveler returns," suddenly came to mind. We had been on the road for almost a month, poking Phoebe into anything that piqued our imaginations. An oppressive heat wave had engulfed the middle section of the country as we entered Iowa and we had become increasingly reluctant to get out of the cool car to wander around. As we stood in Cairo's garbage, we looked at each other and our eyes said, "It's time to go home" before our voices caught up.[4]

176

John Steinbeck once wrote that some trips "are over and dead before the traveler returns." Our 2001 ramble in Phoebe ended here in a litter-strewn park in Cairo, Illinois, on a brutally hot day.

And we did—that day. We crossed into Kentucky, where we ate lunch at Fulton with the Sunday-church crowd in a timeless tradition that dates to long before the 1960s. Several fellow diners noticed Phoebe in the parking lot and because we were the only strangers in the place asked what we were doing driving about in a car that old. Several evinced a tinge of jealousy when we explained our adventure. We left them and cut diagonally across the whole of Tennessee and rolled into Chattanooga about 10 p.m., just in time to pick up some groceries.

For two days I cleaned bugs out of Phoebe's every crevice. Throughout the trip she had bored a tunnel through the nation's insect population. We had never slaughtered so many of God's creatures; perhaps the bugs-to-car ratio on the busier highways is lower because there is so much more traffic. Or maybe there is a greater concentration of winged creatures flitting about blue roads because vegetation grows so much closer to the edges. It could have been the summer of 2001 was spectacularly buggy. Mayhaps the sappy things are attracted to hulking, slow, artesian turquoise automobiles. Every night on the road I used a whisk broom to brush carcasses off Phoebe's radiator and heat exchange unit; some evenings both were solidly covered. It remained a mystery how the insects managed to bypass all the machinery under Phoebe's hood only to die on her firewall, inside her inner fenders, and even underneath her battery. The most perplexing question was how at least one butterfly a day caught one wing in the front crevice between the hood and the body and flapped spastically. I stopped often to free them, but most were too tattered to fly by the time I did.

The trip's length and duration wore on Phoebe, who was unused to such regular exercise, and we had to make some repairs on her after we returned home. At Tawas City, Michigan, less than half way through our trip, I noticed a small puddle of oil under her. I concluded that it was leaking from her rear main seal, which is an endemic problem in Chevrolet sixes; hers has been damp and slightly drippy for almost all of her thirty-six years. She leaked more as we pushed north until finally I had to add a quart of oil, something I never have had to do between changes. In St. Ignace a mechanic confirmed it was a seal problem, not serious as long as I kept her oil level up. During the whole trip she threw out four quarts, enough to coat her undersides all the way to her back bumper. After we returned home, I discovered it was not her seal at all; her plastic oil pressure plug, located just above the starter, had cracked and oil dripped down behind her starter and blew back to the seal where it dripped off. A five dollar plug cured the problem.

In Iowa Phoebe developed the irritating habit of hesitating when I accelerated after shifting gears. At normal speeds, however, she ran just fine. After fiddling with her for a few days I decided the problem was in her carburetor, a part I was unlikely to find in small towns we frequented. To relieve the annoyance I advanced her timing a bit, turned up her idle speed, and experimented with various carburetor settings. This cured about fifty percent of her problem. As usual, however, she brought us home, where her mechanic found that her distributor shaft bearing had worn and the carburetor had indeed "gone bad." After the replacement of both, Phoebe was primed for another extensive adventure.

On the adventure we had just completed we discovered that real America, if such exists, lies along the horrible stretch of strip malls south of Indianapolis on route 31, at the small "resorts" surrounding Buyck, Minnesota, on the flat, bountiful farms in western Minnesota, in Amish buggies with orange triangles on their backs, in the coves of

Appalachia, and on the aprons of mini-mart gas stations along every highway. Real America is exactly what we have at home and we found aspects of it replicated wherever we went. Midwestern America is so diverse and such a pastiche it was impossible for us to squeeze out its simple essence. Moreover, we and Phoebe missed great areas that must be adjudged essential components of the national mix: inner cities, whether Hispanic, black, or Asian; commercial urban downtowns, bus stations, truck stops, airports, casinos, suburbs, or vice strips. We poked our noses, not by any conscious design, into predominately white and mostly rural regions of the continent, thereby missing the important browning of America.

We were only looking for signs of the America that we remembered existed when Phoebe and our marriage were new, the ones we thought we recalled, the ones that had helped to shape our personalities, ambitions, and views. We tacitly assumed that elements of that earlier nation that still mourned recently buried President John F. Kennedy were still out there, aspects of the slower, less technologically connected world where face to face relationships were still the norm, where people and their viewpoints still mattered.

We found ample echoes of the 1960s everywhere: ranch style homes with their picture windows framing important lamps; family farms with their 19th century houses huddled behind their windbreaks; familiar highways retaining their traditional black-white signage; churches still standing in the center of towns; ethnic concentrations still grouped around their churches, cemeteries, and stores; good regional foods; unique state parks; and stop lights galore.

Most noticeable, at least where our blue roads neared the interstates, was the proliferation of the 1960s road icons. Holiday Inns — founded by high school dropout Kemmons Wilson, who built his first one in his hometown of Memphis in 1952 and counted 1,749 more in his corporate empire when he retired after a heart attack in 1980 — were everywhere. We often stayed in Kemmons' motels when Phoebe was young because they were shiny, new, clean, and cheap. Most of them in the twenty-first century are no longer new, although they are generally clean, and certainly no cheaper than many competing motels. As a rule they are in better shape than most of the local motels we frequented in 2001 but lack the myriad idiosyncrasies we enjoyed and endured. Most Holiday Inns, for example, have reliable air conditioning and hot water. Their green and white signs, one of the most recognized brands in the world, are still everywhere. They stand so high along the interstates that we could see them on the back roads.[5]

We did not even have to look that far to find evidence of another 1960s fad, McDonald's. Ray Kroc, a milkshake machine salesman, noticed that a local restaurant where he hustled his devices, McDonald's, always had a line waiting for service. He bought the place and in 1954 began franchising its successful fast-serve operations that promised a "secret sauce" on every hamburger. By the mid–1960s when I was preparing to spend at least four years being poor to prepare for a profession that promised to extend that poverty over a lifetime, the cocktail party conversation in upstate New York revolved around stories of those people prescient enough to have purchased Xerox stock when it sold for two dollars and declamations that a McDonald's franchise was a guaranteed path to becoming a millionaire. Stephen Sears, in *The American Heritage History of the Automobile in America,* got it right when he characterized McDonald's as the Henry Ford of fast food.[6]

In retrospect, McDonald's and Holiday Inns were indicators that the 1960s were a decade perched on the very edge of the great physical changes that swept the nation. The shopping centers that sprouted up everywhere and the multinational corporate merchandisers who competed to "anchor" such complexes symbolized such transformations. The ironic feature of such places was that they were often tagged with rural names; hundreds of such asphalt plains had the word "Village," "Green," "Commons," or "Town(e)" in their names, to add a touch of hometown nostalgia to new ways of doing things. This mercantile sprawl was a post–World War II phenomenon, arising in tandem with the new suburbs built to house returning veterans and defense workers, developments where these survivors of war and depression conceived and nurtured "baby boomers"—and lots of them. In 1946 the United States only had 8 such shopping centers but they were the future; five years before Phoebe's birth that number had grown to almost 4,000. We did not recall ever stopping at such a center driving south in 1965, but we noted the biggest differences between then and 2001 were that the earlier centers concentrated just outside large towns and cities, had not yet spun off the "strip malls" that nestle near virtually all larger shopping plexes, and had not, along with Wal-Mart, Home Depot and others, murdered main street small town merchants.[7]

Even the smaller, less successful remains of forty years ago standing along the back roads are now overlaid with aspects of modernity. Schoolhouses, no matter how old, small, or remote, have computer link-ups, virtually every small town has its own web page — even the Amish can be reached at Amish.com — cell phones are as firmly attached to villagers' ears as they are to those of folks striding through Chicago and not one of them is at the end of an eight party line. SUVs crowd parking lots and line curbs everywhere, restaurants and pubs all advertise Budweiser, the old farm houses sprout satellite dishes on trees, roofs, and sometimes in the middle of their front yards, the smallest crossroads hawks *USA Today,* and every motel has cable TV that offers identical shows. The most noticeable change was the ubiquitousness of credit cards in 2001. Few had them back when Phoebe was new; everyone traveled on cash. Not to have such cards now is to be suspect.

More interesting is what we found missing, things that had been commonplace thirty-six years earlier. Most obvious was the lack of full-service gas stations with "mechanic on duty" signs posted and a pair of bays in which to make immediate repairs. When Phoebe started roaming it was common to find competing gas stations on almost every corner, sometimes four of them at a single busy intersection. Rarely did they advertise their gasoline prices, for gas was cheap; on our honeymoon trip to Louisiana we paid an average of 35 cents a gallon for regular. Instead they touted their rest rooms; Texaco, for example, had small swinging signs outside its stations boasting of "registered rest room." Presumably someone kept a "register" of the nation's public bathrooms.

In 1965 gas stations owners never worried about drivers who pumped their gas and drove away without paying; attendants still filled the tanks and stood there, often in uniform, to await payment, usually in cash. Even the pumps are different. Very few stations have the old, tall pumps, many of which had little swirling propeller devices about eye level to let the customer know that gasoline really was flowing into his tank. Also gone are the globes that stood atop the pumps in

1965, some very clever like Shell's shell, and others with their brand names or symbols, such as Sinclair's dinosaur or Socony-Vacuum's Pegasus, on them. Well-kept stations always had a pyramid of oil cans out front and several tires in metal stands to remind their customers to change their oil and replace their bald tires. Gone too are the free maps, usually marking where the motorist could find other stations of the same brand, glasses, pens, sunglasses, and free air for tires. While stations in Phoebe's youth were not always neat and clean and their level of service varied greatly, they did represent an oasis, a safe place to seek mechanical help, parts, and directions. Gas station attendants knew the best eating places and occasionally had a father-in-law who owned a nearby motel with a picturesque name such as "Shady Rest" or the more prosaic "Fred's Motel." Nowhere on our peregrinations in 2001 did we find a motel that advertised that it had steam heat or telephones; a few still noted that they had TV and the more upscale mentioned their Internet hookups.

The demise of family-owned gas stations highlights the loss of public places used for socialization that marked every village and city in 1965. Gone are the benches that used to lean against gasoline stations' front walls that always attracted groups of men who hoped to catch up on what happened since they had occupied the same bench the day before. They talked and joked with everyone who stopped for gas or repairs, soaked up and passed on the town's gossip, and settled all the world's political problems from local water fluoridation to when the Soviets were going to rain missiles down on the station from their new space satellites. The same gaggles of folks were missing around the shade trees on local courthouse lawns, men who used to be advantageously positioned to see everybody who drove any leg of the town's square. The courthouses are still there, but the trees are not. While we ate lunch in a Bowling Green, Missouri, tavern, we watched as the town cut down all the trees around its courthouse. Tavern patter explained the town fathers were sick of the birds that roosted in them; the benches had been removed earlier.

People must now congregate "to pass the time" in places we did not visit: offices and factories; church basements; sports clubs; malls; and mini-vans. If so, the time they spend in personal chatter is a great deal more fleeting than almost forty years ago. Television and Internet admittedly offer the world at everyone's fingertips, but they have weakened local consensus formation, family ties, hobby organizations, and even social clubs. The electronic marvels are, after all, intrinsically lonely pursuits, excuses for many people to avoid the very social contact that they used to seek.

Drive-in theaters, which once attracted the populations of entire towns on weekend nights, are also as rare as full-service family gas stations. In 1965 the landscape was littered with drive-ins. Almost every town worthy of a name had one and others were located out in the middle of nowhere, between towns to attract their trade. They had the advantages of cheap land and no street lights so there was little glare on the screen and even less on the car windows, behind which few people were watching the movie anyhow. We did see several drive-in relics, screens still standing, with semi-circular furrows waiting to tilt the cars upward towards the picture; one still had the posts upon which the speakers rested. We saw not one still in business, however.

A host of other small businesses that we had patronized in the 1960s have also disappeared. We did not spot a single "five and dime" store, of the type that preceded the modern ones, K-Mart, Dollar Store, Target, and Wal-Mart. The Great Atlantic & Pacific Tea Company, a wonderful corporate name, is still in business but if it had any A&P grocery stores in the Midwest, they escaped us. For those of us raised on groceries bought every week at the A&P and menu selections that depended on the basis of "what the A&P had," it was a sad loss. On a smaller scale, we saw not one popsicle or ice cream truck of the type that used to drive slowly around small towns and suburban neighborhoods with hordes of screeching kids trailing after them.

Minor differences also caught our eyes. Very few towns have a barber pole or even anything called a barber shop. We saw a few, but were startled when we did. The blue roads were also bereft of hitchhikers. We saw not one in almost thirty days of wandering. Kids have their own cars now and skilled thumbing techniques have become superfluous. Nor did we encounter any motorcycle cops on the road; they prefer their safer and more comfortable cruisers, sometimes in disguise. Such unmarked police cars are easy to spot; they are large and clunky, lack sporty accessories and trim, and have blackwall tires. The more unsophisticated departments plant a forest of antennas and bolt government service plates on their unmarked cars.

For obvious reasons we did not find a single town with overarching elm trees lining its streets that gave the impression of driving Phoebe through a bower. Ornamental pears, the decorative tree of choice for elm replacement, are woefully deficient in size and grace and are living advertisements that not so long ago the stately elm was dominant. Phoebe was born just as the Dutch elm disease was ravaging the northeast and preparing to spread across the rest of the country. One of the first photos we took of her was beside the last elm tree in our yard. On this trip we did, however, occasionally find a solitary American elm, usually standing along a fence line in a farmer's field.

We paid an inordinate amount of attention to small eating establishments and yet did not spot a single "real" diner, one built by Budd, Tierney, O'Mahony, Valentine, Kullman, or any of the numerous other companies that were in the business. Likewise we did not see any examples of the generation of diners that were constructed from surplus trolley cars bought and refurbished as the transit companies converted to buses or went broke. The old-time diners, the ones that grew from the horse-drawn lunch wagons and trolley cars, were always more popular in the East, but they did spread into the Midwest where some are still in business. Most are located in large cities, however, so we had no chance to see them.

Scarecrows are as rare as Harriman-roofed, ex-transit company diners. We saw very few and wondered how farmers now protect their gardens. The several we did spot indicated that vegetable garden artistry is in serious decline; they were a pretty sorry lot of straw-men. Likewise, public pay phones are becoming an endangered species. Cell phones have replaced them. Although there still is at least one pay phone outside every mini-mart, they no longer have lines of customers queued up to make calls. We did pass several fruit and vegetable stands along the road, but they stood — often ramshackle, unpainted, and forlorn — waiting for the season to begin. They did not seem as numerous as in 1965, perhaps because so many fewer families cook or eat their meals at home. And nowhere did we spot a single once-ubiquitous, round, blackened, smudge pot set out and lighted to protect construction zones and warn drivers of world-class pot holes, deep water, large mammal road-kill, and collision debris.

We also did not see a long-distance commercial bus on the Midwest's back roads. They stick to the interstates and stop at easy-on, easy-off bus stations located nearby. Citizens of small and medium sized towns all over the country's heartland have lost their bus, train, and airplane service. We crossed few railroad tracks and nowhere did we have to wait for a 120-car freight train to mosey down the rails.

We were not disappointed by the changes. Most are not intrinsically bad and many of them make modern travel safer and more convenient. Had everything remained as it was in 1965, the trip would have been more difficult, not to mention eerie. Bits and pieces of Phoebe's world, however, are still extant and working. Indeed, a few of her siblings even eke out their last years stumbling along back roads. Likewise, we discovered not all of our memories were overblown or fanciful. Good, down-to-earth folks still live along the roads, more than happy to talk, to help each other and wayfarers out, to make lime Jell-o for their church-fetes, and to drive to town at dawn to help prepare for their annual Fourth of July parade. The America of almost forty years ago coexists, sometimes uneasily, with that of the twenty-first century.

We found evidence that some things in the USA had not changed much over forty years. Here Phoebe nudges her nose towards the "Field of Dreams." At the end of the road, in the rolling, rural Iowa countryside, a pick-up baseball game was in progress, the surest indication that some things were right in the country.

Change is never quite as radical or immediate or as all-encompassing was we suppose and sometimes fear. Those who are not on its cutting edge, and certainly we and Phoebe are not, may trail behind, taking the time to lollygag and enjoy our journeys, but we sometimes unconsciously move in its wake because we cannot avoid it. We are saved, however, by the fact that our images of who we are change even more slowly than our realities, especially when we keep driving, wearing, and eating vestiges of our past. That is how we maintain what passes for sanity. And maybe twenty years from now we will climb back into Phoebe for one last tour of middle America to see if we can find evidence of what our memories tell us the good old days of 2001 looked like.

10

Decision Time

Earlier I mentioned that Phoebe seemed to have a sense of just how far she could push me without endangering her chances of joining her sisters in the scrap yard or being sold to one of the people who regularly importune me. In 2004 she crossed that line; everything on her seemed to wear out and break at the same time. She suffered a series of mishaps, malfunctions, and just plain bad luck that left her in the repair shop more than she was at home. More important, for the first time I began to doubt her reliability and worse, no longer enjoyed driving her. She had become a worrisome, burdensome, and exceedingly expensive dependent. Despite our long emotional relationship it was obviously time to get rid of her.

I've always hankered to own a convertible, a car even more impractical than an aged Biscayne. For a couple of years I have had my eye on the new Ford Thunderbird. Not only does it sport a soft top, but it's available in turquoise, which I could easily rationalize as a tribute to Phoebe. Roberta, however, insisted that I get rid of Phoebe first so that we will have a place to garage it. Daughter Anne brought further pressure to unload Phoebe; deep down she really liked the car, probably because she shared a history with it, but she did not want to own it. As decades passed the reality began to strike Anne that the odds were increasing that I would expire while still owning the turquoise lump. She explained, numerous times, at great length, and always with feeling, that the last thing she needed in Niagara Falls, New York, with a husband, two sons, and Archie, their eccentric Jack Russell Terrier, was a forty-plus year old, fragile automobile of doubtful reliability and little intrinsic worth.

Phoebe's downfall started innocently enough in early June 2004 when Roberta and I planned to take her on an extensive, meandering trip north through Kentucky and Pennsylvania state parks to Niagara Falls to see grandson Theodore. Adhering to my sainted mother's admonition that "garbage and guests stink after three days" (one of Benjamin Franklin's favorite aphorisms), we planned to depart just as we began to smell and drive Phoebe into Canada and up the Niagara Gorge to Niagara on the Lake, a most pleasant little village. From there we would motor to Stratford to see a Shakespeare play or two and then west to Lake Huron and up to Tobermory, about which we knew nothing but whose name intrigued us. From there we would take Phoebe on a ferry ride to Manitoulin Island, the largest fresh-water isle in the world, and drive north through a place illogically called Espanola to Sudbury and down the shoreline of the Georgian Bay to Toronto for a peek at its art gallery and museums. Then we'd wander back to Niagara Falls for three more days and home. We already had our play tickets and all summer free.

The plan was ill-fated from the start. The day before we were to

The author's son-in-law, Thomas Chambers, holds grandson Theodore Ward Chambers after his first ride in Phoebe, December 27, 2003. In a couple more decades Phoebe will be his.

leave I caught a bug. But we packed Phoebe anyway, figuring a couple of pre-prandial cocktails would take care of it. They didn't, however, and we postponed our departure; slowly our clothes, one piece at a time, worked their way upstairs again. Three days later, a Saturday, I still did not feel normal, but since Phoebe had not been run for days I drove her to a local Model A Club show. On the way back I pushed in her clutch at a red light and heard a loud clunk and felt a strong vibration ripple up my left leg. Whatever had happened was not good and we limped to our mechanic, who told me that Phoebe's clutch assembly rod, on which the shifting levers, springs, and such hang, had snapped off from her frame. In other words a weld had failed — a structural failure. It was a tricky repair to make because it was tucked out of the way, but he promised to try to get his welder to fix it the following week. We learned his weld-man was out of town, I felt better, and we took Roberta's car and made the planned trip; it was an easier drive but not half the fun it would have been in Phoebe.

The broken weld was vexatious and untimely, although I appreciated it had happened at home, rather than in Tobermory. Phoebe really began her assault on that invisible line that had protected her and my patience, however, the following month when we decided to take her seventy-five miles down to Rome, Georgia, to look over the automobiles at a Horseless Carriage Club of America gathering. All cars in HCCA events were manufactured before 1916, in the so-called "brass era." Their owners trailer them around the country to take part in HCCA meets, where they spend up to a week driving back-country roads at the lower speeds their cars can tolerate. Some of these automobiles have already reached their 100th birthday; they made Phoebe look positively brand new.

It was a beastly hot day and, of course, we got thoroughly lost only a few miles from home and somehow ended up on the top of Lookout Mountain going back towards Chattanooga. But then, Phoebe does not have a compass. Once straightened out I occasionally pushed her up to 60 miles per hour, where I could hear a tapping noise in her engine. It had been there intermittently for several years but only manifested itself between 53 and 65 miles per hour, which presented me with the option of driving too slow or too fast.

I didn't worry much about it because Phoebe always made odd

noises and this one sounded as if it were in the upper part of her motor, perhaps a rocker arm out of adjustment or at the worst a bent or worn pushrod. I knew it was not from a collapsed lifter; she had enough of those over the years so that its distinctive sound had become familiar. And Phoebe had taught me that more or less random noises were not dangerous. When she was about to collapse her groans were loud, long, and always persistent. Moreover, although her engine had been rebuilt twenty-one years earlier, she only had 57,000 miles on it, which augured well for a peripheral problem rather than something fundamental and expensive.[1]

A few weeks before the fall semester began I took Phoebe into the garage that did her initial rebuild with the full expectation that after a bit of tweaking we would be on our way again. The fellow who had owned the garage back in 1983 and had rebuilt Phoebe, Jerry Potter, had since retired. A tall, rangy, stooped fellow with a craggy face and quick, knowing smile when talking about motors, Potter was incapable of doing nothing, however. He started another business out of his home machine shop building racing engines from Cadillac blocks. He also had an arrangement with Marty, who had bought his garage, to use the machine tools still there and to do engine work for Marty if Potter felt like it. All this became important to Phoebe's story.

I took Marty out for a test drive and whisked Phoebe up to sixty miles per hour, whereupon she obligingly started tapping away. This was in contrast to her usual behavior in garages where she purred like a Siamese kitten whenever a mechanic tried to divine her trouble. Marty listened for a couple of minutes and said that he thought the noise was coming from deep down, inside the block. I respectfully disagreed and took his mechanic for a ride; he too thought the tapping was lower. Not good news.

I left Phoebe at the station for Potter to drive when he happened past and he too diagnosed a major problem in the block. I arranged through Marty to have Potter rebuild the motor again and also the carburetor, which had been giving me problems for some time. Potter agreed to the deal, I think, because he could not believe a motor he had built had lasted only 57,000 miles. He was more curious to see what had gone wrong with his work than he was in overhauling the engine. Phoebe certainly was no challenge for him; he said to me later, "I can rebuild one of these with my eyes closed."

10. Decision Time

Potter did not work full time on Phoebe and after a couple of weeks Marty called to tell me that it was going to take longer than expected because Potter had discovered that Phoebe's block was cracked. He later explained that he did not discover it until after he had machined the block and was getting ready to reassemble the engine. He sprayed the block with a cleaner and noticed that in an out-of-the-way crevice by the third cylinder, the cleaner kept bubbling up. He repeated the spray several times until it dawned on him that a sugary substance that could only be anti-freeze must be causing the bubbles. Upon very close inspection he found a barely visible crack along a casting line. In forty years in the business, Potter said he had never known a Chevy six block to crack, an observation that did not make me feel any better.

If Phoebe had been a Bugatti, and at that point I wished she had, as it would have made my decision easier, I would have been out of business. There are some advantages to being common, however; Potter had no trouble finding another block in a junk yard, one which he assured me was solid. He bored it out, put the engine together, and had Phoebe back to me just before classes started. When I picked her up Marty warned me that she was not running very well but he thought that she was just "tight" and needed running in for 1,000 miles or so. He also apologized that his mechanic had not had time to rebuild the carb, but he did guarantee the motor for a year. That was the *exact* moment I should have driven Phoebe to the nearest Ford dealer to trade her in on that turquoise Thunderbird with the black cloth top.

Not running well was the understatement of the new century. In the thirty-nine years I had driven Phoebe she had never run so poorly. She had absolutely no pick-up and missed and bucked every time I lifted my foot from the accelerator to go down hills, a range of which lay between my house and the university. When I retarded her timing to lessen the pulsing, Phoebe would not pull her shadow. I thought it might be the carb and tried three different rebuilt ones without finding one that did not leak or made Phoebe run a whit better. I found that one of the carburetors had been rebuilt eighteen years earlier, ensuring that its leather pump flange and all gaskets had thoroughly dried out. Luckily, however, I had a student who worked in an auto parts store and he found one rebuilt only six weeks earlier. It seeped only a very little, but it did nothing to help Phoebe's performance, which was so anemic that I could only get her up to three miles per hour climbing Missionary Ridge to get home. Even with a cracked block she could top 15 miles per hour on the hill.

I called Marty so many times to complain that his phone number became one of only three I know by heart. He agreed Phoebe was still running poorly and put in a new distributor shaft and different spark plugs. She ran a tad better but was still woefully sub par. And the worse she ran, the fewer miles per gallon she got, only about ten, two-thirds of her historic around-town mileage. Moreover, she puffed great clouds of blue smoke when I restarted her after she had been warmed up, a symptom that indicated problems with her head, probably valve guides.

While trying to break Phoebe in, I stupidly had Marty replace her entire front end which had been under the car for twenty-seven years and over 120,000 miles. During that time it had gotten more than a bit loose until I had to aim her down the road rather than drive her. Afterwards, Phoebe steered much better but unfortunately still ran like a dog. The more miles I put on her rebuilt engine the more oil she burned, using a quart every 500 miles. For the first time I hated to drive her and resented the worry she caused, the time I spent going back and forth to Marty's, which was all the way across town, the rides I had to cage to work when she was laid up, and the mounting expenses. Several times Roberta subtly mentioned that it might be time to get rid of Phoebe and cleverly intimated that a turquoise ragtop might be just the thing to park in our garage. She had my attention.[2]

By October Phoebe had close to 800 miles on her new engine and was still running foully and making me feel the same. Marty protested that I needed to get her out on the road to blow out some soot. So Roberta and I drove her up for a weekend at our favorite state park, about 80 miles away. Unfortunately to get to Fall Creek Falls we had to go up two mountains, which Phoebe had never liked and liked even less on this jaunt. She did run better at 65 and made no noises whatsoever, but it took the better part of a day to get her up to that speed.

By Thanksgiving Phoebe had 1,400 miles on her engine, enough to break in a Mack truck, and still ran no better. I was losing patience and complained to Marty, who was as frustrated as I. His mechanic

We try to drive Phoebe out of town at least once a year to give her exercise. Here she poses at Fall Creek Falls State Park in Tennessee in March 1996. She proudly displays her 1965 Tennessee license plate.

diagnosed bad valve guides and I checked Phoebe into the garage for the work; at least it was free. When I picked her up, Phoebe did run a bit better, but she smoked — all the time. She was getting only about 100 miles per quart and she ran especially bad when she was cold and her motor had difficulty digesting all the oil.

At that point, in early December 2004, I seriously considered giving her away. Congress had just changed the law that regulated donating cars to charity but if I gave her away before the end of the year I could claim a healthy tax write-off. On the other hand, I couldn't think of a charity I hated enough upon which to foist a terminally ill car. The clerk at the liquor store had been pestering me for years to sell her to him and he was willing to pay real money for her regardless of the problems I was having. But I wanted to keep trading there and figured that might not be a good idea. The town is littered with junkyards but the price of scrap was low and I wouldn't get enough to pay for her new front end. But I certainly wasn't having any fun driving her.

I decided to give her one more chance. The day my Christmas

vacation started I drove Phoebe over to Marty's and left her there, telling him to do something, anything. I told him, as I had a hundred times before, that something was fundamentally wrong with the engine. He had been reluctant to call Potter back in on the problem, probably because Potter's time would cost Marty money and Potter was inordinately proud of the work he did, which made him a bit touchy.

Marty finally had Potter check Phoebe and he diagnosed a bad head. Marty's mechanic removed it and Potter took it home where he "reworked" it. After the mechanic reinstalled it the motor it did not smoke, but it had a heavy clunking noise in the block which had not been there before; he thought it was a bad main bearing. I was told all this later or I would have sold Phoebe right then.

Potter claimed that he did not build engines with bad bearings. He suspected that the mechanic had left a washer or something in the motor that was making the noise. Potter tinkered with it and finally asked Marty to remove the head again. After much fiddling Potter discovered that the piston in the 6th cylinder was badly scored and blackened on one side. The only way such a thing could have happened, he reasoned, was when Marty's mechanic filled the radiator after putting the head back on somehow a vacuum developed along that cylinder wall that kept coolant out. Ten minutes after he started the motor the piston burned. The heat did not score the cylinder wall itself, however.

Negotiations, to which I was not privy, ensued between Marty and Potter, the upshot of which was that Potter agreed to rebuild Phoebe's engine yet again and not charge Marty or me for the work. I went down to visit Phoebe the day before Christmas Eve and Potter had every part of her motor laid out, in order, on a huge metal-topped table. She certainly looked forlorn sitting nearby with her nose elevated due to the lack of weight on her front. Potter had already cleaned her block and polished the cylinder walls and was in the process of removing blackened oil deposits from the top of her pistons.

I asked him what caused this disaster. A man of few words, he simply replied, with cigarette dangling from the side of his mouth, "shit happens," a phrase he repeated several times. Then, warming to the subject, he explained how in forty years of rebuilding motors he has had only three bad ones, including Phoebe, and he iterated in greater detail than I really cared to know what had happened with the other two.

He reminded me of the stonemason in Studs Terkel's book *Work-ing*, who after a lifetime of laying stone all over Chicago and dream-ing of making all-stone kitchens with swinging stone cabinet doors, he remembered every bad stone he had ever laid. On Sundays he took his wife out for a ride past buildings on which he had worked and pointed out to her the stones he thought he had mislaid.

Potter is something of that kind of neurotic perfectionist, his shop is pristine, everything is in order, laid out or hung perfectly straight and parallel; he takes failure personally, even if "shit happens." He explained that he was much tougher on himself than his customers were with him. "This is a good car," he said, and promised the new engine would be "perfect" and "purr like a kitten." Even though he was cleaning off Phoebe's pistons he told me he had ordered new ones for this rebuild and had finally found in Memphis a set of chrome rings, the old fashioned kind that he preferred, although they took longer to seat.

What Potter did not tell me on my Christmas visit was that shit *really* had happened to him; it started with Phoebe's cracked block. Unbeknownst to him, the replacement block he picked up in the junk-yard was not a 230 cubic inch one but a 250 cast in September 1966. The difference between the two was imperceptible unless he knew the casting code. Potter could measure it all he wanted; all he would dis-cover is that both the 230 and 250 have identical bores of 3.875 inches. The major difference is in the stroke; the 230 has a 3.250 inch stroke while the 250 has one 3.531 inches. Unfortunately for Potter, virtually everything interchanges between the two blocks — heads, rods, bear-ings, distributors, fuel pumps, valves, valve springs, thermostats, and water pumps.[3]

The crankshafts cannot be interchanged, however, because they determine the stroke. Potter, assuming he had a 230 block, turned my old crank and installed it in the 250 engine, thereby shortening the stroke, lowering the compression ratio, and depriving the motor of power. To make matters worse, he replaced Phoebe's pistons with new ones that featured concave heads, thereby lowering the compression even further. Moreover, the proper pistons for the 250 have longer skirts, which may have contributed to the oil consumption that bedeviled Phoebe all fall.[4]

Potter must have sensed something of this difficulty when I talked to him at Christmas, for he explained that he had found Phoebe's camshaft was what he called "4 degrees retarded." He remachined it and promised that would add some power. He also suspected that the fuel flow from her pump to her carburetor was impeded by kinks that various mechanics had inadvertently formed over the years when they changed out carbs. He bought new tubing and shaped a whole new fuel line.

Potter had Phoebe ready on January 3, 2005, fresh from her second rebuild in five months. But he had been wrong; she did not purr like a kitten. She ran like a scalded cat — albeit an aged one. The old 230 had 140 horsepower; a new 1966 250 cranked out about 150 horses, but Potter's tinkering must have upped that number for the difference in acceleration was astounding; Phoebe could hit 25 miles per hour coming up Missionary Ridge with her air conditioner running. On the downside, however, her fuel consumption fell about 15 percent.

My misery had not ended, however. While I was struggling to break in the under-stroked first rebuild, Phoebe's sending unit from the gas tank conked out, leaving me with a gas gauge that always read empty, even with a full tank. I found an after market replacement which Marty's mechanic installed during Phoebe's Christmas makeover. It appeared to work fine when I picked her up. Two days later, however, I filled her tank and smelled gasoline leaking out around the sending unit. Marty replaced the gasket but it still leaked. Upon his third inspection he found that the unit was faulty, soldered it, and sent me on my way. It leaked again. This time I took it to my everyday mechanic who sent it out to a professional welder who finally fixed it. It did not leak but it was not accurate either; it showed only two-thirds full no matter how much gas I squeezed into the tank and indicated empty when about half a tank remained.

A half a dozen times I came to the point of cutting my losses and getting rid of Phoebe — it was the rational thing to do. Like most people, however, I sometimes make illogical and irrational decisions for reasons I cannot fully explain and I had been making them with this car for four decades. I realize that she's only a machine whose sole function is to serve with a minimum of trouble and expense. But I've never been able to let her go because somewhere in our relationship she had become more than the sum of her mechanical parts, faulty as some of them might be. Despite my anthromorphization of her in this book, she is not human. But selling her would be akin to getting divorced — which people often do for fewer reasons than Phoebe has lately given me. We have shared too much, however; she has long been a joy and I still have a shred of faith she could be one again if she's not too worn out.

Upon reflection I think that writing this book prevented me from disposing of her. I could not have written it without a car that logic dictated I should have sold in 1983. In a curious way I felt an obligation to keep Phoebe as long as I was exploiting her and in that sense she may be the only car a book ever saved. In return she now owes me at least two more decades of trouble-free driving, by which time I will also be thoroughly worn out. Then we will be even and my decisions to keep her will appear rational.

By April 2005 Phoebe was again running well and started on her second forty years.

Phoebe's five months of constant troubles, however, raised the question of just how much of her has to be original for her to still be the 1965 Biscayne I purchased. This probably unanswerable question is hotly debated among antique and vintage car enthusiasts and millions of dollars can ride upon exact the definitions of terms such as "original," "authentic," "restored," and "reproduction." In Phoebe's case, I am not sure what to answer when folks ask me if she still has her "original" engine. The top is, the bottom isn't, and her numbers no longer match. Phoebe is also missing scads of her original parts: water pump, windshield, fuel pump, thermostat, hoses, belts, tires, carburetor, starter, radiator core, several hubcaps, upholstery, front end, most of her paint, shock absorbers, muffler, brakes, right front fender, wheel bearings, bulbs, and alternator, just to name a few. And I have added an air conditioner which is quite different, albeit more efficient, than the original units.

I'd like to believe that she's like many old people who are full of replacement hips, knees, jaws, teeth, hearts, limbs, and various internal organs. Like them, she looks a bit seedy, smells old, leaks a tad, creaks and groans when she moves, has good and bad days, but has retained the essential personality that defines her. She's still hard to steer, stops only fitfully and when she's good and ready, wallows over potholes and bumps, and barely outruns a fit man pushing a loaded wheelbarrow. Unlike old people, however, she's faster than she was when she came out of the Framingham factory and retains her original shape.

We celebrated our fortieth wedding anniversary in the summer of 2005 and held a reunion of our wedding's veterans at the original site. It was also our fortieth anniversary with Phoebe and we planned to drive her from Chattanooga to Logansport to help us commemorate those long-ago events. Given her proclivities of late though, we feared that we might wind up celebrating in a repair shop somewhere gathered around a hydraulic lift. Or if she suffered a terminal break down, we decided we might just leave her on the side of the road, add a postscript to this manuscript, send it off to the publisher — and feel guilty. As it transpired, however, Phoebe won a temporary reprieve because we did not have the time to take her to the festivities.

As further evidence that we are what we drive, however, Roberta

Like her owners' eyes, Phoebe's are not what they used to be, but we are looking forward to seeing more of the USA in her before we become too decrepit to roam.

and I have begun to realize that we too are not as physically reliable or frisky as we once were, although I suspect we would not leave each other alongside the road. Even though we have aged with our car, we remain ever optimistic, laying plans for another trek to prove that we can still strut across the USA in Phoebe and learn something about ourselves and our country in the process.

Chapter Notes

Introduction to Phoebe

1. Lisa Jardine, *The Curious Life of Robert Hooke, the Man Who Measured London* (New York: Harper Collins, 2004), 2.

2. Alfred W. Bruce, *The Steam Locomotive in America: Its Development in the Twentieth Century* (New York: Bonanza Books, 1952), 387.

3. K.T. Berger, *Where the Road and the Sky Collide: America Through the Eyes of Its Drivers* (New York: Henry Holt & Co., 1993), 12 quoted, 13 quoted.

4. *Ibid.*, 13.

5. Lizbie Brown, *Broken Star* (New York: St. Martin's, 1992), 110 quoted, 111 quoted; Edith Hamilton, *Mythology* (New York: New American Library, 1969), 31.

6. William Saroyan, *Short Drive, Sweet Chariot* (New York: Phaedra, 1966), 99–100 quote, 100 two quotes.

7. A.O. Scott, "You Are What You Drive," *New York Times Magazine* (September 29, 2002), 96.

1. Phoebe's Ancestry

1. John Rae, *The American Automobile: A Brief History* (Chicago: The University of Chicago Press, 1965), 26.

2. James J. Flink, *The Automobile Age* (Cambridge, Mass.: MIT Press, 1988), 59–60.

3. *Ibid.*, 60.

4. Ibid, 62–63.

5. *Ibid.*, 64–65.

6. *Ibid.*, 66.

7. *Ibid.*, 66–67.

8. George H. Dammann, *75 Years of Chevrolet* (Sarasota, Fla.: Crestline Publishing, 1986),4.

9. Flink, *Automobile Age*, 67.

10. Dammann, 5.

11. Flink, *Automobile Age*, 67–69.

12. Rae, 75–77.

13. *Ibid.*, 82–84; James J. Flink, *The Car Culture* (Cambridge, Mass.: MIT Press, 1975), 113–21.

14. Flink, *Car Culture*, 97–98; Alfred P. Sloan, *My Years with General Motors* (Garden City, N.J.: Doubleday & Company, 1964), 47–57; David Farber, *Sloan Rules: Alfred P. Sloan and the Triumph of General Motors* (Chicago: University of Chicago Press, 2002), 40–50.

15. Sloan, 63–70; Flink, *Automobile Age*, 231–35.

16. Sloan, 153–54; Automobile Quarterly Editors, *The American Car Since 1775: The Most Complete Survey of the American Automobile Ever Published* (New York: Automobile Quarterly, Inc., 1971), 141.

17. Dammann, 5; *The American*

Car, 140–41; G. N. Georgano, *The Complete Encyclopedia of Motorcars, 1885 to the Present* (New York: E. P. Dutton and Company, 1973), 186, 304.

18. John A. Gunnell, ed., *Standard Catalogue of American Cars, 1946–1975,* 2nd ed. (Iola, Wis.: Krause Publications, 1987), 194, 326.

19. *Ibid.,* 93, 325.

20. *Ibid.,* 134, 142.

21. *Ibid.,* 132, 134, 145.

22. *Ibid.,* 134.

23. Flink, *Automobile Age,* 242.

24. *Standard Catalogue,* 155.

25. New York *Times,* June 29, 1965.

26. *Ibid.,* July 8, 1965.

27. *Ibid.,* July 7, 1965.

28. *Ibid.,* July 10, 1965.

29. All numbers decoded using Dick Washburn, "Numbers Match. What Does That Mean?" *The 1965–66 Full Size Chevrolet Club Publication* (November–December, 1990), n.p.

30. New York *Times,* August 11, 1965.

31. *Standard Catalogue,* 61.

32. Phoebe's Record Book, n.p.

33. *Ibid.*

2. *Storm of the Decade*

1. Chattanooga *Times Free Press,* July 12, 2002; Motel receipt, author's collection; wunderground.com/hurricane/at 196503.asp; Phoebe's Record Book.

2. Baton Rouge *State-Times,* Sept. 1, 1965, Sept. 2, 1965, quoted twice.

3. *Ibid.,* Sept. 3, 1965.

4. *Ibid.,* Sept. 4, 1965.

5. *Ibid.,* Sept. 6, 1965 quoted; wunderground.com/hurricane/at 196503.asp.

6. Baton Rouge *State-Times,* Sept. 7, 1965; quoted; wunderground.com/hurricane/atl96503.asp.

7. Baton Rouge *State-Times,* Sept. 7, 1965.

8. *Ibid.,* Sept. 8, 1965.

9. Phoebe's Record Book.

10. Baton Rouge *State-Times,* Sept. 9, 1965; wunderground.com/hurricane/atl96503.asp.

11. Baton Rouge *State-Times,* Sept. 9, 1965.

12. *Ibid.*

13. Chattanooga *Times Free Press,* Sept. 16, 2003; NOAA Web Page.

14. Baton Rouge *State-Times,* Sept. 10, 1965; wunderground.com/hurricane/atl96503.asp.

15. Baton Rouge *State-Times,* Sept. 9, 11, 1965.

16. *Ibid.,* Sept. 10, 1965.

17. *Ibid.,* Sept. 11, 1965.

18. *Ibid.,* Sept. 10, 1965.

19. *Ibid.,* Sept. 11, 1965, all quotes; New York *Times,* Sept. 14, 1965.

20. Baton Rouge *State-Times,* Sept. 11, 1965.

21. *Ibid.*

22. *Ibid.*

23. New York *Times,* Sept. 13, 1965.

24. Baton Rouge *State-Times,* Sept. 13, 1965, quoted, Sept. 17, 1965, quoted.

25. Baton Rouge *State-Times,* Sept. 14, 1965.

26. *Ibid.,* Sept. 15, 1965, Sept. 17, 1965, quoted.

27. *Ibid.,* Sept. 18, 1965, quoted, Sept. 20, 1965.

28. New York *Times,* September 18, 19, 1965, and October 29, 1965.

29. *Ibid.,* November 13, 1965.

30. *Ibid.,* quoted, November 12, 1965, quoted.

4. The Dairy Queen Klan

1. Patsy Sims, *The Klan* (Lexington, Ky.: The University of Kentucky Press, 1996), 3.
2. *Ibid.*, 292–94.
3. *Ibid.*, 3–4; David Chalmers, *Hooded Americanism: The First Century of the Ku Klux Klan, 1865–1965* (Garden City: Doubleday & Company, 1965), 8–10.
4. Chalmers, 8–10.
5. *Ibid.*, 22–23.
6. *Ibid.*, 24 quoted, 25 quoted.
7. *Ibid.*, 25–26.
8. *Ibid.*, 26–27 quoted.
9. *Ibid.*, 64, 36 quoted, 171–72.
10. *Ibid.*, 64–65.
11. John George and Laird Wilcox, *American Extremists: Militias, Supremacists, Klansmen, Communists & Others* (Amherst, New York: Prometheus Books, 1996), 362.
12. *Ibid.*; Chalmers, 349, 356–65.
13. George, 364; Chalmers, 349, 356–65.
14. George, 365; Chalmers, 354 quoted.
15. *Who's Who in America*, Vol. 31 (Chicago: The Marquis Company, 1960), 290, 2070.
16. George, 366.

5. Long Hot March

1. Baton Rouge *Morning-Advocate*, Aug. 15, 1967.
2. Baton Rouge *Morning-Advocate*, Aug. 14, 1967.
3. *Ibid.*, Aug. 12, 1967.
4. Patsy Sims, *The Klan* (Lexington, Ky.: The University of Kentucky Press, 1996), 197.
5. New York *Times*, Aug. 1, 1967.
6. *Ibid.*, Aug 11 and Aug. 12, 1967.
7. Baton Rouge *Morning-Advocate*, Aug. 12, 1967.
8. New York *Times*, Aug. 11, 1967; Baton Rouge *Morning-Advocate*, Aug. 12, 1967.
9. Baton Rouge *Morning-Advocate*, Aug. 13, 1967.
10. *Ibid.*, Aug. 14, 1967.
11. Baton Rouge *Morning-Advocate*, Aug. 15, 1967.
12. New York *Times*, Aug. 16, 1967, two quotes; Baton Rouge *Morning-Advocate*, Aug. 15, 1967, quote.
13. New York *Times*, Aug. 17, 1967; Baton Rouge *Morning-Advocate*, Aug. 17, 1967.
14. Baton Rouge *Morning-Advocate*, Aug. 18, 1967.
15. *Ibid.*, Aug. 19, 1967.
16. *Ibid.*, Aug. 18, 1967, one quote; *ibid.*, Aug. 19, 1967, remainder of quotes.
17. *Ibid.*, Aug. 18, 1967, quoted; New York *Times*, Aug. 18, 1967.
18. Baton Rouge *Morning-Advocate*, Aug. 19, 1967, one quote; New York *Times*, Aug. 19, 1967, two quotes, Baton Rouge *Morning-Advocate*, Aug. 19, 1967, last quote.
19. *Ibid.*, quote; New York *Times*, Aug. 19, 1967.
20. Baton Rouge *Morning-Advocate*, Aug. 19, 1967.
21. *Ibid.*
22. *Ibid.*, Aug. 20, 1967, five quotes; New York *Times*, Aug. 20, 1967, one quote.
23. Baton Rouge, *Morning-Advocate*, Aug. 20, 1967.
24. *Ibid.*
25. *Ibid.*, Aug. 18, 1967.

26. *Ibid.*, Aug. 21, 1967; New York *Times*, Aug, 21, 1967, quoted.
27. Baton Rouge *Morning-Advocate*, Aug. 21, 1967.
28. *Ibid.*
29. *Ibid.*
30. *Ibid.*
31. *Ibid.*
32. *Ibid.*
33. *Ibid.*
34. *Ibid.*
35. *Ibid.*
36. *Ibid.*
37. *Ibid.*, Aug. 23, 1967.
38. *Ibid.*
39. *Ibid.*, Aug. 22, 1967.
40. *Ibid.*

6. Sugar Boy

1. Robert Penn Warren, *All the King's Men* (New York: Harcourt Brace & Co., 1996), 3.
2. *Ibid.*, 4.
3. *Ibid.*, 396.
4. *Ibid.*, 397.
5. *Ibid.*, 3.
6. T. Harry Williams, *Huey Long* (New York: Alfred Knopf, 1969), 323, 467 quoted.
7. *Ibid.*, 677.
8. *Ibid.*, 864.
9. *Ibid.*, 865.
10. *Ibid.*, 866.
11. *Ibid.*, 873–76.
12. *Ibid.*, 862.
13. *Ibid.*, 876 three quotes; *ibid.*, footnote 8.

7. Road Writings

1. Luigi Barzini, *Peking to Paris: Prince Borghese's Journey Across Two Continents in 1907* (New York: The Library Press, 1973), 251–54, 80–81.
2. Dermot Cole, *Hard Driving: The 1908 Auto Race from New York to Paris* (New York: Paragon House, 1991).
3. Dayton Duncan, *Horatio's Drive: America's First Road Trip* (New York: Knopf, 2003).
4. Curt McConnell, *Coast to Coast by Automobile: The Pioneering Trips, 1899–1908* (Stanford: Stanford University Press, 2000); *ibid.*, *"A Reliable Car and a Woman Who Knows It"; The First Coast-to-Coast Auto Trips by Women, 1899–1916* (Jefferson, N.C.: McFarland & Co., 2000); ibid, *The Record-Setting Trips: By Auto from Coast, to Coast, 1909–1915* (Stanford: Stanford General Books, 2003.
5. Harriet White Fisher, *A Woman's Tour in a Motor* (Philadelphia: J.B. Lippincott, 1911).
6. Melvin Hall, *Journey to the End of an Era: An Informal Autobiography* (New York: Scribner's, 1947).
7. James A. Ward, *Three Men in a Hupp: Around the World by Automobile, 1910–1912* (Stanford; Stanford University Press, 2003).
8. Ilya Ehrenburg, *The Life of the Automobile,* trans. Joachim Neugroschel (New York: Urizen Books, 1929).
9. Henry Miller, *The Air-Conditioned Nightmare* (New York: New Directions Press, 1945), 286.
10. *Ibid.*, 217.
11. *Ibid.*, all quotes.
12. Gilbert Millstein, review of *On the Road* in Jack Kerouac, *On the Road* (New York: Viking, 1997).
13. Millstein's review of *On the Road.*
14. *On the Road,* 307.

15. John Steinbeck, *Travels with Charley: In Search of America* (New York: Bantam Books, 1968).

16. *Ibid.*, 272.

17. William Saroyan, *Short Drive, Sweet Chariot* (New York: Phaedra, 1966).

18. Phil Patton, *Open Road: A Celebration of the American Highway* (New York: Simon & Schuster, 1986).

19. *Ibid.*, 41 all quotes.

20. Susan Croce Kelly, *Route 66: The Highway and Its People* (Norman: University of Oklahoma Press, 1988).

21. Michael Karl Witzel, *The American Gas Station* (Osceola, Wis.: Motorbooks International, 1992).

22. Richard J. Gutman, *American Diner: Then and Now* (Baltimore: The Johns Hopkins University Press, 2000).

23. William Least Heat-Moon, *Blue Highways: A Journey Into America* (Boston: Houghton Mifflin Co., 1982), 26 quote, 3 quote.

24. *Ibid.*, p. 219 two quotes, 316 quote.

25. *Ibid.*, 40 quote.

26. Lesley Hazelton, *Driving to Detroit: An Automotive Odyssey* (New York: The Free Press, 1998), 63 quote.

27. *Ibid.*, 61 quotes.

28. Larry McMurtry, *Roads: Driving America's Great Highways* (New York: Simon & Schuster, 2000).

29. Patricia Leigh Brown, "Is There Room for Kerouac in a Car Pool?" New York *Times,* September 2, 2001.

8. Out on the Blue Roads Again

1. John R. Stilgoe, *Metropolitan Corridor: Railroads and the American*

Scene (New Haven: Yale University Press, 1983).

2. Thomas Merton, *The Seven Story Mountain* (New York: Harcourt, Brace & Co., 1948).

3. Cover, Nauvoo Restoration pamphlet (n.p.; n.d.)

4. Anon., *Menno-Hof: Mennonite-Amish Visitors Center Tour Guide* (Shipshewana, Ind.: n.p., n.d.).

9. Home Again, Lickety-Split

1. Erik Wahlgren, *The Kensington Stone: A Mystery Solved* (Madison: University of Wisconsin Press, 1958).

2. Anon., *Runestone Museum Guide* (n.p.: n.p., n.d.).

3. J.D.B. DeBow, *Statistical View of the United States: A Compendium of the Seventh Census* (Washington, D.C.: Beverley Tucker, 1854), 355, 348.

4. *Travels with Charley*, 272.

5. Kemmons Wilson Obituary, Chattanooga *Times Free Press*, February 14, 2003.

6. Stephen Sears, *The American Heritage History of the Automobile in America* (New York: Simon & Schuster, 1977), 294.

7. *Ibid.*, 296.

10. Epilogue

1. Phoebe's Record Book, n.p.

2. *Ibid.*

3. http://www.raceseek.com/chevy 6 cylinder.htm.

4. http://www.danielstrohl.com/sixinfo3.asp.

Bibliography

Ambrose, Stephen. *Personal Reflections of an Historian.* New York: Simon & Schuster, 2002.

Automobile Quarterly, eds. *The American Car Since 1775: The Most Complete Survey of the American Automobile Ever Published.* New York: Automobile Quarterly, Inc., 1971.

Barzini, Luigi. *Peking to Paris: Prince Borghese's Journey Across Two Continents in 1907.* New York: The Library Press, 1973.

Baton Rouge *Morning-Advocate,* 1965.

Baton Rouge *State-Times,* 1965.

Berger, K.T. *Where the Road and the Sky Collide: America Through the Eyes of Its Drivers.* New York: Henry Holt & Co., 1993.

Brown, Lizbie. *Broken Star.* New York: St. Martin's Press, 1992.

Brown, Patricia Leigh. "Is There Room for Kerouac in a Car Pool?" New York *Times,* September 2, 2001.

Bruce, Alfred W. *The Steam Locomotive in America: Its Development in the Twentieth Century.* New York: Bonanza Books, 1952.

Chalmers, David M. *Hooded Americanism: The First Century of the Ku Klux Klan, 1865-1965.* Garden City: Doubleday & Company, 1965.

Chattanooga *Times Free Press,* 2002-2004.

Cole, Dermot. *Hard Driving: The 1908 Race from New York to Paris.* New York: Paragon House, 1991.

Dammann, George H. *75 Years of Chevrolet.* Sarasota, Fla.: Crestline Publishing, 1986.

Davis, Donald Finlay. *Conspicuous Production: Automobiles and Elites in Detroit, 1899-1933.* Philadelphia: Temple University Press, 1988.

de Beauvoir, Simone. *America Day by Day.* Berkeley: University of California Press, 1999.

de Vries, Clare. *I & Claudius: Travels with My Cat.* New York: Bloomsbury, 1999.

Duncan, Dayton. *Horatio's Drive: America's First Road Trip.* New York: Alfred A. Knopf, 2003.

Ehrenburg, Ilya. Joachim Neugroschel, trans. *The Life of the Automobile.* New York: Urizen Books, 1978.

Bibliography

Farber, David. *Sloan Rules: Alfred P. Sloan and the Triumph of General Motors.* Chicago: University of Chicago Press, 2002.

Fisher, Harriet White. *A Woman's Tour in a Motor.* Philadelphia: J.B. Lippincott, 1911.

Flink, James J. *The Automobile Age.* Cambridge, Mass.: MIT Press, 1988.

_____. *The Car Culture.* Cambridge, Mass.: MIT Press, 1975.

Gabel, Shainee, and Kristin Hahn. *Anthem: An American Road Story.* New York: Avon Books, 1997.

Georgano, G.N. (ed.). *The Complete Encyclopedia of Motorcars, 1885 to the Present.* New York: Dutton and Company, 1973.

George, John and Laird Wilcox. *American Extremists: Militias, Supremacists, Klansmen, Communists, & Others.* Amherst, N.Y.: Prometheus Books, 1996.

Gunnell, John A. (ed.), *Standard Catalogue of American Cars, 1946-1975.* Iola, Wis.: Krause Publications, 1987.

Gutman, Richard J.S. *American Diner: Then and Now.* Baltimore: The Johns Hopkins University Press, 2000.

Hall, Melvin. *Journey to the End of an Era: An Informal Autobiography.* New York: Scribner's, 1947.

Hamilton, Edith. *Mythology.* New York: New American Library, 1969.

Hazelton, Lesley. *Driving to Detroit: An Automotive Odyssey.* New York: The Free Press, 1998.

Heat-Moon, William Least. *Blue Highways: A Journey Into America.* Boston: Houghton Mifflin Co., 1982.

Hyde, Charles K. *Riding the Roller Coaster: A History of the Chrysler Corporation.* Detroit: Wayne State University Press, 2003.

Jardine, Lisa. *The Curious Life of Robert Hooke, the Man Who Measured London.* New York: Harper Collins, 2004.

Kelly, Susan Croce. *Route 66: The Highway and Its People.* Norman: University of Oklahoma Press, 1988.

Kerouac, Jack. *On the Road.* New York: Viking, 1997.

McConnell, Curt. *Coast to Coast by Automobile: The Pioneering Trips, 1899-1908.* Stanford: Stanford University Press, 2000.

_____. *The Record-Setting Trips: By Auto from Coast to Coast, 1909-1915.* Stanford: Stanford General Books, 2003.

_____. *"A Reliable Car and a Woman Who Knows It": The First Coast to Coast Auto Trips by Women, 1899-1916.* Jefferson, N.C.: McFarland & Company, 2000.

McMurtry, Larry. *Roads: Driving America's Great Highways.* New York: Simon & Schuster, 2000.

Merton, Thomas. *The Seven Storey Mountain.* New York: Harcourt, Brace & Co., 1948.

Miller, Henry. *The Air-Conditioned Nightmare.* New York: New Dimensions Press, 1945.

New York *Times*, 1965–.

Patton, Phil. *Open Road: A Celebration of the American Highway*. New York: Simon & Schuster, 1986.

Rae, John B. *The American Automobile: A Brief History*. Chicago: The University of Chicago Press, 1965.

Rubenstein, James M. *Making and Selling Cars: Innovation and Change in the U.S. Automotive Industry*. Baltimore: The Johns Hopkins University Press, 2001.

Saroyan, William. *Short Drive, Sweet Chariot*. New York: Phaedra, 1966.

Scott, A.O. "You Are What You Drive." *New York Times Magazine*, September 29, 2002, pp. 96-98.

Sears, Stephen W. *The American Heritage History of the Automobile in America*. New York: Simon & Schuster, 1977.

Sims, Patsy. *The Klan*. Lexington: The University of Kentucky Press, 1996.

Sloan, Alfred P., Jr. *My Years With General Motors*. Garden City, N.Y.: Doubleday & Company, 1964.

Starrs, James E. *A Voice for the Dead: A Forensic Investigator's Pursuit of the Truth in the Grave*. New York: G.P. Putnam's Sons, 2005.

Steinbeck, John. *Travels with Charley: In Search of America*. New York: Viking, 1962.

Stilgoe, John R. *Metropolitan Corridor: Railroads and the American Scene*. New Haven: Yale University Press, 1983.

Twain, Mark. *Innocents Abroad or the Pilgrim's Progress*. Pleasantville, N.Y.: The Reader's Digest Association, Inc., 1990.

Wahlgren, Eric. *The Kensington Stone: A Mystery Solved*. Madison: University of Wisconsin Press, 1958.

Ward, James A. *Three Men in a Hupp: Around the World by Automobile, 1910-1912*. Stanford: Stanford University Press, 2003.

Warren, Robert Penn. *All the King's Men*. New York: Harcourt Brace, 1996.

Washburn, Dick. "Numbers Match: What Does that Mean?" *The 1965-66 Full Size Chevrolet Club Newsletter* (November-December 1990), 2-3 plus insert.

Wells, Stuart W. "Service With a Smile: American Filling Stations." *Automobile Quarterly*, vol. 37 (March 1998), 42-55.

Williams, T. Harry. *Huey Long*. New York: Alfred A. Knopf, 1969.

Witzel, Michael Karl. *The American Gas Station*. Osceola, Wis.: Motorbooks International, 1992.

Index

Abbey of Gethsemani 160, 161, 165
Albion, MI 156
Alexandria, MI 157, 166–68
Amish 153–54, 164, 178, 181
Ammann, Jacob 164
Anabaptists 164, 165
Anti-Communist Christian Association 92
Apostle Islands 173
Arcadia, LA 116, 117
Ashland, WI 155, 174

Bailey, Mrs. Fred 51, 52, 56, 87
Barthes, Roland 7
Barzini, Luigi 125
Baton Rouge 2, 3; culture of 65–73; Hurricane Betsy 49–60; 1967 civil rights march 98–107
Baton Rouge *Morning-Advocate* 56, 97, 99, 102
Baton Rouge *State-Times* 57, 59
Bayfield, WI 154, 173
Berger, K.T. 7, 11
Billboards 159
Bily Clock Museum 168–69
Biscayne 32
Blue roads 147, 157, 159, 169, 179, 183, 185
Bogalusa 3, 47, 89, 91–93, 104; Voter League 97
Boggs, Thomas Hale 84, 85
Bowling Green, KY 161
Breedlove, Craig 139
Brown, H. Rap 70, 96, 97, 98, 103
Brown, Lizbie 8
Brown v. Board of Education of Topeka 78
Buick, David Dunbar 25
Burbank, Col. Thomas 94, 95, 103, 104

Burger King 138
Buses 184–85
Bush, George W. 2, 34
Buyck, MN 178

Cadillac 26, 29, 30
Cafes 3, 154, 155, 156
Cairo, IL 176
Cajuns 72, 73
Carmichael, Stokely 70, 103
Catholics 72, 73, 77, 78, 160
Chambers, Theodore Ward 188
Chambers, Thomas A. 15
Chattanooga, TN 26, 189, 198
Chevrolet 29, 30, 31
Chevrolet, Louis Joseph 27, 28
Church of Jesus Christ of the Latter Day Saints 163
Civil rights 1, 3, 70
Columbus, IN 170, 171
Congress of Racial Equality 92, 98, 101, 105
Corvette factory 161
Corvette Museum 161
Covington, LA 93, 94
Crocker, Sewall 125

Davis, Pres. Jefferson 75
Deacons for Defense 92
Denham Springs, LA 74, 80, 81, 82, 85, 88, 95, 96, 97
Detroit riots 89, 91, 106
Dewitt, IA 153
Diners 137–138, 154, 174, 184
Dixon, Thomas, Jr. 76
Drive-in theaters 183
Dumas, W.W. (Woody) 57, 59, 91, 104, 105, 106

Index

duPont, Pierre S. 27
Durant, William Crapo 25, 26, 27, 28
Dvořák, Antonín 168, 169

Ehrenburg, Ilya 128, 129

Fall Creek Falls State Park, TN 192, 193
Farmer, James 92
Fast food 138
Ferry, Ping 160–61, 162
Fisher, Harriet White 126
Fisher Body Company 28
Flink, James 32,
Ford, Henry 26, 30, 180
Forrest, Nathan Bedford 75, 76
Fort Mackinac 172
Framingham, MA 6, 9, 35, 198
Frost, Robert 147
Full-service gas stations 181

Gas-A-Teria 137
Gas stations 181–82
General Motors Corporation 25, 26
Grambling College 72
Grand Hotel 172
Grant, Pres. Ulysses 171
Great Atlantic & Pacific Tea Company 183
Great River Road 169
Griffith, D.W. 77
Gutman, Richard 137

Hall, Melvin 127
Hall, William 127
Hamilton, Edith 9
Hammond, LA 94
Hannibal, MO 169–70
Hazelton, Lesley 139–40
Heat-Moon, William Least 138–39, 141, 147
Hemingway, Ernest 134
Hicks, Robert 93
Holiday Inn 154, 179, 180
Home Depot 181
Howard Johnsons 136
Hupp, Robert C. 128
Huron, Lake 172
Hurricane Betsy 2, 46–61, 147, 171
Hutter, Jacob 164

Interstate Highways 17, 148–50
Invisible Empire 75, 78, 79, 82, 86
Itasca, Lake 174, 175

Jackson, Dr. Horatio Nelson 125
Jardine, Lisa 5
Jenkins, Walter Leon, a.k.a. "Big, Black Billy Brooks" 101, 104, 106
Jim Crow Laws 76
Johnson, Pres. Lyndon 2, 47, 57, 85, 89, 90, 92, 98, 101

Kelly, Susan 136
Kennedy, Pres. John F. 101, 179
Kennedy, John F., Jr. 155
Kennedy, Sen. Robert F. 41, 89
Kensington Stone 166–68
Kerouac, Jack 130, 131, 132, 141, 142
King, Martin Luther, Jr. 78, 89
Koufax, Sandy 54
Kroc, Ray 180
Kroll, Marty 190, 191, 192, 194, 196
Ku Klux Klan 1, 2, 47, 73, 93, 95; history of 74–79

Lake Superior 173
Lawn ornaments 159
LeBlanc, Dudley 67
Leland, Henry M. 26
Lincoln 26, 29
Logansport, IN 45, 46, 117, 156, 164, 198
Long, Gov. Earl 116
Long, Sen. Huey P. 60, 67, 78, 111, 114, 115, 116
Long, Sen. Russell 57
Louisiana State University 36, 50, 52, 53, 57, 58, 60, 69, 72, 79, 97
Lynch, Lincoln 98, 101

Mackinac Island 171–72
Malcolm X 70, 106
Malls 178, 180, 181
Marr, Walter 26
McCarthy, Sen. Joseph 132
McDonalds 138, 180
McKeithen, Gov. John 91; 1967 civil rights march 92–107
McMurtry, Larry 140–41, 142
Menno-Hof Mennonite-Amish Museum 164–65

Mennonites 164
Mercury 29
Merton, Thomas 160–61, 162
Michigan, Lake 173
Miller, Henry 129, 130, 132, 139, 142
Minden, LA 65
Model A Ford 29,
Model T Ford 27, 29
Mormons 162–63
Morrison, Jimmy 57, 85

Nash, Charles 27, 60
National Advisory Commission on
    Civil Disorders 89
National Knights of the Ku Klux Klan
    96
Nauvoo, IL 162–63, 165
New Orleans 56
New York *Times* 56, 93, 95, 97, 125,
    131, 141
Newark riots 89, 106
Niagara Falls, NY 187, 188
Nixon, Pres. Richard M. 37, 89

Oakland 27
Old Original Knights of the Ku Klux
    Klan 98
Olds, Ransom E. 26
Oldsmobile 27
Owosso, MI 155

Paige, Leroy "Satchel" 59
Patton, Phil 136
Phoebe: air conditioner 150–52;
    ancestry 25–32; civil rights march
    89, 99, 100; flood 69–70; future
    197–99; gender 6–9, 130; human-
    like 19–21; in Hurricane Betsy 55–
    56; idiosyncrasies 16–19; and insects
    177–78; KKK 74, 80, 86, 87; litera-
    ture 123–24; and Murphy Roden 117,
    119; personality 9–11; production 33–
    36; purchase 36–41; quality 41–43;
    styling 21–22, 43–44; 2001 trip
    133–134, 147–186; 2005 mechanical
    problems 187–96; vestiges of 1960s
    178–86
Phoebe's World 106, 142–43, 185
Police cars 183
Potter, Jerry 190, 191, 194, 195, 196

Protivin, IA 176
Public places 182–83
Pulaski, TN 75

Race relations 49, 71
Rarick, John 85, 91, 92, 106
Reformed Church of the Latter Day
    Saints 163
Rest rooms 181
River Road 66
Roden, Col. Murphy 87, 94, 112, 113,
    114; and Huey Long 115–22
Rome, GA 189

Safety, auto 149
St. Ignace, MI 171–72
Salinger, J.D. 8
Saroyan, William 11, 134, 135, 142
Scarecrows 184
Schoolcraft, Henry R. 174
Sears, Stephen 180
Segregation 3, 65, 73, 75, 87, 88, 90,
    107
Shipshewana, IN 153, 164, 165
Shreveport, LA 65, 74, 78, 112
Simons, Menno 164
Sloan, Alfred P. 28, 29
Smith, Joseph 162–63
Smudge Pots 184
Southern University 57, 58, 72
Spillville, IA 156, 158, 168–69
Steinbeck, John 47, 130, 132, 133, 134,
    141, 152, 176
Stephenson, David C. 78
Stevens, Thaddeus 76
Stilgoe, John 149
Stoner, J.B. 92
SUVs 181

Twain, Mark 169, 170
Two Harbors, MI 176

United Klans 103
Universal Klans of America 98

Viet Nam 34, 37, 89, 90, 101, 148, 170
Villa Nova, IA 153

Wallace, Gov. George C.M. 49, 71,
    107

Index

Wal-Mart 12, 181
Walton, Sam 12
Ward, Anne E. 9, 13, 14, 20, 187
Ward, James A. (father) 37, 38, 39, 115, 116, 117, 119
Ward, Roberta S. 13, 14, 15, 49, 50, 52, 54, 56, 66, 74, 86, 88, 99, 134, 141, 153, 158, 176, 187, 192, 198
Ward, Rose P. (mother) 37, 38, 39, 40, 41, 117
Ward, Sharon E. 38, 39, 41
Warren, Robert Penn 111, 114
Weaver, C. 36, 37, 38, 40, 41
Weiss, Dr. Carl 67, 118, 119, 120, 121
Weiss, Seymour 121

West Union, IA 152–53
White Castle 138
White Citizens Councils 74
Williams, T. Harry 118, 119, 120, 121, 122
Wilson, Kemmons 179
Wilson, Pres. Thomas Woodrow 16, 76, 77
Wise, Gen. Erbon 84
Witzel, Michael 136, 137

Young, A.Z. 93, 94, 95, 97, 98, 106
Young, Brigham 163
Young, R.T. 101, 106

214